POLITEXT 187

The ISPS Code - 4
Intervention of public forces on ships

POLITEXT

Ricard Marí Sagarra

The ISPS Code - 4
Intervention of public forces on ships

EDICIONS UPC

Publication sponsored by the Ministry of Public Works (2009)

First edition: September 2009
Reprint: November 2009

©   Ricard Marí Sagarra, 2009

©   Edicions UPC, 2009
       Edicions de la Universitat Politècnica de Catalunya, SL
       Jordi Girona Salgado 1-3, 08034 Barcelona
       Tel.: 934 137 540   Fax: 934 137 541
       Edicions Virtuals: www.edicionsupc.es
       E-mail: edicions-upc@upc.edu

Production: LIGHTNING SOURCE

Legal deposit: B-36524-2009
ISBN: 978-84-9880-372-3

This work may only be reproduced, distributed, publicly disclosed or transformed with permission from its copyright holders, with the exception provided by the law. If you need to photocopy or scan a part of this work, please contact CEDRO (Spanish Centre for Reprographic Rights) at www.cedro.org.

Index

Introduction 13

        Objectives 14
        Work methodology 15

1. Legislation and organisation 17

1.1	Administrations that are competent in the land maritime public domain 17	
	1.1.1 Ministry of Defence. The Navy 17	
	1.1.2 The Central Maritime Court 18	
	1.1.3 Ministry of the Interior: Maritime service of the Guard 18	
	1.1.4 Ministry of the Treasury. Customs surveillance 19	
1.2	Air-maritime means 20	
1.3	Study and analysis of the model of competence in the land maritime area 20	
	1.3.1 Functional problem 21	
1.4	Centralisation decentralisation of the maritime administration 21	
1.5	Relationships between the administrations of the land-maritime area 22	
1.6	Sector conferences and the associated entities 23	
1.7	The territorial problem of the land maritime area 24	
1.8	Territorial location of the ship 26	
	1.8.1 Territorial sea, internal waters, other maritime spaces 26	
	1.8.2 The contiguous zone (CZ) 28	
	1.8.3 The exclusive economic zone (EEZ) 29	
1.9	Illicit trafficking of narcotics and psychotropic substances 30	
1.10	Right to continuous persecution 30	
1.11	Crimes against public health, confiscation and seizure 33	
1.12	The Constitution and the distribution of competences 35	
1.13	Organic la won smuggling 35	
1.14	The model of the maritime police 36	
	1.14.1 Towards a model of maritime police 37	
1.15	The immediate future of the maritime service of the Civil Guard. Plans. 38	
	1.15.1 From the unification of competences 38	
	1.15.2 From coordination 38	

1.16	Distribution of competences	38
	1.16.1 Ministry of Defence	38
	1.16.2 Ministry of Development	38
	1.16.3 Ministry of the Interior	39
	1.16.4 Ministry of the Treasury	39
	1.16.5 Ministry of Agriculture, Fishing and Food (MAPA)	39
	1.16.6 Autonomous communities	40
1.17	Smuggling	40
	1.17.1 Customs surveillance service	40
	1.17.2 Civil Guard	41
	1.17.3 Salvage	41
	1.17.4 Harbour Masters	42
	1.17.5 Control of crews	42
	1.17.6 Inspection of ships	43
	1.17.7 Port Authorities	43
1.18	Other applications of the Spanish legal area	44
	1.18.1 Malfunctions of the executive area	45
	1.18.2 Official information	45
1.19	Reflections on the tasks of the DGMM and SASEMAR	46
1.20	Coastal surveillance in European countries	47
1.21	Other regulations	47

2. The ship and its realities 59

2.1	Block "A" ships	60
	2.1.1 Accessibility	60
	2.1.2 Access to restricted areas on board	61
	2.1.3 Handling cargo	61
	2.1.4 Supplies	63
	2.1.5 Unaccompanied baggage	63
	2.1.6 Characteristics of the ship with respect to the variables of risk	64
2.2	Block "B" ships	64
	2.2.1 Access to restricted areas on board	64
	2.2.2 Handling cargo	65
	2.2.3 Supplies	66
	2.2.4 Unaccompanied baggage	66
	2.2.5 Characteristics of the ship with respect to the variables of risk	67
2.3	Block "C" ships	67
	2.3.1 Access to restricted areas on board	67
	2.3.2 Handling cargo	68
	2.3.3 Supplies	69
	2.3.4 Unaccompanied baggage	70
	2.3.5 Characteristics of the ship with respect to the variables of risk	70
2.4	Block "D" ships	71
	2.4.1 Access to restricted areas on board	71
	2.4.2 Handling cargo	71
	2.4.3 Supplies	72

	2.4.4 Unaccompanied baggage	72
	2.4.5 Characteristics of the ship with respect to the variables of risk	73
2.5	Block "E" ships	74
	2.5.1 Characteristics of the ship with respect to the variables of risk	74
2.6	Easiness of hiding on board	75
2.7	Summary of conclusions related to the ships	80
2.8	The intervention on board of the Security Forces	82
	2.8.1 Actions that occurred	82
	2.8.2 Situation	82
	2.8.3 Execution	83
2.9	Final observations	85
	2.9.1 MIO Operations	87
	2.9.2 Security force	89
	2.9.3 Maritime Interception Operation [MIO] Teams	90

3. Human factors involved 93

3.1	The ship and its exploitation as a criminal activity	93
3.2	Data obtained from the official statistical sources	94
	3.2.1 General Secretary of State for Security	94
	3.2.2 National Plan on Drugs	95
	3.2.3 Central National Narcotics Office	96
	3.2.4 Tax Office	97
	3.2.5 Spanish Observatory on Drugs	97
	3.2.6 Legal processes	97
3.3	Other sources of information	97
	3.3.1 Analysis of the data recording forms	97
3.4	Approach of the *check list*	101
	3.4.1 Design of surveys	101
	3.4.2 Methodology of survey	102
	3.4.3 *Check list* for merchant ships	104
	3.4.4 *Check list* for concessionaires	111
	3.4.5 *Check list* for commercial ports	115
	3.4.6 *Check list* for fishing ports	121
	3.4.7 *Check list* for sports harbours	124
	3.4.8 *Check list* for high speed boats	125
	3.4.9 Results of the surveys	126
3.5	Human conduct under pressure	135
	3.5.1 Individual conduct	135
	3.5.2 Shock and panic reactions	137
3.6	Drills	139
	3.6.1 Psychological aspects of stress situations	140
3.7	Factors that interfere in the consideration of options	141
3.8	Decision	141
3.9	Reaction phase	142
3.10	The forces of intervention in Spain	142
	3.10.1 Background	142

	3.10.2 Special Spanish units	143
	3.10.3 Interventions at sea	146
	3.10.4 Procedures for boarding	147

4. Prior preventive procedures 151

4.1	Compared equipment and procedures	151
4.2	From regulations	151
	4.2.1 RD 1338/1984, of 4th July on security measures in public and private entities and establishments	151
	4.2.2 Order of 23rd April of ¡1997 which specifies certain Aspects in matters regarding security companies in compliance with the law and regulation on private security	153
	4.2.3 UNE standard 108-131, sections 1 and 2	153
	4.2.4 Regulation on equipment	154
4.3	From protective equipment	157
	4.3.1 New access control systems	157
	4.3.2 New materials	158
	4.3.3 Glass and windows	159
	4.3.4 M.O.H. security glass	163
	4.3.5 Doors	164
4.4	Security systems and access control	168
	4.4.1 Operational security	168
	4.4.2 Verification of threats	168
4.5	Ship / port communications at arrival / departure (case of Barcelona)	169
4.6	Benefits of new technologies in the application to *security*	171
4.7	Operations of snipers boarding ships.	172

5. International policy of cooperation and the fight against crimes at sea 175

5.1	Contents of the requests	176
5.2	Response to the requests	177
5.3	Detaining the boat despite being in accordance with international law	177
5.4	Intervention of the security Forces. Possible procedures	180
	5.4.1 Procedures	180
	5.4.2 Hostile operations on board	183
	5.4.3 Planning the necessary equipment	183
	5.4.4 Special equipment	184
5.5	Preparation of the airplane and the pilot's report	186
5.6	Use of snipers	187
5.7	Treatment of prisoners	187
5.8	Follow up security force	189
5.9	Clearing internal and eternal spaces	190
5.10	Assaulting ships (sub-surface assault)	203
5.11	Possible action of the crew	208
	5.11.1 Hijacking	208

    5.11.2 The assault 211
    5.11.3 Kidnapping people 214

6. Intervention drills on ships 217

6.1   Anchored ship, ship taken by terrorists, and the placing of explosive devices 217

7. Conclusions 245

Bibliography 247

Introduction

The new security procedures established after the terrorist attacks of 11th September try to avoid acts of this nature. Prevention is the objective that all those responsible for security seek the world over. More than 90% of these efforts have gone towards blocking the opportunities that these aggressors look for to attack but, what is the quality of the response to in the case of such an act?

The analysis that followed the recent attacks identified a series of shortcomings in matters of coordination, technical equipment, procedures and operating practice of the personnel responsible for the intervention.

The different terrorist acts on passenger ships may be executed in many different ways and the response from the security forces is slow on most occasions. The reason for this slowness is due to the nature of the ships themselves; when 500 miles from the coast a ship must be self-sufficient in all aspects as the immediacy that this type of intervention requires is not possible in this case.

This reality has led high risk ships to have their own small intervention team as is the case of the Queen Mary II. It is obvious that this measure cannot be adopted by all ships, even some of those with a similar level of risk. For this reason, it is appropriate to work on the preparation of the crews to contain the damage that a terrorist action might cause, in collaboration with the assault forces and within their possibilities.

The intention is not a direct struggle against the aggressors, an action which they have been forced into on more than one occasion, but rather to be able to negotiate, attend the victims, control the panic situations among passengers, etc. Many of these actions, in one way or another, are already carried out by the crews, by they need to be adapted to the new threats.

On the other hand, the security forces, the fire services and the emergency medical services may have to attend an emergency call without the data relating to the ship that would allow them to plan precisely. Universal systems of intervention should be developed that involve these bodies in order to guarantee the expected reply.

At the same time, any intervention will have more guarantees of success if the coordination between the intervening forces and the personnel on board is good. The support of the crew covering accesses, guiding them, can help a great deal in the operations to be carried out.

The intervention in maritime accidents of external help, while by no means routine, can be considered as following logical actions regarding the type of accident considered, the circumstances of the moment, the conditions of the ship, its status, etc.

In complying with the ISPS in security situations that affect the ship, it must be considered that there may be an intervention from units from the State Security Forces. When there is a similar situation on a land facility it is easy to evacuate people and let the external forces act with the freedom their operational intervention needs, without limitations, hindrances, disturbances and without needing the evacuated people to participate in control actions.

On a ship, the crew knows the specifics of the distribution, location, sectioning, etc., of the main parts and elements, while the external forces are immersed into quite unknown and strange surroundings and almost always without the general knowledge required. The success of the intervention is doubtful and the valuable collaboration of the crew could be voided unless they have the necessary knowledge to make their participation efficient.

This study aims to provide positive solutions in the collaboration of the crews with the Security Forces to make possible an external intervention and to minimise the risks for those who are on board.

In this sense, an analysis will be made mainly of the existing relationships between the internal emergency plans, the procedures established in the ISM Code, ship security plan, port facilities security plan, functions of the ship security officer, relationship with the external forces intervening on the ship, etc.

The fields of study shall develop the capacity of:

- Crews in extreme situations, without external help
- Coordination of crews with external assault forces

Objectives

In accordance with the knowledge provided the intention is that there are sufficient rules of conduct and organisation to be able to determine positive directions for each ship, in accordance with the analysis of the distribution of structures, type of transport and other variables, with respect to:

- Marking the access areas to the ship according to the type of ship and the method of approach of the rescue forces.
- Ideal position of the ship for access to it.
- Different types of intervention and evaluation of the pros and cons.
- Tool for evaluating situation marking the ideal system and times required for taking control of the ship and its rescue(according to the function of the ship and the situation).
- Passive and active technical means that facilitate the intervention of the rescue forces.

Work methodology

According to the possible data provided, such as:

- Inspection of different types of ship and of the possibilities of the most common means of access.
- List the devices that can facilitate access to the ship, exclusively by the rescue services, anchorages, standard locks, etc.
- Positioning of the ship depending on sea conditions, existing lighting, approach route for rescue services.
- Trying out recommended actions to be taken by the crew to facilitate intervention.

Make a work approach, summarised as below:

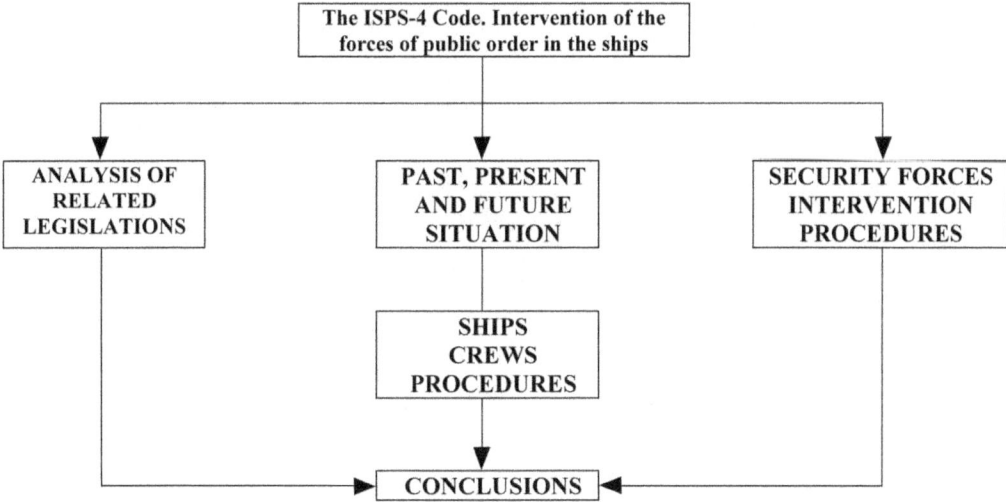

1. Legislation and organisation

1.1 Competent administrations in the land maritime public domain

1.1.1 Ministry of Defence. The Navy

Without forgetting that the Air Force collaborates directly in civil maritime rescue operations through the SAR air rescue service, it is the Navy that has most of the competences of a civil nature.

The organisation of the Spanish Navy was recently remodelled, creating the Maritime Action Force (FAM) through Royal Decree 912/2002 of 6th September, which together with the Fleet, makes up the main force of the Navy. Therefore, all those navy units that are not part of the Fleet are in the FAM and together they carry out the group of activities that the Navy carries out as a contribution towards the action of the State in the sea.

In order to perform this maritime action, it has a series of means made up of naval units, command stations and adjutancies, scientific centres specialised in maritime matters.

The objective of the creation of the FAM is to strengthen the role of the Navy in terms of visibility in the civil area and the consolidation of institutional relationships with those administrations with competence in the maritime area.

The competences that the Ministry of Defence exercises in the civil area through the Spanish Navy and regulated in LPMM RD 145/1989, LC and its RDLC, as well as Royal Decree 1475/2000, are:

a) Until the competences of assistance, rescue, towing, findings and maritime extractions are regulated at the proposal of the Ministries of Defence and Development these competences shall continue to be carried out by the organs of the Navy in accordance with the stipulations of Law 60/1962, of 24th December (LPMM. Art. 86.6 and Transient Disposition 10).

b) Those of assistance, rescue, towing, findings and maritime extractions in military matters or which could affect defence (LPMM. art. 86.6).

c) Ordering and controlling maritime traffic in the waters in which Spain has sovereignty, sovereign rights or jurisdiction that corresponds to the MD for the safeguard of national sovereignty (LPMM art. 86.7)

d) The authorisation of the uses and activities in the area of land maritime public domain that affects National Defence corresponds to the Ministry of Defence through the mentioned Department.

e) At the same time, the Ministry of Defence shall carry out the military surveillance of the coast, making sure that international agreements in this matter are kept. (RDLC art. 206)

f) Dangerous explosive goods: When Division 1.1 explosives are loaded or unloaded in a port as referred to in art. 15.7 of the National Regulation on Admission and the handling and manipulation of dangerous goods in ports as per RD 145/1989 deals with quantities above 400 kilograms per stop, the designation of the special place in the port to carry out the operations corresponds to the Ministry of Defence at the reasonable proposal of the port entity, regardless of the existence of special docks for dangerous goods. (RD.145/1989art.24).

g) Royal Decree 1475/2000, of 4th August, develops the basic organic structure of the Ministry of Development, developing Royal Decree 690/2000, granting in its first article the execution of guideline governing policies related to the management of state services relating to cartography.

1.1.2 The Central Maritime Court

As the competences on maritime assistance, rescue and towing, findings and extraction will continue to be carried out by the organs of the Navy, in accordance with the stipulations of Law 60/1962, of 24th December (LPMM, art. 86.6 and Transient Disposition 10; RD1475/2000 art. 3-c) the administrative organism, the Central Maritime Court, continues to exercise its functions. It depends on the Ministry of Defence and as the central jurisdictional organism in matters relating to maritime towing, assistance and rescue, created by Law 60/62 of 24th December and on which the permanent maritime courts, in charge of the instruction of the corresponding proceedings, depend. The main function of this court is to establish the remuneration corresponding to these services when there is no agreement to that effect between the interested parties, as well as resolving claims against the resolutions of the corresponding judges.

1.1.3 Ministry of the Interior: Maritime Service of the Civil Guard

The Maritime Service of the Civil Guard was created in virtue of Royal Decree 246/91, of 22nd February in compliance with Organic Law 2/86 of the Security Forces and Corps of the State, which until then had not been developed in reference to the competence of the entity of the Civil Guard in Spanish jurisdictional waters. Its development was essentially with the publication of General Order 51, of May 1992 on the Organisation of the Maritime Service of the Civil Guard. Recently the GEAS (Group of underwater activities of the Civil Guard) joined the service. When it is necessary to use other specialities in specific tasks, personnel from the corresponding specialist groups, such as the SEPRONA, Service for the Protection of Nature; Helicopter Group.

The creation of the Civil Guard of the Sea came as a solution to a problem, the lack of a maritime police force in our country. Therefore it was created to fill a legal void and to offer services such as government police, legal police, fiscal police and administrative police and its general mission is to protect the free exercise of the rights and freedom of the Spanish people as well as guaranteeing the safety of citizens through the performance of their duties:

- **Government police:** The Maritime Service of the Civil Guard maintains public safety; the safety of the personalities and installations that require it; offering assistance in situations of serious risk, catastrophe or public calamity in the terms established in the legislation of Civil Protection; custody of ports and coasts; transferring prisoners and detainees and the control of illegal emigration and immigration at sea.

- **Legal police:** Has the function of preventing crimes being committed and investigating events as well as preparing the corresponding technical and police reports,

- **Fiscal police:** As fiscal police they have attributions derived from their consideration as the State Tax Security service and practicing actions aimed at avoiding and persecuting smuggling.

- **Administrative police:** It has functions derived from current legislation on weapons and explosives; make sure of compliance with the stipulations on the preservation of nature and the environment, watch over and protect marine archaeological deposits and in general make sure general laws and stipulations are complied with, by executing the orders that arrive from the authorities in the areas of their competences. Naturally and independently of these functions, as an integral part of the Civil Guard corps, the maritime service also acts in those missions of a military nature given to them.

The Order of 27th April 1992 which establishes the procedure that enables the personnel of the Maritime Service to handle ships. Finally, the Order of 7th April of 2000 regulates the handling of pneumatic or semi-rigid boats by the personnel of the maritime service of the Civil Guard.

1.1.4 Ministry of Economic Affaire and Finance. Customs surveillance

Since the creation of the State Agency of Tax Administration on 1st January of 1992 (article 103 of the Law of General Budgets of the State fro 1991, Law 18/1991 on Income Tax and the Order of the Ministry of Economics and Finance of 25th September of 1991, the Autonomous Body of Customs Surveillance was integrated into its structure within the Department of Customs and Taxes.

The Customs Department was structured through the Order of 27th July 1998 and the Resolution of 28th July 1998 as due to the implementation of the single market in the European Union and the subsequent disappearance of fiscal frontiers, it became necessary to establish the bases of an organisation of the department that makes it possible to adapt the human and material means to the current circumstances of the operations of external trade and special taxes.

The mentioned Order structures the Department of Customs and special taxes and is integrated by the Deputy Management of Customs Surveillance and the following sub-departments to which it will report directly.

a) General Sub-department of Operations

b) General Sub-department of Logistics

Organisation

Its organisation is structured in existing Regional Areas of Customs Operation in all the special delegations of the state administration of the Tax Office. They depend hierarchically on the manager of the Regional Customs Office and are divided into four categories (A, B, C and D) depending on the material and human resources available as well as the work load under the operational responsibility of one of the Regional deputies.

The main functions of the Regional deputy are the management and coordination of the maritime units and bases that have the functions of persecuting, investigating ands discovering fraud in their territorial area.

They have a regional structure of maritime bases and units that cover all the national territory that has a coast. The Regional Air and Naval Unit has the mission to plan, execute and control the air and naval operations that are carried out in its territorial area.

In the local area the Regional Units shall coordinate, direct and promote the work that is carried out at each of the bases and head offices, the name and organisation depends on the circumstances of whether there is only a land or maritime service or both.

Under the management of the Base manager the maritime bases will plan the shifts of the ship resources in their area and shall be responsible for the correct operation of the maintenance processes of the ships in the area, and the direction and control of the personnel on board.

1.2 Maritime air resources

In order to meet its ends the Customs Surveillance has the following material and human resources; 40 ships of a different nature, among which there is a patrol ship which is 64 metres high, with 787 marine personnel apart from 861 people on land, 5 helicopters and 6 airplanes.

1.3 Study and analysis of the competence model in the land maritime area

The functional problem has not been so much a consequence of the promulgation of the Constitution as of its development, which because of political and privatized pressures from the administrations, generated too many generations and even the duplicity of these entities, companies which have taken away the efficiency of the administration or de-regularised it and have led to a greater use of the administrative resources and therefore a lack of human and material resources in the different administrations and the legalisation of the relationships between those administered and administration.

The territorial problem is determined by the huge quantity of functions and administrations that coincide on the same space of competence and are only differentiated by matrices and which require an almost daily coordination of all the administrations and numerous resources of the Constitutional Court to limit its competences.

1.3.1 Functional problem

Among the problems and possible solutions that we could find not only in the land-maritime administration but in all those in which their functions coincide in the same administrative area are:

- The centralisation and de-centralisation of the land-maritime administration.
- The relationships between the administrations in the land-maritime area.
- The Sector Conferences and College Organs, as a solution to the concurrence of competences in the maritime area as it is the main functional problem.

The diversion of functions and competences is one of the main problems which the administration faces and specifically in the land-maritime area:

- Urban concurrences among the State, the autonomous communities and the City Halls., mainly in the territorial area but also in the functional area.
- The dispersion of human resources and maritime police and maritime inspection resources with a loss in the efficiency of the different administrations with competences in the area.
- Concurrences in safety, contamination and maritime rescue.
- The dispersion of maritime titles instead of tending towards unification at a community level.

There has been a trend towards a dispersion among the central administration of the Merchant navy and fishing administrations and in turn from the fishing administrations towards the autonomous communities which have also taken on competences in diving and sporting titles.

On the other hand and common to all the administration is the delay in the modernisation of the administration and the consequent move from public law to private law as a consequence of bureaucracy, work absenteeism, strict contracts, the politicised distribution of resources and non-rationalised by the principles of efficiency, economy and the seasonal problem of a tourist country against an obsolete administrative structure.

1.4 Centralisation and de-centralisation of the maritime administration

When the Constitution was passed the principle of de-centralisation was elevated to the highest level of regulation as it is included among those that will have to direct the organisation of the public administration (CE art. 103.1) as a new manifestation of the desire of our constituents to achieve an approach to the decisions at the lower organic levels which are more in contact with real problems.

Administrative de-centralisation has taken place in Spain in a double sense, legal-administrative and merely administrative, that is, organisational. The former is reflected in article 103 of the Constitution and includes de-centralisation among the principles to which the public administration will have to adapt and to which together with the principles of autonomy of the towns and autonomous communities (CE art. 137) has led to an organisational system based on the idea of an approach between the administration and the administered through the transfer of functions to the lesser territorial entities which act in full capacity of decision with the sole exceptions imposed by the principles of unity and coordination. This first de-centralisation produced, all at the first moment, the duplicity of entities and functions with the subsequent administrative chaos, mistrust in competences and the politicisation of the administration by instrumentalising it.

The second de-centralisation was the creation of a peripheral state administration of delegation of competences in which the opposite effect has come about since 1997; the centralisation in which Law 6/1997, of 14th April, of the Organisation and Operations of the General Administration of the State, configures a new organisation of the peripheral administration LOFAGE and Royal Decree 1330/1997 of 1st August of the integration of peripheral services and structures of the Delegations of Government that is developed in the configuration of the new peripheral services of the ministries of Development, Agriculture, Fishing and Food and of Health and Consumption but does not centralise the majority of the administrations with maritime competences; demarcation of coasts, maritime harbour offices and the Social Institute of the Marine with the exception of the peripheral state fishing administration.

This centralisation of the Lofage has rationalised the peripheral services that had lost their competences through the transfers to the autonomous communities and two peripheral maritime administrations have been created, those depending on the Government delegations and those depending directly in the Central State. Those which do not depend on the Central State may be classified in turn as horizontal centralisation such as that of the harbour masters, port authorities that develop their own competences under the direction and coordination of a central body and another vertical one such as the Demarcation of Coasts which are only administrative and management delegations and only for resolving the temporary authorisations of operations and carrying out projects to be sent for approval to higher bodies.

This non homogenous centralisation and de-centralisation among autonomous communities and peripheral administrations of the State only generate an added difficulty to the administered who do not know it or understand the administration which makes the relationship with it all the more difficult as they never know who is competent in what and through which channels they must proceed and to whom they must make claims. Thus the need for single windows about which so much has been written.

In the land-maritime area there is the added difficulty of not knowing the administrations and what each of them regulates, due to the changes that have taken place in the last ten years, with the decentralisation of competence that concentrated the marine command offices and the State. Therefore it would be desirable form the point of view of those administered to have a new concentration of maritime competences, as was done with the LOFAGE and the Royal Decree that develops it, of the peripheral functions and organs in the land maritime area and an instrument of coordination with the autonomic and local administrations.

1.5 Relationships among the administrations of the land-maritime area

The relationships between the land maritime central administration and the de-centralised entities is very complex due to the existence of a host of public individuals that integrate the indirect administration that makes it necessary to determine the establishment of a series of relationships among themselves and with the central administration which, as soon as there are two or more subjects and they are recognised and covered by law they will be considered as having a legal relationship.

Administrative de-centralisation does not offer us perfectly undefined and unidentifiable competences but rather the public legal personalities that make up the indirect administration act on occasions as superior entities. All of this has an unfavourable effect on the functioning of the administration, as the indefinition of functions and competences, the concurrences and the lack of cooperation make it very difficult to achieve its own targets and those common ones in which it participates.

Only with a legislative development of administrative coordination and efficiency, elevated to the maximum degree (CE 10.3.1) which include a series of duties and obligations for the different public entities (Law 4/1999, of 13th January, on the Legal Regime of Public Administrations and Common Administrative Procedure - LRJAPPA) could the confusion of competences and administrations be resolved, or if not with a new centralization of competences in administrative entities especially at a peripheral level.

On many occasions and above all when the administration is politicised, the divergences that arise between the State or autonomic administration and the de-centralised public entities through the non existence as a rule of a hierarchical dependence of the latter to the former, lead to a collision between the two terms of the conflict which will have to be resolved by the courts through judicial review.

The regulation of these relationships and their principles is included in the LRJAPPA, which states the following in number 1 of article 4: "The public administrations act and relate in accordance with the principle of institutional loyalty and should consequently":

- Respect the legitimate exercise of their competences by other administrations.
- Consider all the public interests involved, in the exercise of their own competences, and specifically those whose management corresponds to other administrations.
- Provide the other administrations with the information that they need on the activity that they develop in their own competences.
- Provide, in their area, the active cooperation and assistance that the administrations may require for the efficient performance of their competences.

This drafting of principles is totally utopian from the political and administrative point of view, as the administrations depend directly on the different central, autonomic and local governments that use their competence with political objectives. As everyone knows, there is also a certain administrative scepticism towards the competences that depend on a same political government with the subsequent lack of collaboration and coordination in an alleged defence of their competences. Although the required assistance and cooperation can only be denied when the entity from which it is requested is not empowered to provide it, does not have sufficient resources for it or when by doing it would cause serious harm to the interests it must guard or to the performance of its own functions. The refusal to provide assistance will be communicated to the requesting administration. This lack of collaboration and coordination increases even more with the concurrence of competences due to the fear of disappearing as an entity.

1.6 Sectorial conferences and the associated entities

It is a mistake to expect that the administrations are coordinated, as the duty to collaborate will be developed through the instruments and procedures that the General Administration of the State and the Administration of the Autonomous Communities establish in common and voluntarily in accordance with Law 4/1999, that is to say that they are not subjected to instruments or procedures previously established by the regulation, but rather that they are free to take on any instrument.

A solution for the decentralisation of competences in the land-maritime area is the development of articles 5 to 8 of the LRJAPPA, sectorial conferences and other associated entities as instruments of coordination. Sectorial conferences, collaboration agreements and consortiums are expected as well as the bilateral commissions of cooperation.

In STC 76/1983, of 5th August, the Constitutional Court maintained that the state legislator may not intervene in the exercise of competence that the autonomous communities have taken on in accordance with the constitutional scheme of distribution. Therefore the sectorial conferences may not replace the entities of the communities themselves nor can their decisions cancel their faculties of decision. The sectorial conferences must be entities who gather to examine common problems and to discuss the appropriate lines of action.

For those administrations with concurrences in certain fields of regulation associated entities may be created with a representation of the different land-maritime administrations and entities or in the same way as the boards of administration of the ports of general interest and the assistance and consultation entities such as the Council of Navigation and Port as a solution of coordination and privatization, with the representation of the private sectors involved.

1.7 The territorial problem of the land maritime area

a) Navigation in internal continental waters

The navigation of ships to enter or leave ports or places located within internal continental waters, communicated with the sea is considered as maritime navigation to public purposes and are therefore regulated by the central maritime administration and the LPMM.

On the other hand, navigation that is circumscribed exclusively to internal continental waters falls outside of the Private Law of Navigation and on those of a public nature are subjected to the LPMM, which, however, co-exist and overlap with those contained in the legislation on waters, Law 29/1985 of 2nd August, on Waters, and Royal Decree 849/1986, of 11th April which approved the Regulation of the Hydraulic Public Domain, declaring that the state hydraulic public domain is constituted by continental waters, both surface and underground, as well as the riverbed and the beds of the lakes, lagoons, surface reservoirs in public courses. In this framework of the use of this domain, and in particular of the waters, navigation (and floating) constitute a special common use and as such, requires prior administrative authorisation (art. 49).

The Regulation carries out the basic control of navigation as a special use (art, 55 to 68). In its virtue, competence corresponds to the Organism of Cuenca, that is, the corresponding hydrographical confederation. However, it is also necessary to take into consideration the possible autonomic competences, in the control of maritime transport (artx. 80.3 and 81.4 of the LPMM).

Among the requisites and conditions for navigation, the regulations include the basic aspects of the use of continental waters for navigation, marking and defining the content that is the objective of the requisites to obtain the authorisation, which in any case are of a regulated nature. At the same time and within it there are different requisites for the vessel, the crews, the areas for navigation and the authorisation itself.

As for the vessel, it should have a standardised registration number with the exception of those that, due to their size and characteristics, may be considered as bathing complements or floating devices and which are used exclusively and sporadically for descending rivers or other sporting events. This specific registration is granted and registered in the organism of the competent hydraulic domain and which operates totally outside the license of the maritime Register.

The regulation specifies that the crew will be required to have a title that is sufficient for handling vessels, referring here to those issued by the "competent organism", referring to the Central Maritime Administration in accordance with the LPMM, art. 86.9 and to RD 1475/2000 art, 4c); the register and control of civil maritime personnel, the minimum composition of the facilities of civil ships with regard to safety, the determination of conditions of suitability, professionalism and the title to be a part of the facilities of civil Spanish ships notwithstanding the competences of the autonomous communities in matters of teaching and titles for handling recreational ships.

The Regulation may establish areas in which navigation is forbidden or restricted. These shall be conveniently buoyed and the authorizations will be precarious and subjected to the payment of a royalty.

As regards the measures for maritime security, navigation will not be permitted until the corresponding authorisation is obtained. Using this formula the regulation makes their beneficiaries responsible for the conditions of stability and safety of the vessels. This formula has little legal significance.

The responsibility incurred by the shipping companies or those who use the ships to sail is determined by the rules of Penal Law and Private Law and is not that of the administration in its role of policing but is that of carrying out precise controls and inspections so that the ship or vessel has a navigability that does not expose those sailing or third parties to risks greater than the normal one of sailing in waters,. On the other hand, the new regulation consecrates a real inhibition of the administrative authorities of the continental waters which apart from not responding to the previous situation, that of the OM of 19-7-1967, abrogated by Royal Decree 2473/1985, which required the application of the SOLAS (*International Convention for the Safety of Fishing Vessels*) and COLREG/72 (Agreement on the International Regulation to avoid collisions) to sailing on reservoirs, contrasts with the large intervention of the maritime Administration in matters of safety in navigation which guarantees that the rules of the LPMM are extended to this matter.

b) The management of the land-maritime public domain

Apart from what has been said in section 2 of this chapter "The relationships between the administrations, under the epigraph of inter administrative relationships in their articles 116, 117 and 118 of the LC and articles 209, 210 of the RDLC, they try to create bases for action for the administrations that have competences in this Law: "The administrations whose competences influence on the spatial area contemplated in this Law will adjust their reciprocal relationships to the duties of mutual information, collaboration, coordination and respect for them" (LC art. 116).

In processing all the territorial and urban approach that controls the coast, the competent body, for initial approval, shall, before said approval, send the content of the corresponding project to the State Administration for them to issue within a month a complete report on the suggestions and observations that they consider appropriate (Art. 117.1).

Once the processing of the plan or standards is concluded and immediately before final approval, the competent Administration will transfer the content of it to the State for it to decide on the matter within a month.

If the report is not favourable in aspects regarding its competence, a consulting period will be opened in order to reach an agreement. If the result of this agreement is substantially modified the plan or standards shall be subjected again to public information and audience of the entities that were obliged to intervene in their elaboration (LC art. 117.2).

The completion of the proceeding mentioned above will interrupt the calculation of the deadlines which are established in urban legislation for the approval of the organisation plans (LC art. 117.3)

STC 149/1991 article 117 clarifies that the approval of the corresponding instruments of organisation (or their revision or modification) is not always subordinated and in any case to the concurrence of both wishes, but only in those situations in which the unfavourable report of the state Administration refers to matters of their competence, that is, on a limited area, in the way we have already explained when analyzing article 112 a). Only in these cases will it be necessary to open a consulting period to reach an agreement. When it is not so, that is when the negative report refers to matters that in the opinion of the Autonomous Community exceed the competence of the state, the search for this agreement is not legally essential and consequently, the Administration that is competent for territorial and urban organisation may adopt the appropriate decision, notwithstanding, of course, the possibility that the state Administration may always offer itself to attack the decision on constitutional or legal grounds.

In order to guarantee the coherence of the action of the Public Administrations in coastal area, the State Administration is attributed the faculty of coordinating the activity of the Local Administration involved in the terms of art. 59 of the Law regulating the Local Regime Bases (LC art. 118). This was declared unconstitutional and consequently null by STC 149/1991 as it did not establish the conditions and limits of the coordination as well as the control formats that must be reserved by the General Courts for the Legislative Assembly of the Autonomous Community. These legally established conditions and limits in each case are naturally essential in order to preserve the local autonomy which is ignored through a general habilitation as that which this precept contains. To this we must add that according to STC 214/1989, art. 59 of the Law of Local Regime Bases is not contrary to the block of constitutionality, precisely because the possibility that is opened in it that the state or autonomic law attributes to the Government of the State or that of the Autonomous Community limited faculties of coordination subjected to the control of the Courts or the corresponding Parliament. This reference to the material sectors of state and autonomic competence, in so far as the precept does not establish any distinction, thus opens the way for the state Administration to take on the task of coordinating the action of the Local Corporations in matters, such as local organisation, which are the competence of the autonomous communities.

1.8 Territorial location of the ship

1.8.1 Territorial sea, internal waters, other maritime spaces

Considering the III Conference of the United Nations on the Law of the Sea, in a brief historical description at the beginning military, colonial and commercial interests prevailed in the Law of the Sea. In those initial moments only two clearly defined spaces were defined: the territorial sea and the open sea, governed by the principle of freedom.

Economic interests took on extraordinary importance as from 1945, and especially those relating to fishing and energy resources. This second phase of the Law of the Sea culminated with the adoption of the Geneva Conventions of 1958 (on the territorial sea and the adjoining area; on the open sea; on fishing and the preservation of the resources of the open sea; on the continental platform) within the I Conference of the United Nations on the Law of the Sea.

Political, economical, strategic and technological factors are those that determine an ample revision of the International Law of the Sea culminating in the III Conference of the United Nations on the Law of the Sea (hereinafter UNCLOS) which we do not doubt to classify as one of the most important international Treaties. Some even go so far as to say it is the most important after the Declaration of Rights.

A significant fact was that the great powers defended the freedom of the seas against the coastal third world states, which wish to preserve and have resources in as wide an area as possible, which would result as something like an exclusive economic area.

After heavy debates the last formula prospered in the 11th period of sessions with the adoption of the Convention, which was signed in Montego Bay (Jamaica) on 10th December 1982.

The territorial sea. The right of innocent passage

This is the area adjacent to the territory of the State which exercises full sovereignty in the terms of International Law. Sovereignty is also extended to the aerial space above the territorial sea, to the sea bed and to the corresponding subsoil. It has the important limitation of the innocent passage of the ships that carry the flags of other states. Innocent passage implies simply crossing the territorial sea and the penetration into internal waters and then leaving them and this points out that it must be quick and uninterrupted although stopping and anchoring is justified for certain causes.

The Conventions relates of a series of cases in which it considers that the passage is not innocent, cases that do not make up a *numerus clausus* as it includes any other activity that are not directly related to the innocent passage, emphasizing among other cases of non innocent passage section c) of art. 19.2; launching, receiving or embarking aircraft.

The extension of the territorial sea is established unilaterally by the coastal State. However this cannot exceed 12 marine miles. Today after long and heated debate we can state the 12 marine miles form part of customary law.

The territorial sea is measured from the baseline. The waters that remain inside this line are called internal waters in which the sovereignty of the state is fully developed. The baseline is the low-water line as indicated in the large scale marine maps officially recognized by the coastal State (art. 5) .The exceptions are, however, very numerous due to the special geographical circumstances such as those with deep notches and openings; or if there is a row of islands along the coastline and near to it, then the method of straight baselines may be used which, in general, do not appreciably from the general direction of the coastline and that the waters that remain on the land side have to be sufficiently connected to the land domain for these to be subjected to the regime of internal waters (art. 7).

In bays the reference is taken from the natural points of entrance which are joined with a straight baseline, always respecting:

- That the bay is not a mere inflection of the coastline, but a well defined and determined notch and in accordance with the rule known as semicircle,
- that the line that closes the bay cannot exceed 24 marine miles.

The exceptions to the low-water line are important and more so taking into account that it is the one that is used as a reference to measure not only the territorial sea but also other maritime zones, contiguous zone (CZ) and exclusive economic zone (EEZ). The tendency of these States is that of extending their sphere of sovereignty and therefore of its territorial sea, either by separating baselines from the coast as much as possible, or by using the resource of the historical bays or by tracing baselines on surfaces that far exceed what a bay is and, which, logically are not accepted by other countries.

When the coasts of two states are adjacent or are located opposite each other, the criterion of the average line and equidistance rules, exceptions apart.

Penal jurisdiction

We will consider three cases from the same perspective as that made by Professor Jose Antonio Pastor Ridruejo in his Course on International Public Law:

"In the case of simple passage through the territorial sea penal jurisdiction should not be exercised to detain a person or to carry out any investigation related to a crime committed on board during the passage, with the exceptions indicated in article 21.1.

"In the passage through territorial sea form internal waters, the coastal State may take any measure authorised by its laws to process to detain and/or investigate (27.2).

Article 27.1 specifically contemplates the exercise of the penal action when, among other things, it is necessary for the repression of the illegal traffic of narcotics or psychotropic substances."

If the crime is committed before the ship has entered the territorial sea, if it has come from a foreign port and does not penetrate internal waters, the coastal State may not, initially, make any arrests or diligences (27.5).

1.8.2 The contiguous zone (CZ)

In Spain, Law 27/92 of Ports of the State and the Merchant Navy is the one that gives a precise definition of the current contiguous zone in its article 71, fourth paragraph: The contiguous zone is that which extends form the outer limit of the territorial sea to 24 nautical miles starting form the base lines from which the width of the territorial sea is measured.

Additional Provision (DA) 20 of the same Law states that in the contiguous zone, the Government may adopt the control measures that are necessary to:

- Prevent breaches of the customs laws and regulations in the national territory or in the territorial sea relating to smuggling, taxes, immigration or health.
- Sanction said breaches.

We consider the inclusion of the rule in the Law of Ports of 1992 as positive, as it increased the possibilities of action of the State in such important and sensitive fields as the fight against drug trafficking and illegal immigration although it must be asked whether the Law in question is the most appropriate for the reestablishment of the Spanish contiguous zone; perhaps it would have been more appropriate to promote a specific law on the matter (Pastor Ridruejo). We totally agree with this opinion that we consider correct and hope that, not only the contiguous zone but also the rest of the maritime spaces are subjected to a specific legislative attention which it already needs, based on what was established in the III UNCLOS, regarding the different material competences of the spaces to which we are referring.

Staying with the III UNCLOS, the width of the contiguous zone is the 24 marine miles measured from the base line. In this area the coastal State may exercise the necessary control to prevent and sanction the breaches of their laws and regulations in customs, taxes, health and immigration committed in their territory or in their territorial sea (art. 33). This article coincides basically with the definition of the Law of Ports of 1992, which adds the term smuggling which we really do not understand. On the other hand, it must be said that in Spain a new jurisprudential trend has started to not differentiate the crimes of smuggling and those against public health; this should not make us lose the international perspective in which, we believe, undoubtedly there is room for the repression of drug trafficking in the laws and regulations of customs, taxes, etc. of article 33 of the III UNCLOS.

1.8.3 The exclusive economic zone (EEZ)

This has its origin in the pretensions of Chile, Ecuador and Peru which were not included in the Geneva coding. In this area the rights of sovereignty to explore, exploit, conserve and administer the natural living and non-living resources of the sea bed and of the subsoil apart from others of a financial nature correspond to the coastal State. It came to light in the III UNCLOS as a result of the demands of the third world coastal states in fishing matters.

A detailed reading of article 59 of UNCLOS. Its content is very subtle and was elaborated after heated debates: In the cases in which this Convention does not attribute rights or jurisdiction to the coastal State or to other states in the exclusive economic zone and a conflict arises between the interests of the coastal State and those of any other state or states, the conflict must be resolved based on equity and in the light of the corresponding circumstances, taking into account the respective importance that that the interests have for the parties, as well as for the community as a whole.

Any comment on the applicability of the article would be daring, but there is no doubt that it could offer other possibilities in a real case of action before the International Court of Justice of the Hague or in arbitration proceedings, as it would be difficult to suppose that an action in matters relating to drugs on a ship from a third country in the exclusive economic zone with positive results would find formal opposition from any state.

That the III UNCLOS should have gone further in matters relating to illegal trafficking and that a certain expansive tendency can be noted in the desire of some States to have protection in matters of drugs in the economic zone is a desire that we have in our cultural area. In any case as the exclusive economic zone would be a surface of around 3,000,000 square kilometres to watch over efficiently this would require an immense police effort if they were to be efficient and effective.

Perhaps the way to find efficient solutions would be to regulate international maritime traffic worldwide once and for all, giving more faculties to the State of the port and limiting those of the State of the flag, as the flag, on many occasions, does not even represent a real link with the sovereignty of the State. In today's globalised and interconnected world in which economical interests do not go hand in hand with the eighteenth century concept of sovereignty, it would not be a bad idea to reduce the degree of sovereignty of a ship, at least when the link is merely one of convenience or administrative and is based solely on the economic interests of the shipowners. While it is true that many shipowners are still serious businessmen it is also true that there is little control on certain fleets which, based on the false sovereignty of countries, lead to shameful interests.

1.9 Illegal trafficking of narcotics and psychotropic substances

Article 108 includes two sections relating to the matter. It must be said that the jurisdiction is exclusive to the State of the flag. In section 1 all states are obliged to cooperate to repress the illegal traffic of narcotic and psychotropic substances by ships ate high sea – once again we are referring to the exclusive economic zone – in violation of international conventions.

Section 2 states that every State that has reasonable motives to believe that a ship that carries its flag is dedicated to the illegal trafficking of narcotics or psychotropic substances may request the cooperation of other states to put an end to this trafficking.

1.10 Right to hot pursuit

The right to hot persecution is a very typical institution of the International Law of the Sea and is widely accepted in the international context. The right to hot pursuit is therefore an unquestionable habitual value. It is a dynamic institution and has been proven to be efficient; this means that we have been able to see recently how it has been incorporated into international treaties with trans frontier land effects.

We are going to analyse it from the point of view of jurisprudential interpretation of the Supreme Court (TS); specifically, from the point of view of the Sentence of the Penal Court of 20th November 1987. This sentence, apart form others not belonging to the case, agreed on the confiscation of the tobacco taken from the ships Ceder and Tessa. An appeal for cassation was lodged against the sentence and the TS declared that the appeal was denied.

Let's see a summary of the legal grounds: Besides the basic types of smuggling described in items three and four of article 11.1 of the Organic Law (OL) of 13th July 1982 (now abrogated), the need to protect the interest of the Public Administration by controlling the traffic of goods subject to Customs duties or of controlled or forbidden goods has inspired the creation of penal subtypes referring to maritime traffic, by using the procedure of sanctioning as perpetrated crimes those which in real penal terms are no more than preparatory or tentative.

Item 71 of article 11.1 refers to carrying or transporting controlled or forbidden goods on a Spanish ship or a foreign ship in any place within Spanish jurisdictional waters and item 81 typifies a double conduct: the shipment or transfer within Spanish jurisdictional waters and the clandestine shipment and transport of any kind of goods or effects in the circumstances described in article 23 of the

Geneva Convention on the High Seas of 29th April 1958. This subtype contemplates the clandestine shipment and transport in the circumstances of the right to pursuit. It must be said that the sentence that we are commenting contemplates the right to hot pursuit in the international regime of 1958. Today, once Spain has ratified the III Conference of the United Nations of the Law of the Sea, we shall analyse it from the perspective of article 111 of the Agreement, also known as that of Montego Bay. The sentence must also be placed in the context of the abrogated OL of 13th July of 1982 on Smuggling without there being substantial changes with the new OL 12/95 of 12th December.

Art. 111.-. Right to pursuit. "Pursuit of a foreign ship is permitted when the competent authorities of the coastal State have strong reasons to believe that the ship has committed a breach of the laws and regulations of that state. The pursuit must begin when the foreign ship or one of its launches is in internal waters, in the territorial sea or in the contiguous zone of the persecuting state and may only continue outside of the territorial sea or the contiguous zone as long as it has not been interrupted."

The article is much longer but now we are in the part that interests us. For the pursuit it is relevant and sufficient that one of the launches be in internal waters, in the territorial sea or in the contiguous zone. It is even applicable to the breaches committed in the exclusive economic zone with respect to the laws and regulations of the coastal State that are applicable in this maritime space (art. 111.2). In this way the ship may be outside, even beyond the exclusive economic zone.

If we intervene by pursuing the speed boat or the launch in the circumstances of the article that we are commenting, and if it does not stop and the rest of the circumstances are present, we may intervene all the ships that form a unit, or better said, that work together, no matter where they are, provided that the ship being pursued does not enter the territorial sea of the State of its flag or of a third country. Obviously, the coastal state must have strong reasons to believe that the ship has committed a breach of its laws or regulations. If it were stopped and detained outside of the territorial sea in circumstances that do not justify the right to pursuit, it will be compensated for all the harm or damage it has suffered because of the detention or capture (art. 111.8). This is a fact to be taken into account given the really high costs that can be generated by the unjustified detention of a ship, which means that the suspicion has to be evaluated before acting.

Returning to the sentence, if the type we commented is to arise there must be an existing interrelation between the conducts of the protagonists of the event, all of them sequences of a preconceived plan and developed in perfectly synchronised time and space which can accept the division of the fact in several conducts. The sentence of the Supreme Court says that there was a transfer at high sea of boxes of tobacco from the merchant ship Tessa to the merchant ship Ceder. The latter is smaller and functioned as a bridge ship or "launch" and also another transfer of tobacco, also in international waters, from the Ceder to thirteen speed boats form the Galician coast which then returned there and just when they entered Spanish jurisdictional waters sailing towards the Ria de Arosa, the persecution of the protagonists of the operation began; the Marine frigate on the Tessa and a navy patrol ship on the Ceder and the auxiliary launch on the speed boats. They managed to stop and detain the first two with a large amount of tobacco on the Tessa and none on the Ceder as it was thrown overboard during the persecution. The speed boats with the help of their powerful motors managed to get away and transfer their load within jurisdictional waters to smaller boats (fishing boats, phantom). Nine boxes were captured on one of them.

The sentence goes on to say that Spanish penal law is subject to the principle of territoriality and respects the principle of the freedom of the seas, with the exception in the right to hot and extraterritorial pursuit.

As these facts are assumed in the legal rule the breach of the Spanish laws by the speed boats is clear. This legitimised the ships and aircraft of the Navy and the Fiscal Control to pursuit and detain the ships that formed a group or team with the speed boats in the open sea with no legal grounds to distinguish the hypothesis of self-propelled boats which form part of the fleet with the "mother" ship (in the Convention of 1982: passing the limit of jurisdictional waters) and smaller launches or ships that come to be supplied by the mother ship in accordance with a preconceived plan, designed together and coordinated in time and space as in both cases the boats "work as a team using the mother ship" to obtain supplies of the goods or effects, which presupposes the right to pursuit in external waters.

Paragraph 41 of article 111 of the III Conference of the United Nations on the Law of the Sea says: *"The pursuit is not considered as started until the pursuing ship has checked with the practical means available to it that the ship it is going to pursue or one of its launches or other ships that work together using the ship to be pursued as a mother ship is inside the limits of the territorial sea, in the contiguous zone, in the exclusive economic zone or on the continental shelf. The pursuit may not begin until a visual or audio signal to stop has been sent from a distance that makes it possible for the foreign ship to see or hear it."*

Paragraph 51 of the same article says: *"The right to pursuit may only be exercised by war ships or military aircraft, or by the ships or aircraft that have clear signs and are identifiable as ships or aircraft at the service of the government and which is duly authorised."*

It must be pointed out that in the case considered the right to hot pursuit has and has had the purpose of extending the Spanish jurisdiction to international waters.

Regarding what has been said to now, we can specify that the breach is caused when the order to stop is ignored and this leads to the hot pursuit. It may continue unto the ship enters the territorial sea or internal waters or those of another country. That is to say that in the sovereign waters pursuit is not possible. If the pursuit of one of the launches or speed boats, is initiated, in reality that of the mother ship or a launch should be started at the same time and without interruptions.

Let us take an example of a case of tobacco smuggling in which the pursuit of the launch or the speed boat is initiated in internal waters or territorial sea. When this boat is detained the pursuit of the launch or merchant ship then begins. This would not be legal. It would be necessary to start the pursuit at the same time. This is what is being done and the courts accept it. It would, to put it bluntly, a domino effect pursuit.

The pursuit may be made by an aircraft – it would be convenient if this were so – which would guarantee the speed and immediacy of the pursuit and besides would be the ideal means for communicating to the mother ship, which normally navigates in open waters, the order to stop and then to check that it does it. It is also useful to prefabricate the proof in audio and video recordings that would be useful and efficient in a court.

Art. 111.6b) "The aircraft that has given the order to stop shall actively continue the pursuit of the ship until a ship or another aircraft of the coastal State, called by it, arrives and continues, unless the aircraft can detain the ship itself. In order to justify detaining a ship outside of the territorial sea it is not sufficient for the aircraft to discover it committing a breach, or to have suspicions that it has done so. If it has not given it the order to stop and has not initiated the pursuit or other aircraft or ships that continue the pursuit without interruption have done so."

The right to hot pursuit is to be found in the sovereign right that it covers. For our purposes it may be initiated when the ship or one of its launches or others coordinated with it penetrate in the contiguous zone, territorial sea or internal waters.

It is nothing new that people question whether the area of protection should be extended for the purpose of illicit traffic. Different authors and especially British ones have started to admit that based on the existence of a right to self-defence that allows a State to adopt limited measures of protection when a foreign ship at high sea carries out activities that create a certain or imminent danger for safety.

Relating to the need to repress illicit traffic, to extending at an international level, even up to 200 marine miles, the possibility of action of the coastal State, this would mean that Spain would have the possibility of action on a surface of approximately 3,000,000 square kilometres. This measure would not be very efficient without a huge policing fleet for surveillance. Of what there is no doubt is that in recent time the maritime areas are in a trend of expansion and that the coastal state exert more and more pressure in the defence of their interests for the creation of new areas and the extension of the existing ones. For the time being, it is probably wiser to specify more and to consolidate the mentioned self-defence at an international level, implement the advances in the conventional right of our area and to be able to involve the countries of origin of the illicit traffic by helping them economically to free them from the large mafia organisations that control their countries.

In recent years there has been a notable increase in international treaties and agreements on the most complex matters and in particular in our cultural area. The matter at hand is not foreign to this phenomenon. At present there are many people who defend that it is necessary to worry much more about their effective compliance than about the conclusion of new agreements.

Today there are more than one hundred and ten agreements which in the area of Public and Private International Law refer in some way to the activities related to the sea, the ships, commercial, sporting, responsibility and activity or of another nature.

This production of regulations which has accelerated in more recent dates, should make us reflect and come to the same conclusion as many of those who are recognized scholars in the matter. The conclusion is as the following:

We are at a point in which it is worthwhile stopping the production of legislation or slowing it completely down and completing, developing, distributing, implementing the mechanisms that make it possible to fulfil what is legislated or recommended.

1.11 Crimes against public health, seizures and confiscation

Crimes against public health: Article 368 of the Penal Code punishes those who "carry out acts of cultivating, elaborating or trafficking, or in any other way promote, favour or facilitate the illegal consumption of toxic drugs, narcotics or psychotropic substances, or who possess them for that purpose."

It is worth mentioning that the prison sentences will be from three to nine years and the fine will amount to three times the value of the drugs involved in the crime but only if they are product drugs which cause serious harm to one's health and one to three years and a fine of double the value in other cases.

As hashish is in the second group and the penalties are of little significance it seems that it is becoming more worthwhile from a penal point of view to transport a large quantity of hashish than a small one of heroine or cocaine because legally hashish is considered not to cause serious damage to our health. Therefore in penal terms it is much more profitable than the drugs that some call hard drugs. To organise a large shipment of hashish and unload it in Spain would cost no more than six years in prison.

The most typical case and indeed the most interesting one is that which contemplates the types of crimes against public health and specifically, those of article 374 of the Penal Code.

11.- " Unless they belong to good faith third parties that are not responsible for the crime, the ships and any assets or items of any nature that have been used as an instrument to commit any of the crimes described in the previous articles will be confiscated......

21.- In order to guarantee the effectiveness of the confiscation, the goods, effects r instruments that the previous paragraph refers to may be apprehended and deposited by the legal authority from the very first moment. Said authority may also agree that, with the appropriate guarantees for their conservation and while the process lasts, the assets, effects or instruments of licit trade may be used provisionally by the Legal Police in charge or repressing the illegal trafficking of drugs.

31.- The goods, effects and instruments that are confiscated in a sentence will be awarded to the State."

There is the possibility of ships being confiscated both preventively (while the process lasts) and definitively.

The concept of ship for the purpose of this case is ambiguous and requires other classifications. We can find this in several laws and each one defines it according to specific ends[1]. The Penal Code puts it in the context of the purpose for which it is used and contemplates it as a means or instrument for committing a crime of drug trafficking, normally when it is used as a means of transport which is a normal circumstance as the drugs are very often transported from high sea (producing countries).

As for launches, which have already been mentioned, it is obvious that they are not ships in the general sense of the word but they are for the purpose of the Code and in specific cases they in the broad sense of the word.

---

[1] Article 8.2 of the LPMM defines the civil ship as "any boat, platform or floating artefact, with or without movement, which is apt for sailing and not subject to the service of national defence."
Paragraph 3 of the same article understands a merchant ship as being any civil ship used fro navigation with a commercial purpose, excluding those used for fishing. .
Article 146 of the Regulation of the Merchant Register of 1956, covering the hollow left by the Code of Commerce states that, for the purpose of the Code of Commerce and this Regulation, ships will be not only those boats used for piloting or high sea sailing but also floating dikes, pontoons, dredgers and any other floating apparatus used or which may be used for services to the industry or sea or river trade."

1.12 The Constitution and distribution of competences

As established in article 149 of the Constitution regarding the matter at hand, the State has exclusive competence in the following matters:

- Immigration, emigration, admission of foreigners and the right to asylum.
- International relations.
- Customs and duties
- Foreign trade
- External health
- Sea fishing, notwithstanding the competences attributed in the sector to regional governments
- Merchant navy and flagging ships
- Illumination of coasts and maritime signals
- Ports of general interest
- Underwater cables and radio-communication
- Public safety, notwithstanding the possibility of the creation of policies by the Autonomous Communities

Article 148 attributes, among other matters, the possibility of the Autonomous Communities assuming competences:

- Ports of refuge, sports harbours, and in general, those that do not develop commercial functions
- Fishing in internal waters, shell-fishing and aquaculture

1.13 Organic law on smuggling

Until recently smuggling was not contemplated as a crime in many legislations of nearby countries but not in ours. Even today many jurists and part of the doctrine question its criminal nature. Unless states that wish to respond in no uncertain terms to the serious threats of the introduction of goods without taxing them so as to compete on equal terms with home made products, it is more often seen in the administrative field and this is really where it belongs, which means that the mere distinction as a legislative technique between the crime and the administrative breach is the economical one, with criteria that are today at 1 and 3 million as the difference between the administrative breach and the crime.

On the other hand, it has been maintained and still is, as a special legislation outside the Penal Code.

A radical change came about with the promulgation of the new Penal Code in 1995. When smuggling was considered as toxic drugs or narcotics and still is in the Organic Law (LO) on Smuggling there was an ideal competition between smuggling and the crime against public health and both breaches were penalized and sanctioned in the sentences. The doctrine of the Supreme Court is that such an aggravation of one same action is not right as it is understood that the penalties of the Penal Code already cover possible crimes of smuggling, or at least that is the intention of the legislator.

If what is being understood is the idea that smuggling drugs is a crime against public health and is not virtually considered as smuggling in Spain, this could lead to the reinterpretation of certain agreements within our country as many of them were signed on previous concepts. We will have to watch the evolution of what has hardly been expressed here. However, the Agreements usually define the terms for their own purposes and virtualities which means that the problem will not be serious.

1.14 The model of maritime police

Since the introduction of LO 2/86, of 13th March, on Security Corps and Forces, in development of article 104 of the CE which entrusts the Security Corps and Forces with the mission of protecting the free exercise of rights and liberties and of guaranteeing public safety and as this LO states in article 11.2b that in performing its functions the Civil Guard has full competence in the territorial sea, as well as stating in article 12.1 that the Civil Guard is also entrusted with the custody of land communication, coasts, frontiers, ports, airports and centres and installations whose interest so requires, the ministries, organisms and institutions related with the sea have been discussing not only the manner and means that were required to carry out these missions but also to which extent and in which matters these competences were going to be exercised and which model of maritime police should be implemented.

At the same time other changes came about and what are today harbour masters (previously marine commanders) fall in the scope of competences of the Ministry of Defence as another responsibility of our Navy. The first intention was to free the Spanish Navy from competences that were not strictly military. Since then many things have moved around the competences and organisms related with the sea, mainly with the Law of Ports and Merchant Navy of 1992 which coincided with two great events that would take place that year: the Olympic Games in Barcelona and the Universal Exhibition in Seville.

These and other circumstances which are not related meant that Royal Decree 247/1991, of 22nd February, regulated the Maritime Service of the Civil Guard and that at that moment arose the need for material and human resources to be able to respond to the functions given them, which were mainly:

- Making sure the laws are complied with.
- Helping and protecting people and guaranteeing the preservation and protection of any assets that are in danger.
- Watching over and protecting building and public installations that require it
- Preventing criminal acts from being committed, etc.

In short, carrying out the functions of judicial, administrative, fiscal, governmental, public order police, etc. as well as those military functions entrusted to them, missions that the RD that created the Civil Guard says will be carried out *"to the outer part of the territorial sea determined in current legislation and, exceptionally, outside the territorial se in accordance with the stipulations of current international treaties."* Thus, the functions of the integral marine police were assumed by the Civil Guard and the first patrols were seen in Barcelona and Seville in the events mentioned above. However, one thing is to award competences by law and another is to create a maritime police force form nothing and overnight.

Nowadays the Civil Guard has fifteen SMP and twenty-six Patrollers covering almost 8,000 km of coastline in Spain. The human and material resources are scarce in comparison with the other European countries around us and for the tasks they have but, on this point, we must indicate that the deployment of the Maritime Service of the Civil Guard was initiated barely six years ago and has not yet concluded and the idea is to create al least one SMP per coastal province and then to move on to other high sea naval patrols which will lead to a greater autonomy in their use and an effective presence, not only in the territorial sea, but also in all the other spaces in which Spain exercises sovereign rights such as the Contiguous Zone and the Exclusive Economic Zone, all of which will depend on the budgetary allowances in coming years and the priorities that are defined, such as the already announced intention for the civil Guard to exercise a stricter control in the Strait of Gibraltar.

1.14.1 Towards an integrated model of maritime police

Spain has opted for a complex model of very varied and atomised competences. Since 1992 when the Maritime Service of the Civil Guard was introduced, this body has assumed only the following police competences, though they do it in an integral manner:

- Judicial police
- Administrative police
- Public order police

They share competences in fishing matters:

- MAPA Inspections. External waters
- Regional Inspections. Internal waters

With the fiscal police

- The share competence with the SVA

The Civil Guard must arbitrate the following aspects in a coordinated model:

- Surveillance and safety of ports as established in article 12 of Organic Law 2/86, of 13.03, on State Security Corps and Forces
- Maritime service
- Fiscal service
- Judicial police service with technical means adapted to marine characteristics.
- Air service with airplanes and helicopters with sufficient autonomy. They may assume SAR missions exclusively.

Perhaps the solution lies in a management of the Civil Guard that is capable of coordinating the different aspects mentioned if finally integration is not opted for.

But one thing is that the law attributes responsibilities and another very different thing is that they have the human and material resources to be able to carry out the competences with a certain efficiency and effectiveness. The Maritime Service of the Civil Guard must be given in coming years resources for the air, qualified personnel and high sea patrols to carry out their tasks in the marine environment in a minimally efficient manner.

1.15 The immediate future of the maritime service of the Civil Guard. Plans

1.15.1 From the unification of competences

Diverse competences in harbour masters, environmental authorities, port authorities, fishing authorities at a national and regional level, different polices, etc. that for the moment mean that the measures of coordination are so weak that they are more like personal impulses than a designed integrated model of maritime control that has become so necessary and ever more so in the matters that are the subject of this study.

1.15.2 From coordination

Nowadays carrying out the competence at sea, in the different areas, is an exercise of good faith on behalf of all those that are involved in resolving the problem that the sea presents.
It is obvious that a policy must be developed to analyse the risks and threats and can be used to establish the proportionate means of response.

1.16 Spreading of competences

1.16.1 Ministry of Defence

Military and defence of the territory competences and those of Law 60/62 in the matters of aid, rescue, findings and maritime extractions. These are residual competences which are pending development to be transferred to the Ministry of Development.

Our Navy also has collaboration agreements with the Ministry of Agriculture, Fishing and Food (MAPA) for the control of the high sea and community fleet. For this purpose, it has two ships from the Ministry which is responsible for maintaining the ships while the Navy provides the crews.

1.16.2 Ministry of Development

General Directorate of the Merchant Navy:

- Harbour masters
- Inspection of ships

State Society of Maritime Rescue and Safety
General Directorate of Telecommunications

Public entity Ports of the State in ports of national interest:

- Port Authorities
- Janitors

1.16.3 Ministry of the Interior

General Directorate of the Civil Guard: several specialities related to the sea which are already under way and coordinated among each other.

Contamination: Maritime service from ships and nature protection service for waste from the land.

Judicial, administrative, public order police, etc., of the territorial sea and exceptionally in other spaces: maritime service and teams of judicial police.

Surveillance from the air: helicopter units. These are basically inadequate helicopter and have little autonomy for sea crossings and surveillances.

Fiscal and drug investigation: fiscal units and groups.

National Police Force: With material competence in narcotics and immigration but without spatial competence in the territorial sea. Help has been given in maritime narcotic operations in the SVA air and sea operations. Together they have carried out important services. This is perhaps because the Civil Guard does not have high sea ships.

1.16.4 Ministry of the Treasury

Customs Surveillance Service: Until the Government opted for a sea police model and awarded these competences to the Civil Guard, the only public service, apart from the Navy that had naval resources was the Customs Surveillance Service (SVA). This service, which has some of the most important naval resources, which at the moment are much superior to those of the Maritime Service of the Civil Guard also has some helicopters and airplanes. Within the naval resources, worthy of mention is a high sea patrol ship which has sufficient capacity and autonomy for transatlantic sailing.

Their competences are basically in matters of smuggling and are exercised both on land and in the sea. Its philosophy of use is to remain on standby and act specifically when there is information o a specific operation. Their ships carry out few preventive missions.

Recently this service which has been questioned by various forums and courts, seems to be shrouded in a certain crisis with respect to the future and maybe the philosophy and its missions should be arbitrated and profiled. There are especially opposing opinions regarding their nature as a judicial police, which many argue about.

1.16.5 Ministry of Agriculture, Fishing and Food (MAPA)

It carries out the inspections of fishing boats outside internal waters and, if they are Spanish, anywhere in international waters. The competences in fishing matters correspond to the State outside the base lines or the straight base lines.

For this purpose the Exclusive Economic Zone has two ships governed by the Spanish Navy. A third ship is being built and will be awarded to and piloted by the Civil Guard. This is based on collaboration agreements.

It has its own body of inspectors to exercise these competences with the specific collaboration of the Navy and the Civil Guard that have been mentioned. The Civil Guard also exercises these competences through the SM.

1.16.6 Autonomous communities

These have exclusive competence in fishing in internal waters, shell-fishing and aquaculture in all areas
Development legislation in matters relating to the fishing sector.

They have their own inspectors with the competences of administrative police in this matter.

Competence in matters of sports harbours, fishing and commercial ports that are not of national interest. Recently competences in the management of ports of national interest have been transferred.

Competence in environmental matters.

They have their own harbour guards.

1.17 Smuggling

1.17.1 Customs surveillance service

As the dependency known as DAVA (Department of Customs Surveillance) has recently been changed this depends on Customs and has the following functions attributed by RD:

Discovery, persecution and repression in all national territory, jurisdictional waters and Spanish air space, of smuggling acts and breaches; to this effect and because of the legal consideration that the service has, it shall exercise the functions of maritime, air and land surveillance that are intended for this purpose.

Maritime surveillance will be carried out in accordance with RD 1002/61:

Actions in those inspection, investigation and control tasks that are entrusted by the Customs inspection services.

Participation in investigation, surveillance and control missions in matters relating to special taxes.

Collaboration with the competent Bodies in the investigation and discovery of infractions in change control.

Any other task that may be assigned by the Ministry of the Treasury.

The recent deployment of the Civil Guard of the Sea represents a certain sensitivity in the Customs Surveillance Service which is currently so due to the lack of maritime police in recent times. Although it was for fiscal purposes, as there was no other, they were supporting the land police and were the only serious naval police at sea. Their resources are far superior to the Maritime Service of the Civil Guard and are irreplaceable today.

Despite the deployment of resources, the philosophy of the service does not support the idea of a permanent presence and the majority of the ships are waiting for specific actions to go to sea. In other countries around us the customs services act as rescue support in the absence of other resources.

Although it is true that the customs services in the developed world have for a long time been the only police in the marine environment, these were the threats to which a response had to be made. Until very recently, large scale smuggling, drug trafficking and illegal immigration were lesser problems with little significance. Nowadays the police forces of the world feel the need to address the sea because the threats to which we are referring come from it and their intention is to intercept or prevent them as soon as possible and before they reach land. Thus, in the light of the problems we are dealing with, the sea is the first frontier that must present a serious filter for organised delinquency when the fiscal phenomenon has been exceeded.

Nowadays, drug trafficking, smuggling beyond the mere concept of customs and illegal immigration demand police responses that require the creation of police services which, taking advantage of the experiences of the customs services that can be used and of their unquestionable specific collaborations that give due response to the defence needs of modern societies in these areas which have at present reached alarming levels and which no serious country can ignore if it wishes to address the criminal phenomenon of the coming millennium.

1.17.2 Civil Guard

The Civil Guard is the Official State Customs Clearance and the police that we find in the ports and airports carrying out these functions in close collaboration with the Customs administrations.

The regulation that governs these relationships is very obsolete and the time has come for the Ministry of the Interior and the Treasury to give a clear response and to establish the duties that the Civil Guard must assume as Official Customs Clearance in a changing world and in which these control figures were designed for cross frontier traffic which at present is practically free of control.

1.17.3 Rescue

In accordance with article 90 of the LPMM of 1992 the objectives of the State Society of Maritime Rescue and Safety are:

- To provide services in maritime search and rescue
- Control and helping with maritime traffic
- Preventing and fighting against contamination in the marine environment, in towing and auxiliary vessels

It is paradoxical that a society with these objectives which has such important economic resources, cannot take on functions of public order. At present, these public resources, managed privately, are the best resources that are available at sea.

We are convinced that among these objectives should be that of controlling certain illicit traffic and of collaborating with the State Security Forces from their areas. It will be necessary to reread article 111 of the LPMM.

Art. 111. *"Prohibition of illicit activities and forbidden traffic. In order to prevent illicit activities being carried out or any forbidden traffic from being exercised, the Government may prevent, restrict or condition the navigation of certain categories of civil vessels in internal waters, the territorial sea or the contiguous area."*

1.17.4 Authorities

The maritime authority shall exercise the following functions among others:

- Authorising or prohibiting the entrance and departure of ships in waters located in areas in which Spain exercises sovereignty, sovereign rights or jurisdiction as well as dispatching ships.

The determination for reasons of maritime safety of anchoring and manoeuvring areas in waters located within sovereign areas.

- It is curious that when the IMO is concerned about the control functions of certain crews and their responsibility regarding certain potentially illicit traffics, the way of providing services of the harbour masters does not contemplate the duty of collaborating and supplying these data nor indeed of even obtaining them. What use is it to have lists of passengers or crews if it not mandatory to transmit the data to the organisms in charge of immigration in Spain?

1.17.5 Control of crews

For the purpose of immigration, but also applicable to smuggling and small scale drug trafficking it can be said that there is nothing reasonably organised in the control of the crews that reach a port, coasts or anchoring points in Spain, or on ships that enter certain areas in distress. The competences are so varied and so diversely distributed that the lists of crew members may or may not be presented to the Harbour Master, that the consignors may or may not give the list to the National Police Force which is responsible for immigration, that generally nobody checks the lists of crews that arrive in Spain and much less the departure of ships from our ports regardless of where in the world they are from, it is no wonder that crew members "drop off" the lists in our ports from time to time. There are cases and several of them.

Other countries with similar problems of massive illegal immigration establish serious controls on crews on their arrival at port and depending on the nationalities and origins, prohibit certain crew members from leaving the ships. Occasionally ships are checked before leaving the port to check on all the crew members.

Crew members abandoning ship in our ports is not a sporadic occurrence where there is an organised illegal immigration under the cover of appearing on the list of crew members. This selective immigration, which we believe continues today, is usually organised by someone responsible for the ship and is not very frequent.

It would not be a bad idea to document ships with foreign crews, both upon arrival and at their departure, for those crews where certain risk factors could be sensed:

- Origin of the crews, type of traffic, country of origin
- Substandarity of ships, crews and fleets.

Leaving the ship should require a control in the form of a written and individualised authorisation and those ships which have had similar events in the past, apart form the heavy economical sanctions that should be inferred upon them, would not obtain permits for a certain time. This would undoubtedly act as a preventive element and would oblige shipowners and charterers to exercise a more serious control on their crews.

1.17.6 Inspection of ships

The inspection of ships is in the hands of the Merchant Navy, at least with respect to the international commitments acquired, and the most significant for us is the one known as the *Memorandum of París*. This inspection, which is carried out on approximately 30% of the ships that come to Spanish and European ports is, in our opinion, the starting point for what in the future has to be the transition of control of the flag State to that of the port State. The concept of sovereignty, which has been used until recently will undoubtedly enter a crisis, with reference at least to the international statute of the ship.

Liberalisation and the consequent transfer of responsibilities to private hands are starting to appear in inspections. The large shipping companies (Lloyd's R, Bureau Veritas, RINA) are beginning to acquire protagonism in these sectors in different but important ways.

The fleets of the great world powers are losing their flags though only apparently so and if shipowners, charterers, insurers and capitals belonging to the first world wish to maintain a minimum of quality in the safety of the ships and a certain qualification and social commitment with the crews, it is time to make a move in favour of the control of the Port State on the flags, especially those known by everyone as convenience flags which do not respect the minimums of quality.

The inspections may be a legal resource in the hands of the authorities of the country of the port to obtain data and information on possible threats such as the one in hand. It is true that very often the only visit to a foreign ship, apart from the protocol visit of the fiscal clearance is that of the MOU Inspector.

1.17.7 Port authorities

The port sector is going through an important management crisis. Many things have changed in a short period of time. The division between ports of national interest and of autonomous communities has in part lost its subsidence, regardless of what our Constitution sys to the effect.

Recent legislative modifications have put the management of the ports of national interest into the hands of the Autonomous Communities and have also left them in the situation, hopefully positive, of free competition which will be brutal and with unforeseeable consequences among neighbouring ports. It must be said though that this has come about at a moment in which the certain structural crises are being overcome and the increase in loads as a result of the increasing standard of living of certain societies seems to have been relaunched.

The port authorities are in a crisis situation in the previous conditions and in a broader sense the port organisation in the current model.

Both private and public security are questioned in port areas as a result of the liberalisation of transits and of the breakdown of levies in our market. Commercial dynamics have greatly exceeded the security response and there is no doubt that all the interests present must be brought together and involve the port authorities in questions relating to security. These must be in a situation to mange security with a commercial profitability notwithstanding the traffic of the security itself. I short, security must be capable of being commercially operative and not hinder commercial traffic beyond reason. Current technical resources must be used boldly for this purpose.

The security of private cargos has to be in private hands but with all the necessary guarantees to avoid breaking the law. Private security will have to be in a situation to collaborate efficiently with the security forces. Private security must take the step from the simple defence of private property to guaranteeing the legality and compliance with certain legal and regulatory requisites of those who provide it. All of this, naturally, under the control of the security forces.

The law of ports and its recent reform which obliges them to compete in market conditions to be competitive and profitable has brought them close to business operation, which will not be easy, given that to date it was practically a supplier of infrastructures and that they were more technical than commercial. The trend observed now is that there is an excess of engineers and a lack of efficient managers.

The private security devices of the various companies that are installed inside the port have to be organised to guarantee the volume of the cargos. It has not yet been done but the security of the traffic has to be guaranteed at other different levels.

1.18 Other applications of the Spanish legal area

Illegal immigration, article 11 and 36 of Organic Law 7/85 and article 75, 76 of Royal Decree 1119/86. Except in the case of asylees crossing unauthorised frontiers is sanctioned by being sent back to the country of origin: the rest of the breaches are sanctioned with fines of 500,000 to 700,000 pesetas.

Drugs, articles, 344 and 344 bis of the penal code. The differentiation in several sentences on hard and soft drugs reduces the gravity of the crime.

Smuggling: Organic Law 12/95 and Royal Decree 1649/98. Quantities below 3,000,000 pesetas are considered as administrative breaches, 1,000,000 in the case of tobacco, and the penalty is a fine of no more than 300% the quantity confiscated, with a minimum of 100,000 pesetas.

1.18.1 Malfunctions of the executive area

- Control of high speed boats. Exclusively organisational decree
- Diversity of administrations intervening in the problem:
    - Civil Guard – Ministry of the Interior
    - National Police Force – Ministry of the Interior
    - Customs Surveillance Service – Ministry of the Treasury
    - General Directorate of the Merchant Navy– Ministry of Development
- Lack of coordination in the judicial, administrative, police, customs information at a national and European level
- Port security is not implemented or organised at an integrated level. Sports harbours in the hands of autonomous communities usually contract private security. Commercial and fishing ports have no legislation regarding port policing, law 27/92 and 6/97.
- Lack of specific training in integrated maritime security.
- Inexistence of the necessary coordination between maritime agents and public and private security.
- Little control of containers in closed areas due to the limited control by the customs authorities.

1.18.2 Official information

Most of it is disperse: without wishing to extend the matter we refer to the Trade Register in

- Ship sales contracts
- Naval properties and mortgages

To the treasury:

- Imports
- Exports
- SVA
- Taxing and port areas: customs documents
- Acts breaching the law on smuggling
- Special taxes
- Temporary and permanent imports

National Fishing: state competence of the Ministry of Agriculture, Fishing and Food:

- External waters
- Basic legislation governing the fishing sector

Regional fishing, competence of the Fishing departments:

- Internal waters
- Shell-fishing and aquaculture
- Development of the fishing sector

Merchant navy:

- Dispatching and administrative control of ships
- Sanctioning regime
- Administrative records: lists
- Ship inspections

The recent trend in Europe is towards privatisation and we already have directives in this sense for the classification societies.

1.19 Reflections on the duties of the DGMM and SASEMAR

As already mentioned, in Spain the two pillars of maritime security are generally formed by the General Directorate of the Merchant Navy (DGMM) reporting to the Ministry of Transport and Energy and by the State Society of Maritime Security ad Contamination (SASEMAR),

The former is responsible for administrative maritime management through the harbour masters located in each port. At the head of this entity is the harbour captain supported by an infrastructure of human and equipment resources and although they do not have an excess of either, may perform the function of control and inspection of the standards relating to the security of the ships. However, as shown during the MARSEC 2 Workshop, only sanctioning functions intervene without using the synergy that could be developed in responsibilities of collaboration and cooperation with the State security forces in the area of the delinquency that uses the sea for its criminal acts.

The possible collaboration procedures of the DGMM with the Police forces, Civil Guard, Customs and any other must undergo a period of trial and reflections to achieve the maximum use and efficiency of the management. We do not believe that this is the place to structure ties, relationships and agreements which have to be articulated at a governmental or institutional level, but whatever the method used, it will surely lead to an important step in the fight against crimes and criminal organisations which still operate in the maritime area.

SASEMAR is responsible, among other things, for the control of maritime traffic through an important network of control towers installed in ports and points of intense maritime traffic which are equipped with modern technology in the positioning and monitoring of ships (RADAR, ARPA, communications, goniometers, etc.) and which should, in our opinion, be part of a possible network of remote stations that could control any type of ship that approaches our coasts, many of which need not be done at a great distance but simply at a close distance, before the disembarking of illegal immigrants, narcotics and smuggled good and alerting the State security forces that are nearest the place,

It is obvious that the two functions mentioned for the DGMM and SASEMAR would cover the land and maritime part in which the constant factor is the ship or vessel, a little known element for land authorities in the same way that maritime authorities do not know the land elements. We believe that in a modern State we cannot do without supports, especially the two existing ones to achieve the preventive objectives in the fight against all types of crime. The responsibilities and competences should not be a cause for discrepancy between the two areas. With special reference to the maritime part, they must do their duty in the inspection and control of ships, SASEMAR on those in movement and DGMM for those stationed in ports (docked or anchored) in compliance with the stipulations of international entities, including IMO, and consisting mainly of the collaboration in alerting the corresponding police authority of irregularities.

1.20 Coastal surveillance in European countries

The responsibility of the surveillance of the coastal waters varies from country to country and is sometimes even shared by marine units of Customs and Coast Guards, the Navy or local police forces, while air support also comes from a variety of security forces.

The coastal surveillance vessels are of varying size and even the scope and patrolling distance of the interception vessels is highly varied which means that the costs generated in the surveillance of the coastal areas cover a wide span. For a risk level, the equipment deployed should reflect the levels of needs at the scenario; thus, if fishing boats are the main problem, more than speed it will be the navigating conditions that will determine the type of vessel needed. On the other hand drug traffickers can obtain and use the most powerful high speed vessels available and the Customs ships must be able to catch them in the case of having to intercept them.

In ideal circumstances, the marine and air units will work together. Current surveillance of suspicious targets is visual, or on radar screens and sending ships to intercept.

Italy's very long coast line provides a huge challenge in terms of police surveillance and the *Guardia di Finanza* (Customs) has a large fleet of ships, the latest of which is the Giorgio Zara, which is 51 metres long and was built in the Fincantieri Muggiano shipyard.

Following the reunification of Germany, the COSAT Guard was formed by joining the Ship Administrations, Frontier Police, Customs Service and fishing authorities. The new organisation has 28 patrol ships and a large number of helicopters at their disposal.

Although there are several high speed interception vessels of different designs at the disposal of the police that control the coastal waters, most of them have the disadvantage of not being very manoeuvrable at high speed. Some of them have bee adapted from ocean racing vessels capable of reaching speeds of 60 knots or more.

1.21 Other regulations

The possible participation of members of private security companies in interventions, either from the beginning or at a later stage, in collaboration with the other intervening forces, makes it possible to quote other regulation available for consideration and analysis when appropriate, mainly in the coincidence of several organisations in the event.

The most directly related extracts to the matter of this study are:

Order of 23rd April 1997 by which certain aspects are specified in terms of security companies in compliance with the law and regulation on private security.

Law 23/1992 of 30th July, on Private Security, and its Regulation entrust the Ministry of the Interior with the specification of certain aspects related to security companies.

The current order develops requisites of a technical nature that are required for the authorisation of private companies, such as the security measures of the shipowners, the common security system for all of them and the specific systems for those dedicated to the deposit, custody and treatment of coins and notes, title values and valuable and dangerous objects: the characteristics of vaults, of explosives deposits, of the vehicles used for transporting funds, values and valuable objects and of the vehicles used for transporting explosives and metal cartridges and the security system and technical requisites of the alarm centres.

The regulations that govern the operations of the security companies, among which is the limit for which the transport of money must be in armoured vehicles, the protection of said transport and that of other vehicles and the characteristics of the systems that are to be connected to the alarm centres are also complemented in order to check the reality of the attack or intrusion from the central unit.

In order to be able to carry out their activities, the security companies must request their authorisation by registering with the corresponding Register, through an application sent to the General Directorate of the Police, General Commissionaire of Public Safety or, if the case may be, to the corresponding entity of the autonomous community that has competences for the protection of people and goods and for maintaining public order, in accordance with the statutes of autonomy, and the stipulations of Organic Law 2/9186, of 13th March on Security Corps and Forces, when they have their registered office in the autonomous community and their scope of action is limited to it.

In their main offices and in the delegations, the security companies will have a physical and electronic security system comprising, at least:

- Reinforced armoured access door or doors, with security locks and magnetic contacts with at least average power.
- Windows or spaces protected with fixed solid or embedded grids, in accordance with UNE standard 108-142
- Volumetric protection or image capturing and recording equipment or systems in the interior and exterior respectively
- Control unit and connection with an alarm centre

1. The armourers that have security companies at their head office or in their delegations or branches must have the following security measures at least for the custody of the weapons:

- Passive: Minimum degree of safety B, in accordance with the classification established in UNE standards 108-110-87 and 108-112-87, when dealing with a safe and in the case of a vault it must have a reinforced wall with a minimum degree of safety A, determined in standards UNE 108-111-87 and UNE 108-113-87 with reinforced doors and hatches, with the same degree of security and with locks belonging to group 1R of the standard ANSI/UL-768 and which allows the choice of at least 10 combinations.

  The walls of the enclosure in which the armour is located must stop any attack with mechanical equipment (saws, drills, etc.) and the access door must be reinforced and must also have security locks.

- Active: The armours will have detectors such as those classified in Standard UNE-108-210-86 which make it possible to detect any type of attack through the door, walls, ceiling or floor.

The reinforced door of the private enclosure will have detectors that alert of the unauthorised opening of the door or the detector, and there will be standardised volumetric detectors inside protecting the weapons.

These alarm systems will be differentiated from other systems located in the installation and their signals will be sent to an alarm centre.

2. The armours installed in places referred to in article 25.1 of the Regulation of Private Security must meet the followings security measures:

- Passive: Minimum degree of safety B, in accordance with standards UNE 108-110-87 and UNE 108-112-87 and shall have an IR type lock in accordance with ANSI/UL-768 with a minimum of 10 combinations. If there is a permanent surveillance service with continuous observation of the safe-armour, the place will have a vault, the minimum degree of security will be type A and in the case of the latter, it will be installed in the interior.

    Its location will be in a discreet place out of the view of the public.

- Active: The will be permanently protected with standardised volumetric detectors and the door will have a device that detects the unauthorised opening and/or breakage of the door.

    When they are not installed inside a vault and are authorised for the custody of more than three weapons, they shall have the measures determined in the first paragraph of number 1b) of this seventh paragraph,

    The technical characteristics of these measures will be included in the protection plan for the places referred to in article 25.1 of the regulation of Private Security.

3. The number of weapons that can be authorised in deposit will be that corresponding to the volume of the armour, taking into consideration that the average volume of a weapon is 3.5 litres.

With respect to cartridges, whose storage will be independent from the weapons must take into account that a capacity of 1.5 litres will be needed froe ach 100 cartridges.

4. In the offices or delegations in which there are weapons, the security companies will have a protection plan, with a contract for the installation, maintenance and revision of the electronic system, installed by an authorised company form the sector with a certification that as a minimum the safety measures contemplated in number 1 of this seventh section are complied with.

5. In the cases of article 25.4 of the Regulation of Private Security, in which the armours may be replaced by a safe, this must be a point of activation for an alarm signal, differentiated from the rest of the alarm signals that exist in the establishment or on the premises.

The safe must not custody more than one weapon, unless the circumstances of the place and the security measures of the establishment guarantee the custody of more weapons, in the opinion of the supervisor of weapons and explosives, in which case each weapon must be kept in independent metallic boxes.

6. In the cases contemplated in article 90.4 of the Regulation of Private security, when the escort cannot guarantee the custody of the weapon, as established in article 144 of the Regulation on Weapons, it must be delivered in an authorised weapons deposit, in a safe that meets the conditions described in number 5 above or in the post of the Civil Guard.

The deposits of self protected explosives of the security companies registered and authorised for providing this type of services, notwithstanding the stipulations of the Regulation Explosives, must meet the following minimum requisites:

A) Physical means of protection: Regardless of the type of construction, the resistance of concrete will not be more than 250 kilogrammes per square centimetre on all side of the deposit.

Except on the facade, the minimum thickness of the concrete will be 20 centimetres, and must be adhered with steel bars with a diameter equal to or greater than 12 millimetres with a maximum separation of 20 centimetres between the centres of the horizontal and vertical rows.

The use of corrugated steel is admissible on igloo type structures though their characteristics will be subject to definition in each specific case.

The facade will be concrete, with a thickness equal to or greater than 30 centimetres, with a double steel grill with a diameter equal too r less than 12 millimetres. The separation between the two will be 10 centimetres and the squares of the mesh will have a side equal to or above 20 centimetres.

The door of the deposit will be one or two slabs assembled on external hinges which make it possible to open to 180 degrees.

The maximum dimensions of a slab will be 3 metres high and 1.5 metres wide.

The chassis will be made of steel and will be reinforced to allow it to be installed and integrated with the concrete of the façade.

The structure of the door will be made up of the following elements at least:

- Front steel plate, at least 6 millimetres thick.

- Extra hard refracting cement agglomerate, with a high abrasive power, complementary framework in tordbar or a similar product, minimum resistance to the compression of 500 kilogrammes per square centimetre (rilem method) and a thickness equal to or less than 100 millimetres..

- Inner steel plate, with a thickness equal to or less than four millimetres.

- As these are exterior doors, the finish will be stainless steel with 18/8 chrome-nickel.

- The closing mechanisms will be built with two high security locks, one of them with a combination with at least 10 combinations and with radiological protection (standard 768 1R). The key will be anti-picklock and inimitable. The two locks will be duly separated to make attacks more difficult.

- It shall have an automatic blocking device, in the case of an attack on the locks, as well as condemnation areas on all the sides.

The ventilation ducts will not be more than 150 by 150 millimetres if they are open on the structured and their section is straight and they must be protected internally and externally to prevent objects from being introduced into them.

The arsenal, with the exception of the head wall or facade, will be covered with compacted soil with a thickness of at least one metre, measured from the ceiling or keystone.

The fill material will be clean, cohesive and free from stones (maximum diameter 20 millimetres). It will be filled in batches whose thickness will be in accordance with the type of soils and machinery used. Minimum compacting will be 85 per cent of the normal proctor.

The soil face will be as smooth as possible and in no case less than 1.5:1.

A clear coloured layer or ant-erosion will be spread over the whole covered surface, with a base of gunite, cement or similar.

The meshing on the perimeter fencing, in the lower part, will be anchored to a concrete slab, using wing bolts or a similar procedure, embedded in it every 30 centimetres.

The minimum distance between the fencing and the exterior limit of the area covered by the intrusion detection system that is furthest from the deposits or buildings will be three metres.

The main access will form part of the perimeter fencing and will be perfectly observable in all its extension from the control post located inside the deposit.

It will have a sliding door, whose manual opening and closing will be done by remote control form the control post.

B) Electronic protection measures: The electronic protection system will comprise the following systems:

Perimeter detection system, made up of a minimum of two subsystems of perimeter detection for the exteriors, not attachable to the fencing with a different operating system and no correlated false alarms, one on the surface and the other in the subsoil or buried, both duly overlapping each other and with correspondence between their areas.

In order to reduce the FAR, the two systems will have an integrated Y logic and a time window of 15 seconds.

The selection of the systems and their distribution will be made by taking into account the climatological characteristics of the area, the topography of the land, the organisation of the area of the arsenal and the location of the constructive or auxiliary elements (post, lighting, fencing, etc.).

Once installed, the systems will be evaluated separately. The Pd of each of them must not be less than 90 per 100 with a confidence index of 95 per 100.

Both systems will credit an MTBF better than or equal to 20,000 hours.

Interior detection system, composed of the following groups of detectors:

- Seismic or electronic vibration detectors, of a piezoelectric type, embedded in the structure and doors of the arsenal, capable of generating an alarm in the case of any attack perpetrated on them with a hammer / chisel, drill, percussion, grindstone, torch, thermal lance or explosives.

- Detectors of the open/closed situation of the doors of the arsenals, of the ant-deflagration limit switch type.

- Passive infrared detectors (PIR) for inside the arsenals, with a minimum of three detection beams in the vertical plane or an angle of less than or equal to 60 degrees in the same plane. Its number will be necessary to detect any movement inside the arsenal.

Communication lines supervision system, whose circuits will provide an adequate level of security to the signal transmission lines, between detectors and the local alarms reception unit and between the latter and the control unit located in the offices of the Civil Guard.

The supervising units will depend on the type of transmission and whether it is digital or tone (classes A and AB); CA and CC, transmission by cable (class B) or transmission via radio (class C). The values to be required will be similar to those determined in the *Interim Federal Specification* W-A-00450B (GSA-FSS).

Control system, made up of two units, remote in deposit and local in offices which will communicate with each other, either by cable or radio.

The remote unit will supervise the status of the perimeter and interior sensors and shall compose a message based on them to be sent to the local central office for analysis and interpretation.

The local unit, based on a PC computer, will receive and interpret the message sent by the remote unit and shall present it on the screen.

The link shall send the digitalised information, guaranteeing that the message is not repeated, by including a pseudo random code in it with a repetition rate of no less than three years based on a message every ten seconds.

The information relating to sensors shall include the identification of the sensor and its status.

This information will be individualised:

- In the perimeter detection system, by perimeter areas.

- In the internal detection system by arsenal and type of detector.

When the link between the remote unit and the local unit is made via radio, the loss of four consecutive messages will provoke an alarm due to the loss of the link, in the case that a message is sent every thirty seconds.

If the link is by cable, the supervision of the line will be in real time.

Auxiliary systems

- The remote unit and the local unit of the control system and if the case may be, the unit of communications will have a UPS in the case of a failure in the ordinary power supply. The UPS of the arsenal will keep the equipment activated for sufficient time for the emergency power group to enter into service.

    The start up of the UPS system will transmit a pre-alarm

    The UPS of the remote unit will keep this in operation for a period of time of no less than one hour.

- Anti-deflagration alarm buttons will be installed next to the doors of the arsenals. Two will be installed in each arsenal, on the outside and another on the inside. The alarm buttons may only be activated while the system is in the status of access.

- The room here the remote unit is located will be protected by PIR and magnetic contact in the door. The number of elements to be installed will depend on the size and shape of the room.

    The building in which this room is located will be inside the area protected by the perimeter detection system.

    If there are windows, these will be physically protected with grills.

    The door will be reinforced with a security lock.

- The deposit will have an access control unit, to enable authorised personnel to enter without generating an alarm. The changing of the system from a safe status to access and vice versa will be carried out from the unit. The changes of status will always generate an alarm.

    The time window for access and departure will be sixty seconds. The change of status will be made with a magnetic card and personal code or biometric device.

Statuses of the system

- Access: in this status, all the sensors, except the alarm and seismic buttons go to access to allow work in the deposit. The radio link and the supervision of the lines and anti-sabotage functions of all the detectors are maintained.

    The status of all the sensors will be known in the local unit and will only generate alarms in the case of the failure or activation of the line supervision units, anti-sabotage devices, alarm buttons, seismic sensors and loss of link.

- Safe: All the sensors are activated and in a safe position, with the exception of the alarm buttons.

The vehicles used for the transportation and distribution of valuable or dangerous objects must meet the following characteristics:

a) Division of the vehicle in three compartments:

- The front compartment in which only the driver will be located, with the access door on the left and the door on the right will only be able to be opened from the inside and separated from the central compartment by a shielded screen without access.

  The key that gives access to the internal security device of the driver's door will be deposited in the main office or delegation of the company where the armoured vehicle gives its service.

- The central compartment in which the security guards will travel with a door at either side, will be separated form the back compartment by a shielded screen which will have a reinforced door with access to the cargo area, with a hatch system to open the sides of the vehicle in such a way that they cannot be opened simultaneously.

  In the area of the central screen which limits the compartment where the security guards travel from the collection area, a system or mechanism will be installed to permit the introduction of objects and to prevent them from being taken out and it will have a reinforced door that can only be opened form the main office of the security company.

- The back compartment, for the cargo, will be divided into two areas, delivery and collection areas, separated by a reinforced screen. The back compartment may have an external door at the back of the vehicle which will be shielded and with a security lock which will only be opened in the maximum security hatch areas to be able to access the vehicle.

The key for the door mentioned in the above paragraph will always be deposited in the main office or delegation of the company where the vehicle provides its services.

b) The following levels of resistance of the shieldings, determined by UNE standards 108-131 and 108-132 whish will be replaced, if the case may be, by the European standard UNE EN 1063:

- External perimeter of the central front compartment and front screen: A-30.

- External perimeter of the back compartment and the floor of the vehicle: A-10.

- Separating screen between the central and back compartments: A-20.

- Separating screen between the cargo areas: A-10.

c) Small windows distributed on the sides and the back of the vehicle.

d) Device that makes it possible to locate the vehicle permanently from the main office or delegations of the company. Installation of a radio and mobile cell phone communication system to permit communication among the members of the crew with the company as well as the intercommunication of the transportation and protection security guards with the driver of the vehicle.

e) Installation of an external aerial in the reinforced vehicle in order to transmit and receive any communication through the mobile cell phone equipment.

f) Electric or mechanical locks on the doors, fuel tank and access to the motor which can only be opened form inside the vehicle.

g) Alarm system with an acoustic device that can be activated in the case of an attack or the entrance of an unauthorised person in the vehicles.

h) The fuel tank must have sufficient protection to prevent an explosion if it were hit by a projectile or a fragment of explosion as well as to avoid the chain reaction of the fuel located in the tank should the vehicle catch fire.

i) Protection against obstruction in the motor exhaust.

j) Air conditioning and fire detection and extinguishing systems.

k) Unique number and identifier of the vehicle which will be located on the outside of the roof of the vehicle in adhesive or reflecting paint and large enough to be visible at a great distance. This number shall also appear on the sides and back of the vehicle.

l) Vehicle aptitude card or certificate, indicating the registration number and motor and chassis numbers and a certificate from the manufacturers, body-makers or technicians that have intervened in the preparation of the van that it meets the characteristics required in this section. This card will be deposited in the main office or delegation of the company where the van has its base.

m) Vehicle control card which includes the revisions that must be made quarterly. No more than four months should elapse between successive revisions and the card shall indicate: name of the company, number and registration of the vehicle and numbers of the motor and chassis as well as the elements under revision such as: communication equipment, alarms, doors, hatch, locks, fire detection and extinguishing system and al those that could be of interest for the security of the vehicle or its cargo. The card will be kept in the vehicle itself and the conformity of the revision will be signed and dated together with any corrections there may be by the technician responsible for it.

1. Notwithstanding compliance with any of the other requisites of conformity in the stipulations of the legislation for road transportation and especially in the National Regulation for the Transportation of Dangerous Goods on the Road (TPC) approved by Royal Decree 74/1992, of 31st January, the vehicles dedicated to transporting explosives and metallic cartridges must meet the following requisites:

a) Security

Vehicle blocking system, comprising a mechanism which when activated directly (by pressing the button) or indirectly (by opening the cabin doors without deactivating the system), fuel injection to the motor cut off and acoustic and light alarm. The system must have a maximum delay of two minutes between its activation and action.

A metallic grid inside the vehicle fuel supply tank pipe to prevent foreign elements from being introduced.

Fuel tank protection system in accordance with the eleventh section letters e) and g) of this order.

Special closing device for the vehicle safe, with a padlock or security lock.

b) Signals:

Panel on the ceiling of the vehicle cabin with the requisites specified in annex 3.

The General Directorate of the Civil Guard may dispense the requirement of this requisite in special security circumstances.

c) Transmissions:

Cell phone installed in the vehicle that can memorise the telephone numbers of the Service operating Centres (COS) of the circumscriptions of the Civil Guard Commands where the transport takes place and whose aerial is installed and duly protected in the upper part of the vehicle safe.

2. The requisites described above must be inspected by the Civil Guard sufficiently in advance of the transport requested and a note must be mad that the vehicle meets the requisites in the circulation guide or similar document that accompanies the transport.

3. Notwithstanding the fact that the transportation of explosives and metallic cartridges meet the above mentioned conditions when the circumstances so require in the opinion of the Civil Guard it may be necessary for the transportation of said materials to have an escort, either public or private, in compliance with the stipulations of the Regulation of Explosives.

The communications to the Security Corps and Forces referred to in article 14.1 of the Regulation on Private Security will be made to the competent Corps in accordance with the distribution of competences referred to in article 11. 2 of Organic Law 2/1986, of 13th March on Security Forces and Corps and articles 2.0 and 18 of Law 23/1992 of 30th July on Private Security, or if the case may be to the corresponding local police.

4. The communication to the Security Forces and Corps referred to in article 36 of the Regulation on Private Security or if the case may be, to the corresponding body of the competent autonomous region will be made when the value of the transported goods exceeds 400,000,000 pesetas.

5. The obligation to carry out the transport in armoured vehicles referred to in number 2 of this section will also be applicable to works of art which in each case is determined by the Ministry of Education and Culture and to those objects that generate value, risk or expectations of the General Directorate of the Police of Civil Governments, by considering prior circumstances and cases relating to these objects.

6. When the characteristics or size of the objects prevent their transportation in armoured vehicles, this may be done in other types of vehicle with the protection of at least two security guards whose

exclusive function will be the armed protection of the objects as referred to in number seven of the twenty second section.

7. The guard or guards who protect the goods will carry a calibre 12/70 repetition shotgun with 12 shot cartridges.

2. The ship and its realities

The following are the aspects of the Ship Security Plan that constitute the essential measurements from which the efficiency levels in terms of the protection of a ship can be determined, as specifically detailed in Section 9.8 of Part B of the Code[1]:

- Accesses
- Restricted areas
- Handling of cargo
- Delivery of provisions
- Unaccompanied luggage
- Vigilance over vessel protection

These can be grouped according to the degree of structural vulnerability (type of vessel), operative vulnerability (traffic) and degree of rigour of their crews (speciality), in the following block by block observations:

A. The passenger vessel, which in diagram 2.1, includes ferries, cruise-ships and Ro-Ro, due to the fact that they carry on board persons other than those that form the crew, cannot be treated in the same way in certain aspects since there are clear differences between the procedures and objectives of each type of maritime transport.
B. Vessels that usually transport loads in tanks, such as petrol, chemicals and gas tankers, make up a single group with similar characteristics and considerations.
C. General cargo ships, such as refrigerator ships and bulk carriers can also be grouped into a unified category.
D. Ro-Ro ships with transport carried without drivers or passengers, container-ships and car-carriers make up another block.
E. Finally, vessel-types such as fishing-boats, tug boats and recreational craft will be considered and treated as a block of vessels from the port environment.

---

[1] Practically compulsory on the EC level, under the specifications of the Regulation, in section 4.1.12 (Revision of ship security plans) of Article 3.

2.1 Block "A" Vessels

2.1.1 Accessibility (Fig. 2.1 and 2.2)

At sea and from it, a ferry is difficult to access, given the height and verticality of its freeboard above the waterline. Access through its doors is only possible if these are opened from inside, in sheltered waters and with the vessel detained.

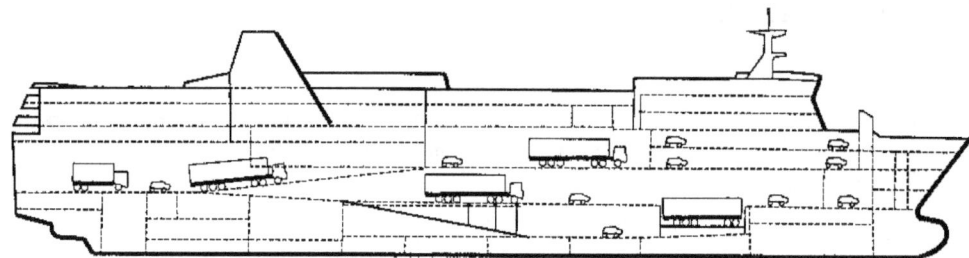

Figure 2.1

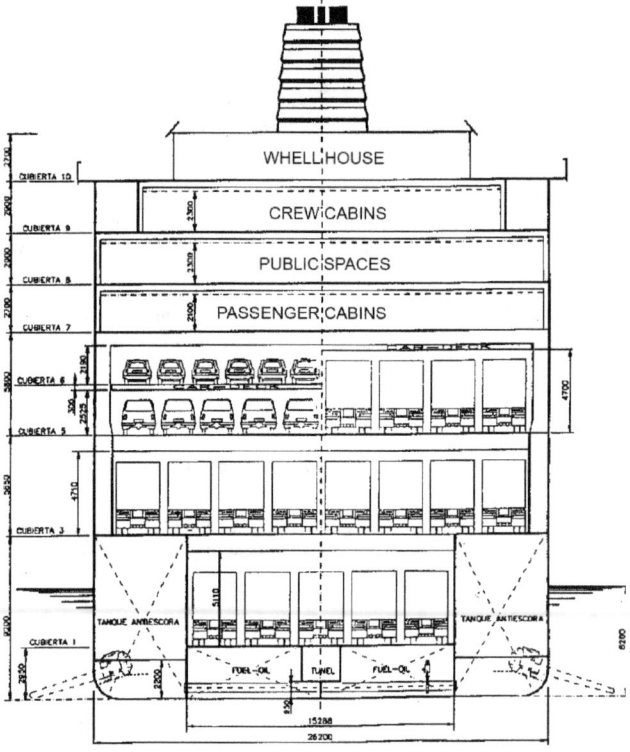

Figure 2.2

Boarding from the sea will only be possible if there is an occupying support force already on board, so that access to the open decks can be made with the vessel stationary or at very low speed.

2.1.2 Access to restricted areas onboard

Table 2.1

ASPECT	FERRY	CRUISER	RO-RO
Control areas and posts	Easy	Difficult	Easy
Areas with surveillance equipment	Easy	Difficult	Easy
Ventilation system areas	Easy	Difficult	Easy
Drinking water tank areas	Easy	Difficult	Easy
Areas with dangerous goods	None	None	Easy
Loading/unloading pumps	None	None	None
Crew quarters	Easy	Easy	Easy

At present, except for cruise-ships, the rest of the vessels of this block offer a certain ease of access to especially relevant restricted areas, with internal consequences for the vessel and external ones for port facility environments. Figures 2.1, 2.2 and 2.3 show the layouts of the cargo and passenger areas and the ease with which one can pass from one to another.

The existence of ship protection procedures on cruise-ships constitutes a significant advance in this field, since the control of these spaces is preserved, with greater or lesser efficiency, against the meddling and the intentionally devious manipulation of the teams and services located therein

Areas dedicated to dangerous cargoes, according to their nature and classification in the IMDG, are not normally found on passenger vessels, or only a small amount is allowed in a safe and highly-controlled means of transport.

2.1.3 Cargo-handling

Except on cruise-ships, for which the application of this variable is non-applicable, (N/A), on ferry-type and Ro-Ro vessels this cargo is accepted as long as the existing controls are passed in the corresponding concession, authorising its embarking.

The stevedoring operations are carried out on board. Due to the nature of the roll-on cargo embarked, this is limited to the positioning of vehicles on the corresponding decks, ensuring the minimum possible surface occupation depending on the volume of each unit.

Table 2.2

ASPECT	FERRY	CRUISER	RO-RO
Systematic inspection of cargo	Normal	N/A	Normal
Inspection outside port	Null	Frequent	Null
Check on contents	Null	Frequent	Null
Inspection of vehicles prior to embarking - Visual means - Devices - Dogs	Scarce Scarce Scarce	N/A N/A N/A	Scarce Scarce Scarce

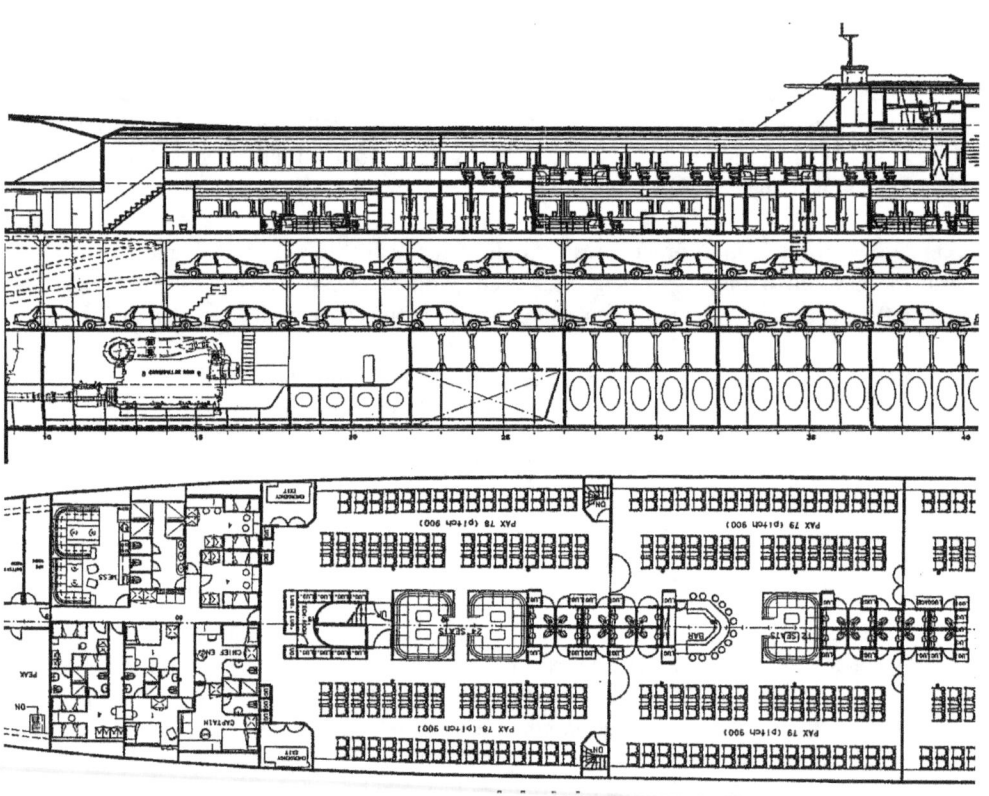

Figure 2.3

When palletised loads are embarked on these vessels, attention on board is focused on their placement on the decks in such a way that they do not impede and are not affected by the movement of the roll-on units, so that they are not damaged in any way and do not get in the way of the vehicles.

2.1.4 Provisions

The reception of all types of provisioning can be considered as positive and acceptable as carried out in most of the vessel types in this block. The appearance and quality of the provisions received is given a certain priority, especially on cruise ships, which is important since it is not good practice to allow on board articles that do not coincide with the specifications of the order.

The rejection of packages with signs of damage is a measure which is in keeping with the degree of rigour that should be applied on a vessel. A broken box might be accepted, if it still has all its contents, without thinking of the possibility of changing the identification of the contents. The consideration of the principles of protection should change the way of thinking in the application of the criteria on accepting or rejecting goods on board.

Table 2.3

ASPECT	FERRY	CRUISER	RO-RO
Damaged packaging	Yes	Yes	Yes
Rejection without prior inspection	No	Yes	No
Undue handling	Yes	Yes	Yes
Only requested items	Yes	Yes	Yes
Order and delivery documentation	Yes	Yes	Yes

2.1.5 Unaccompanied luggage

Table 2.4

ASPECT	FERRY	CRUISER	RO-RO
Inspection prior to acceptance on board	No	N/A	No
Prior inspection in port	No	N/A	No
Security after inspection	No	N/A	No
Stowage in closed storerooms	Yes	N/A	Yes

On cruisers, this variable has no application since the luggage is well-identified, with its owners on board; otherwise it is disembarked, as it has no use on board. Nevertheless, the luggage on these vessels, which is always accompanied, does go through each of the aspects mentioned in the table.

At present, however, there is no control on the other two vessel types, the luggage being accepted as it is, trusting that any anomaly will have been detected in the inspections conducted on land. Once the luggage has been received, it is taken to storerooms where it will remain stored until unloaded on arrival at the port of destination. One aspect to be highlighted is the degree of impenetrability of the systems for closing or locking these storerooms, over which doubts may be held regarding their efficiency of resistance and the technology applied in these systems.

2.1.6 Characteristics of the vessel with respect to the risk variables

Table 2.5

ASPECT	BY EXPECTED FREQUENCY OF VARIABLE		
	FERRY	CRUISER	RO-RO
Accesses:			
- At sea	Difficult	Difficult	Difficult
- In port	Easy	Easy	Easy
Restricted areas	Several	Many	Few
Cargo handling	A lot	Very little	A lot
Delivery of provisions	High	Very high	Normal
Unaccompanied luggage	Little	Very little	Little
Surveillance of vessel protection	Little/average	High	Little
Degree of concealment	High	High	Average

While Tables 2.1 to 2.4 analysed the routine procedures applied by the crew to this block of vessels, Table 2.5 illustrates the opportunities offered by the vessel due to its specific structure, without considering the crew, even though this will eventually be a decisive factor.

As regards establishing a criterion on the possibility that the distribution of spaces on board provides opportunities for the concealment of illicit materials, this is very high on all vessel types, in direct relation to the number of spaces accessed by the passengers.

2.2 Block "B" Vessels

2.2.1 Access to restricted areas on board

This variable is of routine compliance on board the vessels contemplated in this block. The specific, well-defined characteristics of nearly all of the terminals, docks or the location of the mooring lines, are normally in safe areas of port installations, access to which is protected by security checks and surveillance at the point of connection with the port.

Table 2.6

ASPECT	PETROL	CHEMICALS	GAS
Control areas and posts	Normal	Normal	Normal
Areas with surveillance equipment	Normal	Normal	Normal
Areas with ventilation systems	Normal	Normal	Normal
Drinking-water tank areas	Normal	Normal	Normal
Areas with DG	Normal	Normal	Normal
Loading/un pumps	Normal	Normal	Normal
Crew quarters	Normal	Normal	Normal

The operations required for the specific cargoes of each of this type of vessels facilitate the free access of the crew, particularly those working in the machine rooms and on deck. Only the outer accesses are rigorously closed for security reasons related to the risks of the cargo, in order to avoid the introduction of the inflammable or toxic vapours emanated in the unprotected rooms and areas.

Most of the restricted areas on board these vessels must be easily accessible for reasons of operative security. Only the inner watertight doors whose purpose is to separate decks in the mode of a firewall will be closed, and in any case, these do not have permanent locks nor are they difficult to force; indeed, quite the opposite is true.

2.2.2 Cargo-handling

Table 2.7

ASPECT	PETROL	CHEMICALS	GAS
Systematic inspection of cargo	N/A	N/A	N/A
Inspection outside port	N/A	N/A	N/A
Check on contents	N/A	N/A	N/A
Inspection of vehicles prior to embarking - Visual means - Devices - Dogs	N/A	N/A	N/A

Due to the characteristics of the cargo and the procedures of closed transportation of the special products carried on the vessels of this block, none of the applications common to all the other vessels are applicable in this case.

2.2.3 Provisions

Table 2.8

ASPECT	PETROL	CHEMICALS	GAS
Damaged packaging	Yes	Yes	Yes
Rejection without prior inspection	No	No	No
Undue handling	Yes	Yes	Yes
Only requested items	Yes	Yes	Yes
Order and delivery documentation	Yes	Yes	Yes

The same comments as those referring to ferries above apply to this variable, as the routine is the one widely accepted by the maritime community. Provisions, whether these are the best or most desirable or not, are always taken, as long as they coincide with the order, there being no procedures for alerting of criminal intentions. This situation should, however, change substantially with the training provided as a consequence of the Code and its implementation on board.

2.2.4 Unaccompanied luggage

Table 2.9

ASPECT	PETROL	CHEMICALS	GAS
Inspection prior to acceptance on board	N/A	N/A	N/A
Prior inspection in port	N/A	N/A	N/A
Security after inspection	N/A	N/A	N/A
Stowage in closed storerooms	N/A	N/A	N/A

Nor does this variable have any application to this or any subsequent block of vessel type, since the absence of any passengers rules out any possibility of unaccompanied luggage, the only luggage on board being accompanied by its owners (the crew members).

Nevertheless, at times, part of the luggage of a crew member might remain on board, because of his prompt incorporation or enrolment or because he is to be picked up in the next port, Then, for the purposes of protection, some procedures must be established to guarantee that this luggage is inoffensive and does not represent a threat to the vessel.

2.2.5 Characteristics of the vessel with respect to the risk variables

Table 2.10

ASPECT	BY EXPECTED FREQUENCY OF VARIABLE		
	PETROL	CHEMICALS	GAS
Accesses:			
- At sea	Easy	Easy	Regular
- In port	Closely supervised	Closely supervised	Closely supervised
Restricted areas	None	None	None
Cargo handling	None	None	None
Delivery of provisions	Normal	Normal	Normal
Unaccompanied luggage	None	None	None
Surveillance of vessel protection	Normal	Normal	Normal
Degree of concealment	Low	Low	Low

Due to the characteristics of its freeboard, structures and superstructures, the chances of suffering attacks at sea is quite high, as can be observed in the acts of piracy in some well-known areas of maritime navigation in the Far East.

Due to the operative scope of the vessels of this block, taking into account the specialised training and awareness of its crew members (in general terms) and the obligations in view of the requirements of the substances normally transported as cargo, it can be assured that the corresponding aspects of industrial safety have a high degree of fulfilment.

But while the vessels remains in the port installations, the confidence in the access controls, surveillance and the personnel specifically devoted to maintaining these means that their preventive routine in matters of prevention is practically non-existent except, of course, when there is a specific warning requiring special measures on the part of the crew. In relation to the implementation of the Code, this is considered in the application of levels 1 and 2, for which the crew must be specially trained and drilled, a condition which applies to all vessels, whatever their type or load.

2.3 Block "C" Vessels

2.3.1 Access to restricted areas on board

Even though the vital functions of the vessel are specified, clearly identified and well-known, as is their importance for the security of the vessel, the peaceful and civil purpose of these vessels leads to a routine behaviour that makes this type of vessel highly vulnerable.

Table 2.11

ASPECT	GENERAL C.	REFRIGERATED	BULK CARRIER
Control areas and posts	Normal	Normal	Normal
Areas with surveillance equipment	Normal	Normal	Normal
Areas with ventilation systems	Normal	Normal	Normal
Drinking-water tank areas	Normal	Normal	Normal
Areas with DG	Normal	Normal	Normal
Loading/un pumps	Normal	Normal	Normal
Crew quarters	Supervised	Supervised	Supervised

Most of the restricted areas on board these vessels are usually of easy access due to an excess of confidence. Attention is paid only to the inner watertight doors whose purpose is to cut off decks in the mode of a firewall, or to impede the entry of concentrations of dust from the cargo operations and in any case, these do not often have permanent locks which make them impenetrable; indeed, the truth is quite the opposite.

As break-ins are quite common on this type of vessels in the accesses of the port facilities with little surveillance and easy access, the crew members pay special attention to the closing of access to their quarters or rooms with their belongings. Many cases of robberies by the stevedore teams or by passers-by on the docks have been reported. In any case, it cannot be said that the locks can be included in the matter of security since they are quite easy to open.

It is quite clear that the implementation of the Ship Security Plan on each vessel would transform this confidence into interest, making all of the areas on the vessel as safe as those given the greatest attention.

2.3.2 Cargo handling

The aspect concerning vehicle inspections is treated as a cargo in relation to each vessel type.

All the criteria expressed in the table refer to the operative security of the cargo and not to actions intended for the purpose of protection. With the implementation of the protection procedures, the coincidence or not of the objectives (safety and security) can be observed, as well as the substantial change involved in the adaptation of the routine methods to those imposed by the Code.

Table 2.12

ASPECT	GENERAL C.	REFRIGERATOR	BULK CARRIER
Systematic inspection of cargo	Average	High	Low
Inspection outside port	Normal	Normal	Normal
Check on contents	None	Average	None
Inspection of vehicles prior to embarking			
- Visual means	Yes	No	No
- Devices	No	No	No
- Dogs	No	No	No

Refrigerator vessel cargoes register a higher level of control and inspection due to their nature and the phytosanitary requirements, although these do not differ greatly from the routine inspections on other types of vessels.

As regards the bulk carriers, the nature of their bulk cargoes, the means used to load the cargo on board, the closing of the holds and the danger of the atmospheres surrounding them for human life means that the need for protection on this type of vessel can be foreseen to be quite low.

On general cargo vessels, any alteration detected is registered as damages, with a view to making claims for these damages, which would otherwise be attributed to the vessel in the port of unloading.

Palletised loads or loads unitised by other systems allow the detection of breakages in their packaging of plastic, sack-cloth or canvas etc., but up to now, attention has focused on the state of the cargo and not on its illicit contents, as in the mate's receipt the safe-conduct document still has the expression 'I do not know the weight and content', the load being accepted and embarked.

2.3.3 Provisions

Table 2.13

ASPECT	GENERAL C.	REFRIGERATOR	BULK CARRIER
Damaged packaging	Yes	Yes	Yes
Rejection without prior inspection	No	No	No
Undue handling	Yes	Yes	Yes
Only requested items	Yes	Yes	Yes
Order and delivery documentation	Yes	Yes	Yes

For this block of vessels, the criteria identified for any type of merchant ship are applicable, using the procedures outlined above.

In all of these aspects, the crew acts according to the widely accepted routines which, though not necessarily the most adequate, do constitute the normal practice in normal conditions, and are only modified when required by circumstances, returning to normal once these are over.

2.3.4 Unaccompanied luggage

In this section, all of the above comments referring to all types of vessels that do not have passengers can be applied, as the luggage is always accompanied by the crew members except for the occasional specific case mentioned above.

Table 2.14

ASPECT	GENERAL C.	REFRIGERATOR	BULK CARRIER
Inspection prior to acceptance on board	N/A	N/A	N/A
Prior inspection in port	N/A	N/A	N/A
Security after inspection	N/A	N/A	N/A
Stowage in closed storerooms	N/A	N/A	N/A

2.3.5 Characteristics of the vessel with respect to risk variables

Table 2.15

	BY EXPECTED FREQUENCY OF VARIABLE		
ASPECT	GENERAL C.	REFRIGERATOR	BULK CARRIER
Accesses: - At sea - In port	Normal Easy	Normal Easy	Easy Normal
Restricted areas	None	None	None
Cargo handling	Very high	High	Low
Delivery of provisions	Normal	Normal	Normal
Unaccompanied luggage	None	None	None
Surveillance of vessel protection	Normal	Normal	Normal
Degree of concealment	Low	Low	Low

The structural configuration of bulk carriers, quite similar to tankers in the dimensions of their freeboard and their great length, facilitate the boarding of the ship from smaller crafts, quite unlike the other two types of vessels in this block.

In the port, however, the methods and means used in the handling of bulk cargoes, the absence of the need for the presence of security personnel and the nature of the cargo itself mean that bulk carriers are less likely to be the object of incidents related with protection.

In the rest of the aspects, no great differences are observed in the handling of threats related with protection in the vessels of this block.

2.4 Block "D" ships

2.4.1 Access to restricted areas on board

In all aspects referred to in this section, the same observations as those made for the above blocks are applicable, as these vessels will always remain merchant ships, with crews that enrol on one vessel or vessel type one day and another one the next. Thus, as it is not a specialised vessel, the routine behaviour is directed only at the requirements of navigation and those that correspond to the nature of the cargo, without any special measures being adopted except for those arising in ports or areas of known danger.

Table 2.16

ASPECT	RO-RO	CONTAINER	CAR-CARRIER
Control areas and posts	Normal	Normal	Normal
Areas with surveillance equipment	Normal	Normal	Normal
Areas with ventilation systems	Normal	Normal	Normal
Drinking-water tank areas	Normal	Normal	Normal
Areas with DG	Normal	Normal	Normal
Loading/un pumps	Normal	Normal	Normal
Crew quarters	Supervised	Supervised	Supervised

2.4.2 Cargo handling

Although these three vessel types have been grouped together in this block due to their similarity of appearance, the nature of the cargoes and the procedures used for loading them on board are quite different, which incidentally facilitates the detection of irregularities related with protection.

Table 2.17

ASPECT	RO-RO	CONTAINER	CAR-CARRIER
Systematic inspection of cargo	Average	Low	Low
Inspection outside port	Normal	Normal	Normal
Check on contents	None	None	None
Inspection of vehicles prior to embarking			
- Visual means	Yes	Yes	Yes
- Devices	No	No	No
- Dogs	No	No	No

Nevertheless, once the results are analysed, whatever the method used, reality shows that there are no big differences and that they all show the same vulnerability on board and that protection, should there be any, depends on the measures taken at the terminals, without any further procedures for embarking directly on the vessel.

2.4.3 Provisions

Table 2.18

ASPECT	RO-RO	CONTAINER	CAR-CARRIER
Damaged packaging	Yes	Yes	Yes
Rejection without prior inspection	No	No	No
Undue handling	Yes	Yes	Yes
Only requested items	Yes	Yes	Yes
Order and delivery documentation	Yes	Yes	Yes

The comments repeated in the above sections are also applicable to the aspects here.

2.4.4 Unaccompanied luggage

The same comments as those for the previous vessel blocks apply.

Table 2.19

ASPECT	RO-RO	CONTAINER	CAR-CARRIER
Inspection prior to acceptance on board	N/A	N/A	N/A
Prior inspection in port	N/A	N/A	N/A
Security after inspection	N/A	N/A	N/A
Stowage in closed storerooms	N/A	N/A	N/A

2.4.5 Characteristics of vessel with respect to risk variables

Again, the characteristics of the vessels as regards their structural particularities show certain differentiating details, according to whether the vessel is considered to be in port or at sea, and in turn according to the nature of the cargoes and the operating procedures for loading these on board, to the traffic generated on board, to the number of persons intervening and to the steps taken to inspect the cargo.

For example, considering the aspect of cargo handling, the higher frequency of trips made by the Ro-Ro vessels and car-carriers results in a greater probability of incidents than for container ships.

Table 2.20

	BY EXPECTED FREQUENCY OF VARIABLE		
ASPECT	RO-RO	CONTAINER	CAR-CARRIER
Accesses: - At sea - In port	Difficult Easy	Normal Normal	Difficult Easy
Restricted areas	None	None	None
Cargo handling	High	Low	High
Delivery of provisions	Normal	Normal	Normal
Unaccompanied luggage	None	None	None
Surveillance of vessel protection	Normal	Normal	Normal

No differentiating circumstances are observed for the other aspects among the three vessel types that make up this block.

2.5 Block "E" Ships

The vessels in this block are not considered in the strict fulfilment of the specifications of the application of the Code, and thus it would seem that they should not be dealt with under the protection criteria of any Ship Security Plan, but they are considered in the Port Facilities Security Plan.

These vessels lead to an intense traffic in the internal waters of any port installation, and often avoid any minimum security inspection, despite having been used in the past in terrorist and other criminal actions. Only tug boats are treated differently, since their exploitation is an indirect port management service, so that the port can control it closely, both in terms of the units themselves and the crews, who have more or less stable, permanent work contracts. However, the location of tug boats in port areas makes them extremely accessible, facilitating their boarding and use in precisely those actions which the Code and its specifications are designed to avoid.

Hence, this vessel type has to be considered, not because of their owners or their objectives and activities, but for the ease with which they can be used by third parties to cause damage. Moreover, it is clear that fishing ports and marinas are open to the outer part of the port facilities, with few control mechanisms and if there are any inspections, these are highly vulnerable to criminal actions.

It is considered unnecessary to apply here the procedure followed for the rest of the blocks since, while the aspects in question are extremely precarious in relation to the protection requirements in a far more rigorous operative domain, no positive aspects can be found in this block that might constitute a brake, a control or a filter to the first steps of piracy with terrorist aims from taking place.

Only the frequency table is presented, as the values expressed require no further explanation, but these should be taken into account when considering the overall protection of the port.

2.5.1 Characteristics of the vessel with respect to risk variables

Table 2.21

BY EXPECTED FREQUENCY OF VARIABLE			
ASPECT	**FISHING B.**	**TUG BOAT**	**LEISURE CRAFT**
Accesses: - **At sea** - **In port**	 High High	 Easy Easy	 High High
Restricted areas	None	None	None
Cargo handling	Low	None	None
Delivery of provisions	Low	Low	Low
Unaccompanied luggage	None	None	None
Surveillance of vessel protection	None	Normal	None

2 The ship and its realities   75

2.6 Ease of concealment on board

The distribution of the spaces, holds, store-rooms, quarters, chambers, rooms and work areas on all vessels, whatever their type, endows them with a great number of possibilities for use in the concealment of illicit materials, for smuggling goods, hiding persons and, in relation to security, for hiding arms and explosives.

The concealment could be carried out by two groups: on the one hand, the members of the crew itself (there is a low probability of this happening), and on the other hand, thanks to the ease of access to these hiding places, some of the passengers or the on land work-teams used for the loading operations.

In general cargo vessels, the possibility of accessing empty spaces in bulkheads, side panels and false floors, will depend largely on the level of efficiency of the following (Figures 2.4, 2.5 and 2.6):

- ✓ Surveillance of holds maintained by crew members
- ✓ Inspection of hand luggage taken on board
- ✓ Inspection of contents of cargoes loaded

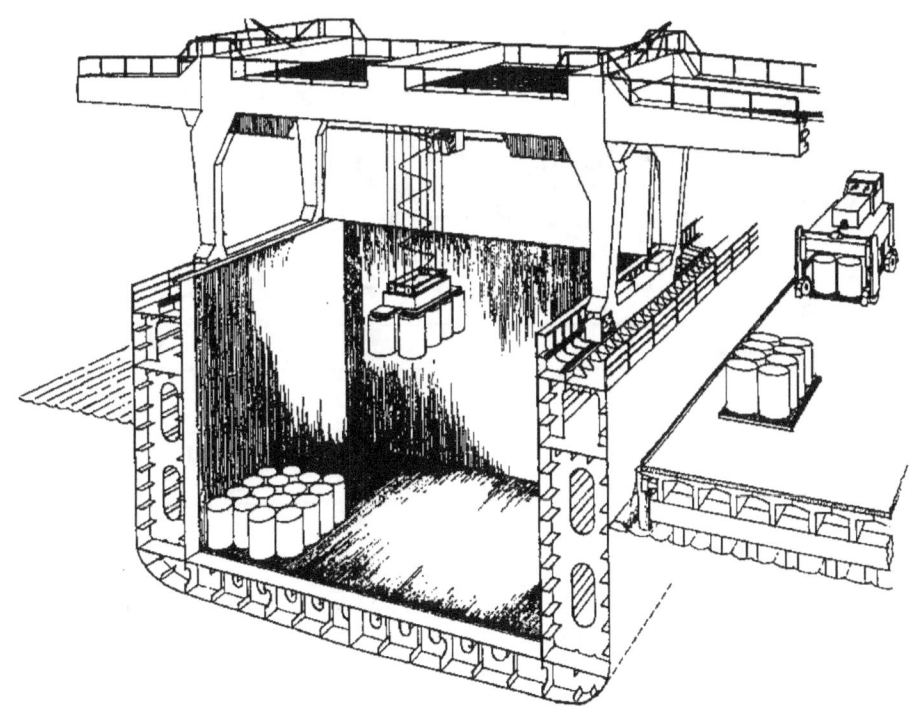

Figure 2.4

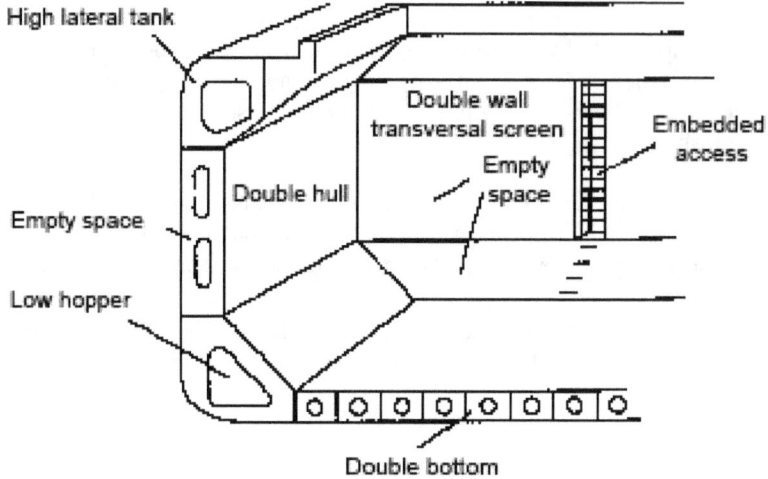

Figure 2.5

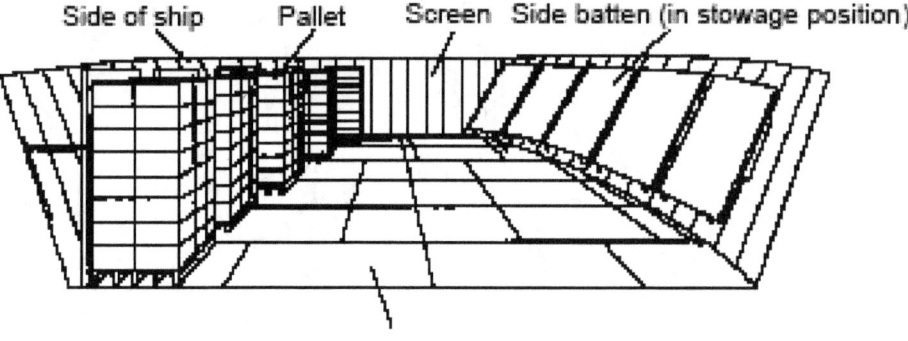

Figure 2.6

Container ships offer other hiding alternatives although it may appear at first sight that the cargo bays do not offer or allow any possibilities for concealment. Hence, these spaces must receive more inspections than just the routine ones (Fig. 2.7).

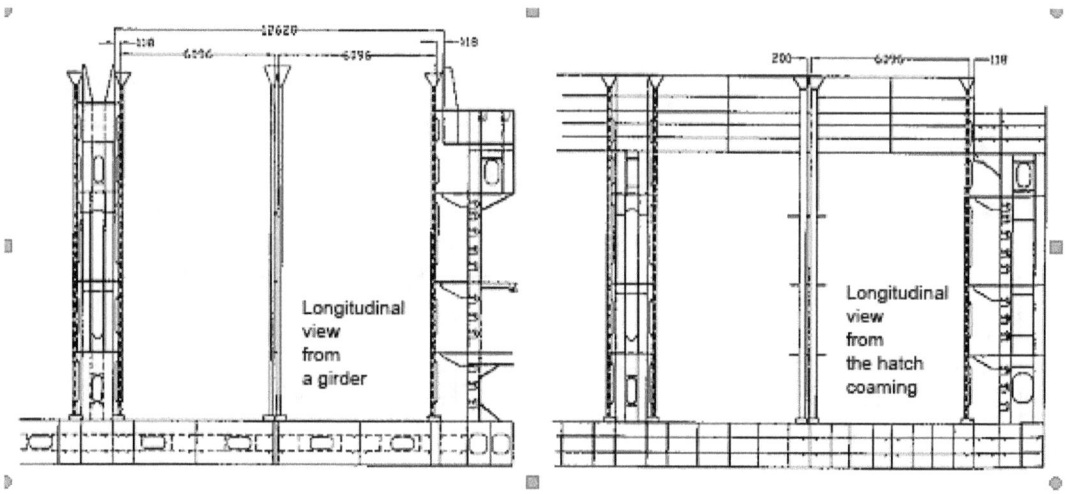

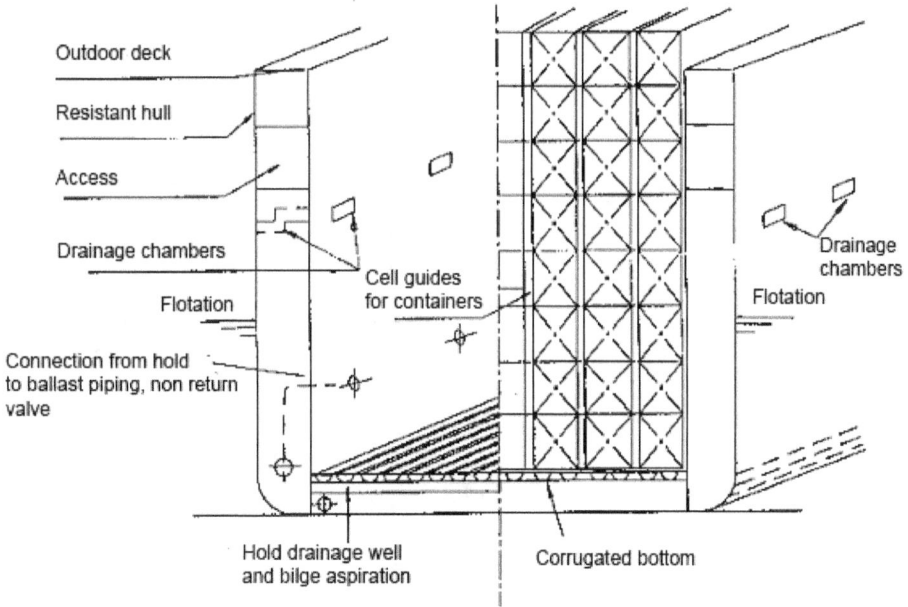

Figure 2.7

Ro-Ro ships offer ease of access to many areas that offer possibilities of concealment, some of which belong to the restricted area category and others which are of free access (Fig. 2.8).

It is clear that, in this case, control of access to restricted areas must be exhaustive, although the vehicles themselves embarked as cargo can often be used for criminal purposes.

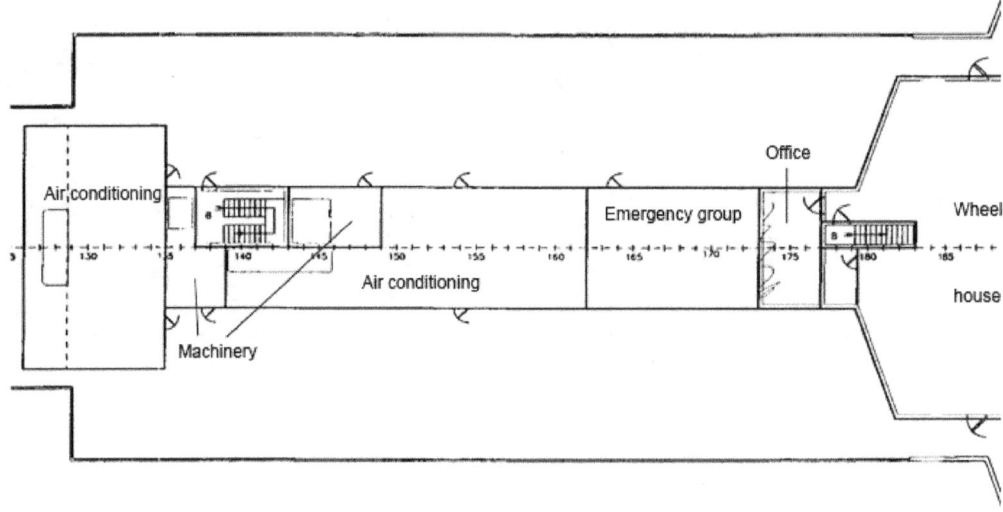

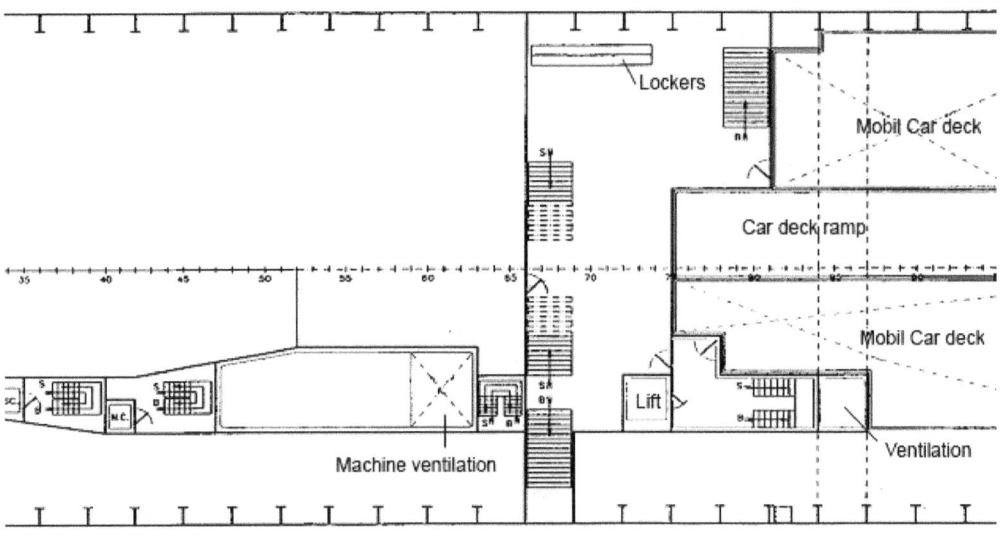

Figure 2.8

The areas dedicated to the crew or those which are freely accessible to the passengers, but at certain times of day are vacated by their usual occupants, such as bars and service points, can also be selected for concealment (Fig. 2.9).

2 The ship and its realities 79

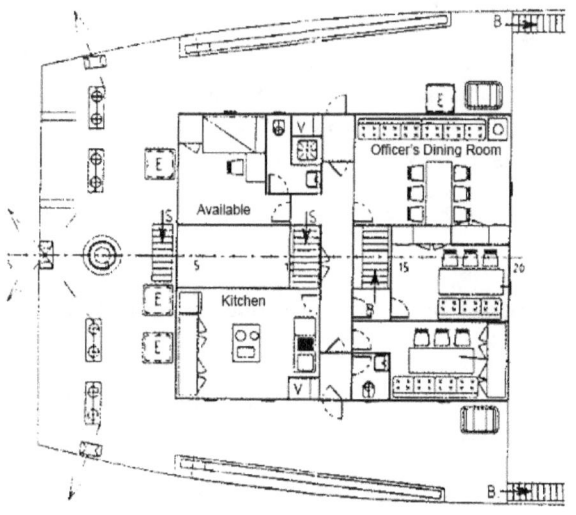

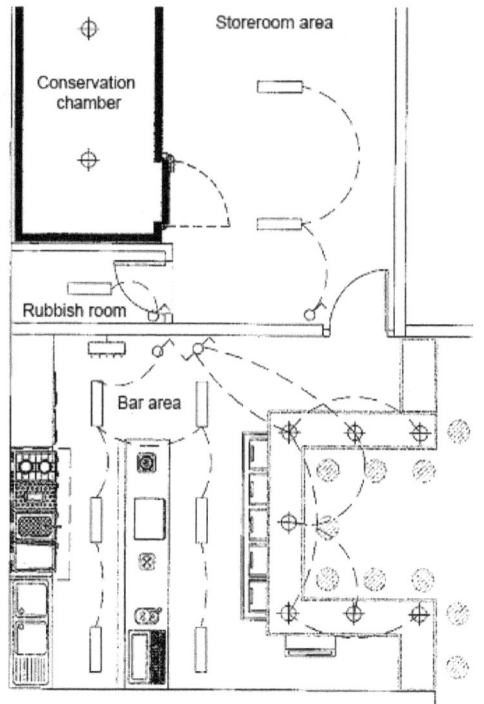

Figure 2.9

2.7 Summary of conclusions on vessels

Table 2.22 presents a summary, by characteristics and vessel type, in such a way that these are qualified by risk category for each aspect considered, allowing a final assessment to be made (right column). This assessment, although it is made with the objectivity applied throughout this analysis, must be interpreted as orientative, since any type of vessel or craft can be used in the event of a terrorist attack, whatever the nature of its cargo. Nor does this depend on the size of the vessel, but on the possibilities of boarding and the ease of use.

Identifying the vulnerability of each vessel type to the risks listed in the Code leads to three possible lines of action:

- Facilitating the relations of the Port Facilities Security Officers with the Ship Security Officers

- Providing the Port Facilities Security Officers with a reasonable knowledge of the security risks on board the vessels.

- Assisting the Port Facilities Security Officers with the implementation of the Port Facilities Security Plan in those aspects which are directly related to vessels.

Finally, we must not overlook that fact that one of the most vulnerable points of the vessel in port may not be the port side where it is tied up, but the sea side where there is always far less surveillance and over which, unless level 3 comes into force, there is insufficient control to provide the required protection. For this reason, even when the vessel is in the port facilities, all threats of this type must be detected, identified, controlled and neutralised by the protection systems managed by the Port Facilities Security Plan assisted, in all likelihood, by the support, collaboration and intervention of the special forces, as well as by the use of any electronic means the port installation may be equipped with.

Table 2.21

Ship	Characteristics of the ship			Characteristics of cargo		Characteristic of land			Characteristic of crew		Evaluation
	Sea access	Land access	Category	Type of cargo	Category	Cargo Oper.	Type handling	Category	Crew origin	Category	Risk category
Cruise	N	S	2	N	1	N	N	1	N	1	1
Ferry	N	S	3	S	3	S	S	5	S	2	3/4
Tanker	S	N	2	S	5	N	N	1	N	1	2
Gas	N	N	1	S	5	N	N	1	N	1	2
General	N	S	3	S	4	S	S	5	S	3	4
Cold storage	N	S	3	N	2	S	S	3	S	2	2/3
Bulk carrier	S	S	3	N	1	N	N	2	N	2	2
Ro-Ro	S	S	3	S	4	S	S	5	S	4	4
Container	N	S	3	S	5	N	N	4	S	4	4
Car carrier	N	S	2	S	3	N	N	2	N	1	2
Tug boat	S	S	4	N	1	N	N	1	N	1	1/2
Fishing boat	S	S	4	S	1	N	N	1	N	1	1/2
Leisure boat	S	S	4	N	1	N	N	1	N	1	1/2

Encoding:
- 1 … Possible
- 2 … Low
- 3 … Normal
- 4 … High
- 5 … Very high

2.8 Intervention on board by FCSE ('State Security Forces and Corps')

2.8.1 Previous Actions

Operation SOCOTORA[2]

For its interest, below is a transcription of the article that describes as far as possible the events that make up Operation Socotora:

"Members of the Naval Brigade (TEAR)) of the Marine Infantry undertook yesterday morning the boarding of a vessel in the Indian Ocean which carried, among its cargo of cement, fifteen Scud missiles. The operation was completed without any casualties, although the United States returned the missiles to Yemen, to whom they apparently belong"[3].

The above clearly states that the action had two clearly distinct phases, one military and a subsequent political phase. This article will deal only with the military phase, which I intend to describe with the maximum objectivity which the data available allows. But before entering into action, let me first make three general remarks on the information appearing in some of the media, both military and civil.

1. The Navy Brigade (TEAR) is a unit in which all of its subordinate units have the same configuration and the same level of training, the only differences being those due to the specific task for which each of these is expressly conceived. It makes no sense, therefore, to talk of a part of the TEAR units as an elite force, as is often the case. The elite force, as it is now fashionable to say, is the TEAR in full.

2. The TEAR, like all of the units of this corps, is a naval unit, with naval doctrines and mentalities. And when units of the Marine Infantry embark or join Navy vessels to engage in an amphibious operation or any other mission, the resulting force is a Naval Force with the capacities corresponding to the components integrated in it.

3. And thus, in the case we are concerned with, the frigate 'Navarra', or the combat support ship 'Patiño', since they carry units of the Marine Infantry, have certain operative possibilities that they would not have without these units, and without these the mission commended to them could not have been conducted as it was; that is, through the use of the means available, each one for the purpose for which it was conceived, with firmness and in an impeccable and synchronised fashion.

2.8.2 Situation

Very simply, the general situation in which the action took place can be described by stating that Spanish naval units, integrated in a coalition, intervened in the Operation 'Lasting Freedom', planned after S-11 under the auspices of the United Nations and led by the United States to fight against

---

[2] José Gil Gundín. Colonel Marine Infantry (Ret.)
[3] Diario de Cádiz, 12-12-02

international terrorism and prevent the illegal trafficking of arms in the highly sensitive zone of the Persian Gulf.

On December 5th, 2002, the US intelligence services reported the presence in the area of a suspect vessel sailing towards some point of the Middle East and which was believed to be transporting illegal arms. The vessel, a cargo-ship, was heading towards the zone of responsibility of Task Force-150, in the Gulf of Aden, which, since November 1st, had been under Spanish command (C.A. Moreno Susana), its flag being hoisted on the frigate 'Navarra'. This operative force comprised Spanish, American, German, French and British vessels.

The suspect vessel was identified as the So San, and appeared on NATO's military intelligence list as susceptible to be used by hostile adversaries. Once located (a significant role was played here by a plane of the sea patrol, Orion P-3, of the Spanish Air Force), it turned out that it was sailing without any nation's flag, was registered in Phnom Pemh and the last port it had visited was Chinese.

The operative force (TF-150) was the closest naval group to the course pursued by the So San, which was around one hundred miles east of the Straits of Bab el Mandeb, separating Djibouti from South Yemen and giving access to the Red Sea. And due to this proximity, the supreme naval command of Operation Lasting Freedom alerted the CTF-150 on December 5th "... to carry out surveillance actions on the MV So San and to be ready to make a review and inspection". To fulfil this request, Admiral Moreno Susana sent the Spanish vessels of the TF (the frigate Navarra and the combat support ship Patiño) to the zone. Embarked on these vessels were two helicopters and two units of the Navy Brigade, one of the 3rd Group of the Special Operations Unit (Patiño) and another of the SERECO (Reconnaissance Section) of the 2nd Disembarkment Battalion (frigate Navarra). The naval formation, under the command of Rear Admiral Moreno Susana, was made up, then, of three elements of the Navy: vessels, helicopters and units of the Marine Infantry. All three were of the same mentality and doctrine and this allowed this unexpected situation to be approached and solved in a synchronised way, in the minimum time and without problems.

A register and inspection operation at sea does not represent any difficulties. It is performed in a routine way, in accordance with the international regulations and normally the collaboration of the vessel is total. But it becomes quite complex when the vessel refuses to be inspected or even does everything at its disposal to flee; or when the vessel has no country flag and it is difficult (due to its characteristics and attitudes) to board; when the crew is excessive for this type of vessel (thus making it suspicious); or when the action takes place in an environment of international terrorism and thus, the attitude of the crew may be dangerous. In this case, all of these characteristics were in place. The American intelligence services warned that "the behaviour of the crew may be unfriendly" and thus might resist boarding. It was even not too far-fetched to think that, on being captured, possible members or sympathisers of Al Qaida might perform some dangerous act with the Spaniards on board, etc.

2.8.3 Execution

On December 8th, a photograph of the So San was received showing the existence of some cables in diagonal towards the centre of the deck which prevented the insertion of units by means of helicopters and which would consequently have to be eliminated if these means were to be used.

The boarding action began on the dawn of Monday, December 9th. On this day, the merchant ship sailing without a flag in international waters was intercepted. The legal protocol was initiated and the vessel was urged to reduce its speed in order to be inspected. The merchant ship's captain refused to do this, increased speed to more than 11 knots, informed that it only transported cement and even tried to prevent the nationality of the crew, which turned out to be North-Korean, from being discovered. In the face of this refusal and after several hours of urging the Captain to stop and even after threatening him with opening fire if he did not do so, Rear Admiral Moreno Susana took the decision to enter into action. The frigate Navarra fired some deterrent shots, with prior warnings of several minutes in advance in each case, so that the vessel should stop but, far from obeying, it even increased its speed, making it necessary to perform a definitive boarding action. This was conducted in several phases:

Phase 1

Faced with the evasive action of the vessel, and to force it to stop, several warning shots were fired from the frigate (at two hundred and a hundred metres from bow, including some shots at the hull and funnel). The cargo ship continued forth, so the Rear Admiral proceeded to the next stage. As the vessel would not stop, the boarding would be executed by means of helicopters, since conducting it from rubber dinghies was too risky given the speed of the vessel and the state of the sea.

Phase 2

The sniper shots were fired from around two hundred metres, from the deck of the frigate Navarra, with the ship sailing in parallel to the So San, despite the swaying movements of the ships and with the cargo ship at full steam. They found their mark, however, on some very small targets.

Phase 3

Once the deck was cleared, two helicopters approached the vessel, their pilots showing great resolution and bravery. One helicopter, the Sea King SH-3D of the 5th Squadron, protected by an SH-60 from the Navarra, transported from the Patiño an assault group made up of seven men who reached the deck in twelve seconds using a fast rope, and in a rapid action took the bridge, captured several members of the crew and forced the captain to stop the ship (photo 2.1)

Phase 4

Once the ship was detained, a control group, made up of five men from the Special Operations Unit approached by means of a semi-rigid launch and embarked to locate and control the rest of the crew.

But before initiating the boarding, the cargo-ship deck had to be cleared, as the cables of the masts and spars area made the approach and stationary flight of the helicopters very dangerous, as can be seen in photograph 2.1.

This operation was conducted by means of shots fired from the machine-guns of the Navarra and by two snipers of the Marine Infantry (SERECO). The snipers used Accuracy AW and Barret M95 precision rifles.

Finally, once the vessel was secured, a review and inspection team from the Navarra embarked to verify the nationality of the crew and the documentation and to inspect the cargo.

The inspection revealed fifteen full bodies of Scud missiles, fifteen HE warheads, twenty-three hoppers of nitric acid, used as a propeller fuel for missiles, and eighty-four drums with chemical products. All of this war material was camouflaged among 40,000 sacks of cement. The ship's cargo list declared that it only transported cement and the captain of the cargo-ship changed his declaration several times with reference to the port of destination.

Photograph 2.1

Phase 5

On December 10th, the American vessels arrived in the zone. An inspection team from one of the coalition vessels joined the Spanish team for a detailed inspection of the cargo. Once the inspection was completed, with the appearance of the material mentioned above, the So San was placed at the disposal of the command of the Lasting Freedom coalition.

This was the end of Operation Socotora, efficiently completed as part of the international cooperation responsibilities assumed by Spain.

2.9 Final comments

The action was acknowledged by the highest American authorities as being carried out with great professionalism, clarity, efficiency and brilliance. And, independently of the final destiny of the vessel, the Spanish naval force did what it had to do and did it impeccably.

The operation, which is not at all difficult in normal situations, turned into a very delicate and dangerous one in this case due to the hostility of the cargo-ship. However, it was performed brilliantly with ingenuity in the approach and resolve in the execution.

Some comments:

"It was an operation of enormous difficulty and great danger due to the complete refusal of the vessel to collaborate and because we did not know what the response of the crew of the So San would be once we boarded the vessel...".(Commander of Frigate Navarra, CF Rodríguez Garat. Diario ABC 13/12/02).

1. William Zafire, in one of his regular columns in *The New York Times* on 19/12/02 : "...a true ally who, at our request, put the lives of its men at risk...".

2. "... It corresponded to Spain, through its participation in the organised fight against international terrorism, to undertake the far from easy task of detaining the vessel, occupying it, inspecting its insides, discovering the hidden and mortal cargo and delivering it to the command of the coalition of countries that supervise the illegal traffic of arms ('The Pirate Ship'. J. Campany).

3. Maj. General USMC (Commander of the 2ª division USMC, and designated Combined Joint Task Force (CJTF) from the USS Mount Whitney) sent the CJTF 150 the following message:

   "Yesterday we followed your highly professional interception, boarding and detention of the vessel, So San. A great day for Spain and its navy, for the CTF-150 and the global war against terrorism. Its sailors and navy soldiers, facing a situation of great danger, resolved it heroically..." .

4. These quotes (others could be added) are mentioned as a sample of the praise the action deservedly drew. The operation was reported by all the communications media, both national and foreign.

   - The personnel of the SERECO had embarked in Rota on the frigate Numancia, on September 4 and the action took place three months later. This fact speaks for itself as regards the level of training at the time of embarking and of the maintenance of this level for prolonged periods of sailing. The same can be said of the personnel of the Special Operations Unit.

   - The arms used by the snipers were an "Accuracy AW rifle, calibre 308, and a Barret M95 of 12.7 millimetres. This weapon, with a tremendous recoil that the sniper has to withstand, fired more than eighty shots. There were two snipers on the helicopters, from the Special Operations Unit and the SERECO, as well as medical personnel.

- The action of the units of the Marine Infantry was no surprise to me, as I know the TEAR very well. But I was pleasantly struck by the calmness with which the personnel that participated in the action evaluated their performance, as if it was a question of a routine exercise and the natural fruit of a hard, continuous training.

- And this action took place while other navy soldiers participated in other missions with no less bravery and enthusiasm: some fighting against the oil stains on the beaches of the North of Spain, others on peace missions in the Balkans and all of them fulfilling their motto "Brave on land and at sea" members of a Corps with a cost/efficiency ratio which is difficult to beat.

2.9.1 MIO Operations

Under the name of Maritime Interdiction Operations (MIO) can be found a series of NATO procedures designed to enforce an embargo supported by resolutions of the international organisms.

This type of procedures are quite in fashion these days due to the proliferation of international embargo operations in the framework of the fight against terrorism or the fight against the traffic of materials and weapons of mass destruction.

Thus, at the beginning of 2003, we witnessed the assault that forces of the Spanish Navy conducted on the North-Korean cargo-ship, So San, or the one that towards the middle of that year, Greek special forces carried out on a vessel loaded with explosives with an unknown destination.

Background of MIO operations

Throughout history, the various naval powers have established review and inspection mechanisms for vessels suspected of undertaking illicit activities or activities which go against the international treaties. For this purpose, the vessels of the respective navies established the appropriate mechanisms for intercepting suspect vessels and reviewing their documentation and cargo.

Obviously, the attitude of the merchant ships subjected to these review and inspection activities could either be one of cooperation or one of non-cooperation. In one or the other case, the response of the vessels responsible for executing these operations would depend on the degree of resistance.

Present state of MIO operations

Today, it is assumed that there are terrorist conflicts and interests that have no place in international law and order. Hence, the international organisms have equipped themselves with certain tools to prevent the sea from being used for the traffic of weapons of mass destruction or of materials susceptible to be used by international terrorist gangs.

These tools are validated by international security organisations, such as NATO. This body establishes through its permanent or non-permanent operative naval organisations, the aerial and naval means capable of locating, identifying and, if necessary, inspecting, with cooperation or not, vessels which are suspected of breaking the rules of these embargoes.

Similarly, in the framework of the anti-terrorist security or international security operations, the allied countries also establish procedures designed for the same ends of review and inspection of suspect vessels.

How is a maritime interdiction operation conducted?

Without getting involved in detailed explanations, it is enough to know that the air and sea spaces where these actions take place in the framework of international agreements are 'shared' between different operative organisations, made up of vessels and, sometimes, airplanes. A high Command coordinates the operations of the various operative groups.

The confluence of information from the intelligence services, electronic listening devices, detection systems and others will lead to and locate the so-called 'Contacts of Interest' (COI). At a given moment, these COI will be intercepted by the air and sea forces and invited to collaborate by answering a series of questions asked by the naval authorities, aimed at verifying nationality, port of origin, destination, cargo and shipping company. Normally, there is full cooperation and it is simply a matter of a brief check.

At times, mistrust or an excessive wariness will mean that some merchant ship may be unwilling to collaborate, but the presence of naval units close by will mean that the majority of these will end up collaborating.

In very few cases, suspect merchant ships try to dodge these units. A procedure is initiated designed to execute the so-called 'Rules of Engagement', consisting in a series of measures implemented, in the final extreme, in order to take control of the vessel by force, should the attitude be uncooperative.

It may be necessary to fire some warning shots to make the merchant vessel obey. Normally, if an inspection on board the suspect merchant ship is necessary, the review and inspection team should be sufficient. These will approach the COI, protected by the warship, by means of a RIB-type craft to get on board and inspect papers and cargo. This review and inspection team will be made up of personnel of the General Corps of the Marine Infantry who will provide security to the team.

If there is active resistance on the part of the suspect vessel, it may be necessary to take control of the vessel by force. To do this, it will be necessary to insert on board a Marine Infantry operative team, which will quickly take control of the bridge and machines and will capture the crew in order to then bring on the review and inspection team.

The insertion may be through the use of helicopters with the fast rope technique, or using crafts. The former is faster, but extremely dangerous if the merchant ship decides on armed resistance. The warship will order the merchant ship to adopt a certain heading and a low speed so that the MIO team can approach.

The warship will situate itself at a distance that allows its collective weapons to neutralise any violent resistance, and an order will be sent for nobody to appear on deck. The approach to the ship will be covered from the helicopters by snipers while the operative teams descend and take control.

Once the bridge and machines are taken, the crew gathered at a visible point and the vessel under control, the review and inspection team goes on board. Then, it is the authorities that decide what to do depending on what is found on board.

This operation is not as simple as it may seem. To begin with, there are hundreds of ships sailing through the areas where the operative groups have to conduct their mission; of these hundreds of ships, many have no crew members who can speak English to a minimally acceptable level, making any connection or communication with them extremely difficult. Indeed, an error in the interpretation of the orders given may result in aggressive actions being taken by the warship.

Similarly, in the case of boardings without the cooperation of the merchant ship, one single crew member armed with an AK 47 might prove fatal for the helicopters or the RIB. Obviously, the response would be overwhelming, but the primary objective in these operations is the respect for the basic rights of persons and to avoid any unnecessary violence.

2.9.2 Force Protection Team

However, the blatant threat posed by terrorism in the western world today makes it necessary to take measures to protect these priceless naval units from attacks such as that suffered some years ago by the USS Cole.

Hence, the so-called Force Security teams often join the units of the Spanish Navy in international missions. Their mission is to collaborate in the protection of the vessel through the use of their weapons and of the collective armour of the warship. This is a response to aggressions by vessels that use high-speed crafts loaded with explosives, attacks from land once moored in foreign ports, or even attacks by hijacked aircraft (helicopters, etc.).

How does the Marine Infantry train for these missions?

As always, the training begins in the barracks, with practice in mounting and insertion by fast rope from the walls of the military tracks. The individual and collective techniques of movement and neutralisation of hostile persons are also worked on in the barracks. Next, the training is completed with techniques in insertion by helicopter or crafts in special areas on Navy vessels, both in port and sailing in manoeuvres.

This gruelling daily work means that, when it comes to tackling a situation like that of the merchant-ship So San, they know how to react adequately and brilliantly.

Which units of the MI undertake these missions?

The MI units that undertake these missions are the Special Operations Units (who will normally handle MIO missions without the cooperation of the corresponding merchant ship), the SERECO of the disembarking forces, the rifle companies normally provided by the Force Security teams and the review and inspection teams. In Operation Socotora (boarding of the So San), the team that boarded the ship belonged to the Special Operations Units, but the team that provided security to the review and inspection teams that went on board immediately came from the BD-II, as did the snipers who fired at the frame of the Korean vessel.

2.9.3 Maritime Interception Operation (MIO) Teams

Since the end of the combat operations in support of Iraqi freedom in May, MIO teams continually board and check the traffic of merchant ships in the Persian Gulf in order to ensure that nothing illegal enters or comes out of Iraq.

Although the sanctions in place before the war have been lifted, there are still banned products that leave the country. When the interception teams board the ship, they are specifically looking for weapons or objects that could be used as bombs. Each interception is different for each team. They never know if the mission will be incident-free and routine or if they will find contraband.

The crew of the USS Chosin (CG 65) have learned that being ready for anything can help their work immensely. When the words "Man the boat deck!" are spoken, the MIO team gets ready. The MIO team on board the Chosin wait on the boat deck for the rigid hull inflatable boat (RHIB) while they concentrate on what they will have to do when the mission begins. As the RHIB moves away from the Chosin, its captain receives a report from the bridge with his target. They need to know everything about the vessel they are to board: its course, vessel-type, who the leader is thought to be and what is suspected to be on board.

On many occasions, the crew has no idea what to expect. The challenge may range from simple linguistic hurdle to the risk of being shot at. They need to be ready for everything. The MIO teams do not board all vessels in the Persian Gulf, only those that do not respond to their calls.

"The reason why we perform MIO is to help stabilise the maritime environment and to ensure the ordered flow of traffic in and around the port of Umm Qasr", said Captain Mark Kellam, commander of Task Group 55.1, of the Maritime Interception Force (MIF) task group.

The American army and coastguard and the navies of Australia, Great Britain, Poland; Spain and Holland all participate in the MIO, returning security and stability to the port of Umm Qasr.

"We are all, in reality, in the same organisation. We work together, and we are a team", says Kellam.

At present, the Chosin serves as the command platform for the MIF commander, although this position is occupied by the Australian captain. When the Chosin leaves the Gulf, another ship will take its place, and its responsibilities will be passed on to that vessel. The US coastguard cutter, Baranof (WPB1318) and the MIO teams of the Chosin keep the Gulf under control.

There are currently three MIO teams on board the Chosin. The first two keep watch over four-hour periods but they do not board the ships. They will call the third team, or the boarding team if necessary. There are three teams in the boarding team, one security team and two search teams, as well as a boarding officer and an assistant boarding officer.

"Normally, if you take a team of eight men, there will be two persons per group: two in search team one, two in search team two, two in the security team, one boarding officer and the assistant officer," says Cameron Alexander, third deck officer of the Chosin and member of the search team.

Boarding procedure

The first team to board is search team one. It begins on the top part of the ship, moving down towards the cabins making sure it makes an Initial Security Investigation (ISI). This includes a quick check of the vessel to ensure that nobody is hiding anywhere, or that no suspicious actions are taking place.

Search team two is the engineering team. They go down into the machine rooms and talk to the head of machines. They verify how much fuel there is on board and exactly what type of goods. After completing the ISI, search team two secures the machines room and returns to the main deck.

The security team takes all of the crew to the forecastle. Depending on the size of the craft there will normally only be one or two members of the security team, led by a first-class officer.

Once the crew is gathered and a thorough inspection of the ship has been made, the boarding officer will talk to the ship's captain or skipper.

"Sometimes, the crew does not understand what is happening, because we talk to them in English", says Alexander. "But on other occasions we have interpreters and then they obey with no problem".

The MIO teams of the Chosin and the Baranof have not encountered serious problems with any ships.

"At the beginning, I was really nervous about boarding all the ships, because I thought they were all bad guys", says Alexander, "but then I realised that they were only trying to get by, and they are not bad people really. They want to secure their jobs, just like us".

When the sailors abandon the ship after a successful, problem-free MIO, they are proud to know that their presence in the Gulf is making it a safer place.

3. Human Factors Involved

This chapter focuses on the human factor in a security situation, and in particular two of its main aspects: the crew, as civil elements unaccustomed to the circumstances threatening their survival, and the special forces who will intervene in the vessel boarding to free the hostages (crew and passengers).

3.1 The vessel and its exploitation for criminal activities

Few activities escape the attention of organised crime gangs, whatever their objectives or criminal methods.

The vessel and its activity, due to the internationality of this means of transport, the great volume of traffic, the conflictive countries visited, the intermodality of the various means of transport which are more and more interrelated, constitutes a channel for criminal activity, the most common offences being drug-trafficking and smuggling in terms of goods and illegal immigration in terms of persons.

A clear picture of the reality of the situation is painted by research studies, surveys, quantifications of the fulfilment of the current norms by the crews, their levels of awareness in the constant battle to prevent and to avoid being the object of, and party, to crime.

From 1998 to 2000, a research project was carried out for the EU[1] which provided an overview of maritime activity with respect to crime, culminating in a forewarning of several dramatic events which have occurred recently and in the confirmation of the threat that intelligence services have singled out whereby vessels become the vehicle for criminal activities.

Below are presented some of the conclusions reached, presented and accepted in the Falcone Programme of the EU, as these provide a picture of the crews, their manner of thinking and acting, tested out in Italian and Spanish ports, under the rigorous and systematic system provided by the use of check lists, based mainly on the OMI Resolution A.872 (20) of 28.11.97 on Guidelines for the Prevention and Suppression of the Smuggling of Drugs, Psychotropic Substances and Precursor Chemicals on Ships Engaged in International Maritime Traffic.

---

[1] "Identification and analysis of the influence of the maritime dimension (ports and vessels) in the state of organised crime". European Commission. Task Force for Cooperation on Justice and Home Affairs. Police and Customs. FALCONE Programme. UPC, October 1999/July 2000.

3.2 Data obtained from official statistical sources

The Spanish data on maritime provinces from the Ministry of the Interior have made it possible to pinpoint where the greatest incidence of certain illegal trafficking linked either fully or in part to certain aspects of maritime navigation or traffic has occurred.

3.2.1 State Secretary General for Security

Concerning smuggling and the type of vessels involved:

- In cargo vessels, it was observed that Barcelona, Valencia and Vizcaya are the three Spanish provinces that stand out from the rest. It is clear that Barcelona and Valencia are two conflictive provinces as regards tobacco-smuggling.
- As regards fishing vessels, which can also play a major role, the southern provinces of Cadiz and Malaga account for 88% of the total in this type of smuggling.
- As regards passenger vessels, Almeria makes up 50% of the incidence of all provinces as the main port of entry for this type of vessels.
- As for recreational vessels, the greatest incidence is in the provinces of Almeria, Cadiz, Ceuta and Melilla in the south of Spain, accounting for over 95 % of the total.

As regards drugs trafficking, the same statistic gives these results:

- In cargo vessels, the provinces of Seville, Valencia and Vizcaya make up 50% of all the offences involved.
- In passenger vessels, it is again the south that has the greatest incidence, the provinces of Almería and Cadiz accounting for 50%, while the Balearic and Canary Islands reach 23%. The rest, 27%, is distributed among the remaining Spanish maritime provinces.
- As for fishing vessels, the southern provinces of Cadiz and Malaga have 88% of the total number of infractions.
- In the case of private recreational vessels such as yachts, it is again the maritime provinces of the south, Almería, Cadiz and Malaga, which account for 66% of the total.

This information is of great value for focusing and channelling any future analysis, survey, etc.

For Spain, the countries involved in this illicit trafficking are Morocco, with 96% of the total, while for the American continent, Columbia and The United States make up 37%, and finally, for Europe, the United Kingdom also accounts for 33%, as it is also a source or entry point, a country of origin. In the list of countries with drugs, Morocco has 98% and Columbia 78%.

As for the number of arrests related with smuggling, especially tobacco-smuggling:

- The ports of Melilla, Alicante and Gerona have 5%, Valencia alone has 20%, the most western province of Spain, Pontevedra, 28%, and Vizcaya stands out with 47%.
- Offshore, that is, outside the port, the provinces of Cadiz, Malaga, and Algeciras are the three most relevant. Cadiz stands out, with 91% of arrests through preventive detection before reaching land.

For drug-trafficking:

- With respect to cannabis-based drugs, the south of Spain again has the greatest incidence, with 97% of the total, while the offshore trafficking is shared between Algeciras, Cadiz, Almería and Malaga, also provinces of the south of Spain.
- For opiate drugs, the maritime province of Barcelona stands out together with Gerona, although it is not clear whether it is the maritime channels or recreational vessels that are the most used. Another entry point is the Canary Islands province of Las Palmas.
- For cocaine-based drugs, Valencia heads the list with 67%, followed by Barcelona, with 13%, and Cadiz with 5%, while outside the ports, offshore, Barcelona reaches 42%, followed by La Coruña and Pontevedra, with 25% each.

As regards illegal immigration:

- The information gathered over a period of six years, ranging from 1992 to 1998, provides a register of 3,837 immigrants, 38 stowaways, and 182 crew members, who make up the main body of the immigration detected.
- This illegal immigration leads in turn to drugs-trafficking accounting for 527 kilos of drugs and 369 vessels charged under the crime of immigration itself and also in the collateral trafficking of drugs.

It can be concluded that the information available on this aspect is scarce. There is a lack of any analysis by year or of the ports with the greatest incidence or relevance.

In general, the source of the State Secretary General of the Ministry of the Interior is considered adequate for determining the maritime provinces which represent the greatest risk, providing impoundment percentages and a breakdown of the type of vessels involved in the process, but if any other variables are required, the information provided does not allow any further conclusions to be reached.

The above observation can be applied further still to the other statistics available, where the information is gathered to fulfil other objectives than their possible relation with the maritime dimension. It is practically impossible to use such information for a rigorous scientific study, since there is no way to quantify the detentions, typology of offenders, actions leading to the discovery of the offence, procedures for detection, hiding places, special persons and equipment used or any other type of incidence that might be adopted as a repetitive, and thus significant, variable.

It can be considered, therefore, that the information provided by the current presentation of the data through these statistics might fulfil the objectives required for the internal functioning of the State security forces, but are of little use to those outside the State's own institutions or security forces.

3.2.2 National Drugs Plan

For example, offering some constructive criticism of the information obtained from the National Drugs Plan of the Ministry of the Interior, this limits itself to drawing up statistics on drugs consumption. It focuses on the age of the consumers, quantities, forms of consumption, medical treatments, and police and prison indicators. From this information, statistics are extracted on the detainees, the amounts confiscated, the value of these, the attention received by drug-addicts as users of these drugs and, finally, the preventive activities in the different fields such as school, the workplace, etc. It is clear, therefore, that this information, valuable as it may be for the internal government of a country for finding social solutions to the problem, has no direct relationship with maritime activity.

Civil Guard Fiscal Service

With respect to the statistics provided by the fiscal service of the Civil Guard, an evaluation is made quantifying drugs captures, vessels and tobacco; however, there is no way of knowing, from these data, if there is any relation between the tobacco and drugs captures and the vessels. This relation, then, is far from explicit and thus no conclusions can be drawn regarding the maritime dimension, or the two may be completely independent, in which case there is no way of linking them together. They do, however, list the most conflictive provinces.

From the same source, there is an interesting statistic on foreigners detained for drugs trafficking, specifying the most significant nationalities involved, which are the Moroccan, Columbian, French or British nationalities, but again there is no relation with the maritime dimension.

Also in the case of immigrants at border crossings, it can be concluded that there is no information taking into account specifically the maritime dimension, nor can the risk factor be determined for this type of activity. Again, then, there seems to be a lack of information on the relation with the maritime factor.

3.2.3 National Central Drugs Office

The National Central Drugs Office (OCNE) has some statistical tables listing quantities of pills, hashish, cocaine and heroin captured in Spanish waters, differentiating between beaches, territorial sea, international waters and the bodies that have intervened. Of particular interest are the percentages of hashish and cocaine captured in the maritime environment. These statistics should be of some use, then, but they do not indicate whether the captures, specified under the heading of other customs centres, correspond to the port customs service, something which is specified in the case of airports.

Table 3.1

REGIONAL	APREHENS.	HACHIS (gr.)	TOBACCO	VESSELS	DETAINEES	IMMIGRANTS
CATALONIA	3	9.025.880	3.979.690	2	8	0
BALEARIC	1	1.004.366	0	3	8	0
VALENCIA	8	8.362.055	1.733.000	8	11	0
MURCIA	2	5.506.400	0	2	7	0
ANDALUC.	90	71.460.658	193	100	216	148
TOTAL	104	95.358.359	5.712.883	115	250	148

3.2.4 Tax Office

The Tax Office provides results on the customs controls in the form of an evaluation of the captures in the different provinces, but not by maritime provinces, so that we do not know whether Lerida (an inland province) or Barcelona (a maritime province), both of the Community of Catalonia, are the main culprits of the crime. An example of can be seen in Table 3.1.

3.2.5 Spanish Drugs Observatory

The Spanish Drugs Observatory, dependent on the Ministry of the Interior, meanwhile, gathers information from the different public and private government offices, showing it in tables which indicate the control of drug consumption and aspects of consumption and sociological indicators considered. For the purposes of this study, however, it has been of no use whatsoever.

3.2.6 From legal cases

Trial procedures, obtained from the Aranzadi data base, which gathers the jurisprudence in High Court sentences and others related with imposed sanctions and juridical intervention in aspects of drugs trafficking and smuggling provide little more than the legal procedures, with no description available on the operating procedures, detection, or any actions carried out by the state security forces which might have led to the success of the operation.

This source might have provided police and operative procedures which could then have been used effectively in training courses, or simply as information for all of the state security forces.

All of the above circumstances, objectively justified, lead to a loss of information which might have been of great value in its application to conclusions or to institutional actions aimed at the prevention of, or the fight against, crime at sea.

3.3 Other sources of information

In any type of accident investigation, one must turn to the information provided by the parties involved and their reports, which reflect data, conditions and circumstances which can then be processed more rigorously than a simple exposition of events. Thus, an analysis will now be made of the forms used by the Ministry of the Interior.

3.3.1 Analysis of data registry forms

The current forms for Ministry of the Interior security statistics are too generic in their treatment and registry of the offences related with the legislations on the merchant navy, smuggling and the clandestine passage of immigrants, so that most of the sections and subsections are inappropriate or insufficient for clearly defining the facts and circumstances surrounding the offences committed in the maritime environment.

From a detailed study of the forms currently used without any great variations for the different Spanish security bodies, a large number of data can be observed which are not applicable to the marine activity and, similarly, a complete lack of any specific variables for this field is observed.

The excess of data on a form, which it might not be possible to fill in as it does not correspond to the topic, is not a cause for great concern. However, all the data not requested in the list and register of specifically significant variables will be lost if no place is found for them on a form specifically devised to cover the particularities of criminal activity.

Thus, as well as the data that each body considers it necessary to maintain on the current forms, it is considered essential to extend the number of variables in order to ensure the specific statistical analysis, systematically reflecting the most significant events and the intervention undertaken by the police agents according to the analysis below.

- With respect to the official registry form used for police actions, blocks A, B, C and D are valid, since they describe the action and the environment.

- Block E should be replaced by certain terminologically accepted variables such as the following:

On the geographical location of the action:

- International waters (>24')
- Exclusive economic zone
- Adjoining zone (12÷24')
- Territorial sea (<12')
- Inland waters
- Coast and beaches
- Rivers, estuaries
- Port
- Commercial port
- Fishing port
- Recreational port
- Geographical situation (φ, λ)

This block, in its new form, should be amplified to include data on the location of the event, if it occurred on board or in coastal waters, substituting Block N of the form.

Nature of the place:

On board:

- Deck
- Bridge

On land/port:

- In the sand
- Afloat

- Machines
- Lodgings
- Holds
- Tool cribs
- Galley
- Storerooms
- Containers
- Pallets
- Vehicles
- Adjoined to the hull

- Submerged
- Caves
- Among rocks
- Storage sheds
- Vehicles
- Lorries
- Vans
- Buildings
- Cellars

- Block F of the current form should be discarded for actions in the maritime field.

- We consider it necessary to specifically distinguish the offence and the special legislation applicable.

Type of offence

- Drugs trafficking
- Smuggling
- Illegal immigration
- Arms trafficking

Special legislation

- Theft of vessels
- Ports and Merchant Navy Law
- Other legislations and regulations

- We consider that Blocks G, H, J and K of the form analysed are perfectly valid, but not Blocks L and M.

- Block S should remain as it is, as this may be a consequence of police actions.

- Block T should continue as it is, as it has an application to the offence of smuggling in its various guises, especially those considered for tobacco, arms, vessels, drugs and explosives.

- Block U should be replaced by an identification which is more in keeping with the medium:

Vessel Typology

- Navy Vessel
- General Cargo Vessel
- Container ship
- Roll-on Roll-off Ship
- Tanker
- Cruisers, ferries
- Auxiliary vessels
- Fishing vessels
- Yachts
- High-speed crafts

- Blocks V, W, X and Y can remain unaltered as they provide useful information, although there may be some repetition in the following blocks.
- The following blocks will provide a data registry that enhances the knowledge of the criminal activity through the intervention and the actions carried out by the security forces.

On the method of detection:

- Boarding
- Inspection in port
- Detection on coast/beach
- Continued persecution
- Inspection of packages
- Inspection of containers
- Inspection of holds

On the intervention:

- Resistance, violence
- Quick to surrender
- Casualties in delinquents
- Casualties in security forces
- Persecution at sea
- Persecution on land
- Various security bodies
- Special assault units
- Special diving units
- Special units (dogs, etc.)
- Coordination from land
- Use of special vessels
- Special detection teams
- Special search teams
- Suitable external conditions
- Aerial means
- Lighting means
- Night vision means
- Use of light weapons
- Use of heavy weapons
- Blinding lamps
- Paralysing light/sound grenades
- Gases
- Data transmission/reception equipment
- Access to data base from the high seas
- Transmission disturbing devices
- Mini-planes tele-controlled from the vessel or from land
- Survival kits

On the procedure of capture:

- Opening of closed spaces
- Breaking of ship's containers
- Breaking of cargo containers
- Personal luggage
- Breaking of homogenised goods
- Mixed in with cargo
- In the machinery of the vessel
- Hidden on persons

On the human intervention team:

- Sufficient number of components
- Several intervention brigades
- Adequately equipped
- Adequate communications system
- Failures in communications
- Availability of plans of the vessel
- Difficulties in co-ordination

3.4 Check list approach

The OMI Resolution A.872 (20) of 28.11.97 on "Guidelines for the prevention and suppression of the smuggling of drugs, psychotropic substances and precursor chemicals on ships engaged in international maritime traffic" has been largely forgotten since its implementation; many of those in positions of responsibility on board did not know of it and few complied with it in terms of its philosophy and operative application.

The design and development of the check list presented here has at all times followed the text and contents of said resolution, with a view to making it an objective, impartial tool which could be answered by any officer or crew member, maintaining their anonymity, and allowing them to express freely their impressions or overview of the circumstances they experience on board or in the port environment that they frequent. Practically all of the procedure is perfectly applicable to the requirements of the ISPS Code, and thus, it is described in full.

3.4.1 Design of the surveys

Two options were considered in order to obtain the opinion base required:

- Make a subjective survey considering future criteria.
- Use an internationally acknowledged document, with data gathered up to the present.

The former possibility, though more aggressive as it contemplates complex aspects of the organisational type, should be based on consolidated foundations, something which one suspects is not the case since there are no such foundations in maritime security matters.

The second alternative might allow the current state to be verified in order to establish the procedures to be followed in the future.

Obviously, this latter option was chosen, using as a basis for the formulation of the sections the recent IMO Resolution A.872 (20) of 28.11.97 on "Guidelines for the prevention and suppression of the smuggling of drugs, psychotropic substances and precursor chemicals on ships engaged in international maritime traffic".

While the Resolution is intended for application in the area of international traffic, it was assumed that it could be applied to any other kind of traffic, such as that between the peninsular ports and the Balearic and Canary Islands, Ceuta and Melilla.

The procedure for the design of the surveys was a meticulous breakdown of the IMO Resolution A.872 (20), as it was considered that a document of this nature and source has undergone the appropriate modifications and filtering to be judged to be important and irreplaceable in all its parts and precepts.

Also, with the same application criteria, different blocks were developed from the resolution according to subject areas, so that check lists could be obtained for vessels, shipping companies, concessionaires, commercial ports, fishing ports and leisure ports. This approach made available information related not only to vessels but also to the vessel-port interface and its internal organisations.

3.4.2 Methodology of survey

When it came to selecting the methodology to be used, quantitative analysis was considered the most appropriate. A questionnaire type survey would be suitable for the gathering of the information. Since it is the objectives that determine the most suitable method for the study, systematic questions were judged to be the best way to assess the protagonists involved.

A basis was provided by the definition of a survey as an investigation performed on persons, representative of a wider collective, using standardised questioning procedures in order to obtain quantitative measures of a wide range of characteristics of the population.

An initial phase was undertaken in which the objectives and the topics to be investigated were more clearly defined, in order to identify and delimit the significant aspects.

An exploratory phase was devoted to revising and analysing the various theoretical contributions to the subject matter, focusing on the resolution.

A research design was established in order to devise the hypotheses of the study, delimit the most interesting variables and define the population and the sample.

Finally, the fieldwork itself was carried out, formulating the questions using the previously elaborated questionnaire.

The research concluded with the analysis of the information and the interpretation of the results.

The questions used were of the closed type, due to the advantages these offer for a simpler and faster decoding, which is the ideal situation when dealing with an object of study which is not very structured, as is the case with maritime matters. This method is also suitable for verifying the level of knowledge of those surveyed on these matters and their motivation for telling us about it.

Within the closed system, the dichotomy of the YES-NO questions was preferred, sometimes with multiple choice questions. Given the ease with which these can be decoded, the most advanced version of the SPSS informatics package was used.

As a result of this planning, the total number of questions prepared for each survey, without taking into account the sections with multiple choice, was:

- Commercial vessels   440 sections
- Shipping companies   58   "
- Commercial ports   331   "
- Leisure ports   94   "
- Fishing ports   297   "

The surveys were presented to be filled in just as they were exposed in the Workshop of April, 1999, and also as they are registered in this report.

3.4.3 Check list for merchant ships

	YES	NO
APPLICABLE TO PERSONS IN CHARGE OF VESSEL		
Do you know the IMO Resolution A.872 (20) of 28.11.97 on "Guidelines for the prevention and suppression of the smuggling of drugs, psychotropic substances and precursor chemicals on ships engaged in international maritime traffic?"		
Do you collaborate with it only because the law so requires?		
Do you collaborate with the customs officers to facilitate the ship inspection?		
Do you use all means available to you to collaborate in the inspection?		
Do you consider adequate the means made available to the customs officers when they come on board?		
Do they have free access to all parts of the ship and cargo areas?		
Do you think they have free access to all the cargo?		
Do you consider it appropriate that they can mark and lock up any goods found on board or in containers?		
Do you know that a customs officer can issue detention orders to any offender?		
Do you agree with this measure?		
Do you know that the customs office can require of the captains information on the crew-members, numbers of people embarked or disembarked and on the cargo prior to your arrival on board?		
Do you know that any lack of integrity or abuse of power of the customs officers must be notified to the national authorities?		
Do you know that the customs office can designate information points in ports where drugs-related incidents can be reported?		
If you knew of some drugs-related incident, would you go to the said point?		
Do you believe in the effectiveness of these points of contact in the ports?		

	YES	NO
PREVENTION DURING NAVIGATION		
At high sea, would you be suspicious of a vessel that attracts your attention?		
In this case, would you refuse to respond to it?		
If this is justified and is possible, would you,		
increase speed?		
turn off the sailing lights?		
turn up the lights on deck?		
Should all vessels behaving strangely be identified?		
Should this behaviour be communicated immediately?		
Should the deck and the sides of the vessel be lighted at night or in low visibility while on route?		
Do you have lights to light specific zones in response to an alarm?		
Is the lighting system complemented by portable or fixed projectors?		
Are reflectors used to illuminate suspicious persons or vessels approaching the vessel?		
Is vigilance kept to detect bubbles, swimmers or small crafts?		
Are the crafts that approach your vessel interrogated?		
Are they prohibited from sailing alongside your vessel unless they identify themselves?		

	YES	NO
ON SAFETY MEASURES		
Do you consider that the continuous training of the crew-members will complement safety on board?		
Do you consider that the officers have sufficient knowledge of:		
the safety plans on board and the corresponding emergency procedures		
the determination of risk, threat and vulnerability		
Do you also consider that they are trained as regards:		
methods for conducting safety inspections		
the techniques used to escape safety inspections		
the functioning of technical security aids, if these are used		
the characteristics and behaviour of suspicious persons		
the detection and recognition of illicit substances		
methods of physical inspection of persons and their equipment?		
Do you think that the coordination between the police, the customs service and the port authorities for determining a threat is good?		
Do you think that the safety precautions on board are effective?		
Do you think that the best deterrent is for the personnel to be aware of the threat?		
Do you think that the presence of security on land can determine the security on board?		
Do you think that control of access to the cargo areas prevents the use of the vessel for illicit purposes?		
Is there a security patrol?		
Is there a procedure for examining empty containers and those sealed off by customs?		
Is there a procedure for sealing off empty containers?		
Is there a procedure for registering the number of sealed items?		
Is there a procedure for notifying of broken or torn seals?		
Is there a procedure for the issuing of seals?		
Is there a procedure for preventing unauthorised access to the containers?		
Do you think packages can be concealed on board?		
Do you think the crew controls entry onto the ship?		
Do you think that all the means of access to the holds and the tool cribs are taken into account?		
Are the tool cribs locked up when not in use?		
Does the security system on board have the adequate staff?		
Do the areas of the vessel which overlook the sea have means of security?		
Are packages without documentation or unsealed packages allowed on board?		
Are the cargo nets ever inspected before lowering them into the hold?		
Are there procedures governing access on board?		
In the case where persons other than the crew are allowed on board,		
are all packages or bags taken on or off the ship checked?		
is it set out that they have access to specific areas?		
and not to restricted areas?		
Are there restricted areas on board?		
Are the internal accesses on board locked with a key?		
Does the captain control the vessel's master keys?		
Do the personnel responsible for the disembarking board have a list of crew members, land officials and expected visitors?		
Are the guards complemented by alarms and security devices?		
Are all the spare parts taken on board examined?		
And the provisions?		
Are full unannounced inspections made of the items taken on board?		
Is entry to high risk areas on board not allowed to visitors?		

Are employees who demand to go on board examined?		
Is entry not allowed to persons without their security documents?		
Is a report made to the authorities when these persons try to board the vessel?		
Are vulnerable compartments kept under lock and key?		
Are random inspections made of these to ensure that there are no suspicious signs?		

	YES	NO
ON CONCEALMENT ON THE VESSEL		
Which of the following factors do you consider to be the weakest link in the security system for preventing the concealment of drugs on board?		
the ports of call and the routes of the vessel		
the origin and destination of the cargo		
the level of control applied in the coastal installations and services		
the level of control applied in relation to access to the vessel		
the vulnerability of the crew to the pressures of drugs-dealers		
Do you think that drugs can be taken on board by means of:		
- cars, loading vehicles, trailers, etc.		
- persons visiting the vessel		
- suitcases placed on the luggage trolleys		
- provisions for the vessel		
- subcontracted staff (e.g. cleaning teams, etc.)		
- as part of the personal belongings of the crew		
- concealed in the machinery of the hull of the vessel		
- in the cargo or in the structure of the cargo containers		
- in the packaging/wrapping of the cargo		
Do you think that a drugs trafficker could take a package on board and hide it and not be discovered?		
Do you think it is possible for members of the crew to conspire to take drugs on board?		
Did you know that a package can be placed on the hull by divers?		
Do you now that the responsibility for safety lies with the company and the captain?		
Do you think that the level of security should depend on the drugs risk in each specific area?		
If suspicious packages or substances are found:		
is handling them without protecting your skin and without a mask avoided?		
are hands washed after handling to avoid any contamination?		
is it ensured that there is sufficient ventilation and lighting in confined areas?		
are suspicious substances wrapped in sheets or plastic bags?		
are all persons who show an excessive interest in the incident watched over?		
On finding a suspicious package, is a witness asked to confirm its position?		
Are photos taken of the package just as it is found?		
Do you know that all findings of packages must be recorded in the ship's log?		
Do you know that the discovery of a package should not be announced, rather the information should only be given to the adequate person?		
Do you know that you should prevent the crew members from disembarking until they are interrogated by the police?		
Do you know that you must write a report immediately after the event?		
Do you know that you must include yourself in this report for it to be of use?		
And that at high sea the report should be signed by the person who found the package, the functionary in charge and the captain as witnesses?		
Do you know that the date and time must be included?		

	YES	NO
PROCEDURES FOR CONDUCTING REGISTERS		
Are inspections made on board with a certain regularity, especially on leaving port?		
Do you consider the inspection plan to be sufficiently detailed?		
Does the inspection plan detail the routes to be taken by the inspectors?		
Does the inspection team have sufficient equipment?		
Do you know that during an inspection, one's own living quarters cannot be inspected?		
Do you know that it is preferable to conduct the inspection in pairs?		
Does the team know which measures to adopt if a suspicious package is found?		
Do you know that the machine room is the place normally chosen to hide packages?		
Do you know that the discovery of a package does not mean the end of the inspection?		
Do you think that, on some occasions, all visitors should be subjected to a inspection?		
Do you think that the points of access to the vessel should be controlled?		
Do you consider that passengers and equipment should be examined on land?		
Do you think it should be allowed to leave the vessel without inspection?		
Do you think the method of inspection depends on the danger of each situation?		
Do you consider that the physical inspection is still the best method?		
Do you think that, in order to be effective, a physical inspection of the packages should be made?		
Do you know that an apparent imbalance of weights can justify a new inspection?		
Do you know that special attention should be paid to any patch, grease stain or hole on the outside of the package?		
Do you know that the passengers should be questioned about the origin of their luggage?		
Do you know that passengers' luggage should be examined in search of excessive weight?		
Do you know that the x-ray check is less effective for identifying drugs?		
Do you know that dogs can be highly effective in car and ship inspections?		
Do you know that the examination of some items of cargo may present problems due to their nature?		
Do you know that the unexpected package is the one that requires the most attention?		
Do you think that some form of identification of the personnel helps to counter the risk?		
Do you think the following are common places for hiding drugs?:		
places rarely entered into		
rudder tunnel		
under the electricity panels		
in idle cargo spaces		
near the funnel		
in passenger cabins		
in store rooms		
in the spare provisions		
deck storage tanks		
crew quarters		
places with restricted access to unauthorised persons		
oil tanks		
cargo tanks		
floor boards		
open air		
ventilation tubes		
control panels		
bilges		
funnel passages		
cargo cages or containers		
oil drums		

double-based paint cans		
lifeboats		
sickbay		
inside fire extinguishers		
inside hoses		
water tanks		

	YES	NO
POSSIBLE INDICATORS OF IRREGULARITIES		
Do you consider the following circumstances suspicious?		
Crew members and unknown persons found in unfrequented places (vessel in port)		
unknown persons with packages who want to access the vessel		
Teams working without supervision on something unnecessary, at strange times and without any justification		
Unplanned work, especially on structures		
Crew members showing undue interest during inspections		
Passengers outside the public or passenger areas		
Unexpected events (e.g. full ballast tanks when these should be empty)		
Things out of place		
Evidence that some package has been opened		
Disorganised stocks		
Closed spaces		
Pipelines that lead nowhere		
Missing keys		
Unexplained failures in mechanical or electrical parts		
Signs of handling or forcing of tank lids		
High readings on pressure gauges		
Unfastened lifeboat covers		
Do you think the habits of the crew members should be known?		
Do you think that any deviation form the normal routine should be examined?		
Do you think that surveillance should be maintained on the gangplank?		
Do you think any object which is out of place should be examined?		
Do you think that evidence of undue handling of luggage on board should be searched for?		
Do you think that access to keys should be controlled?		
Have you considered whether the cargo has its origins in a drugs-producing country?		
Have you considered whether the cargo would seem appropriate as regards the origin, route of the vessel, destination and value of the goods?		
Is it ensured that the cargo is adequately described in the documentation?		
Do you take pains to ensure that weights/measurements are in harmony with the item?		
Do the staff handling the cargo look for torn safety seals?		
Do the staff handling the cargo look for false floors and ceilings in the containers?		
Have blocked cavities been found in the structure of the containers?		
Have perforations been found in the body of the containers?		
Is special attention paid to the refrigerated containers?		
Do you know that these containers offer additional opportunities for hiding drugs?		
Do you know what to do on finding drugs on the high seas?		
Should the nearest port be notified before entering its territorial waters?		
Do you know that if you do not do this, you may be charged with drug-trafficking?		

	YES	NO
CONTROL OF MEDICINE STORES ON BOARD		
Do you know that medical supplies on board are subject to the corresponding international legislations?		
Do you think that these legislations are taken into account?		
Do you think that these legislations are known?		
Do you know that the Captain is the person responsible for drugs and the medicine store?		
Do you know that the medicine store should be kept under lock and key?		
Do you think this store is normally kept under lock and key?		
Do you know that the first-aid kits on the lifeboats should be inspected frequently?		
Are these inspections often carried out?		
Do you know that in port these first-aid kits should be taken to the medical store?		
Do you think that this precaution is fulfilled?		
Do you know that a list of the drugs in stock should be handed over to the customs office?		
Do you think that it is common practice for ships to provide this list?		
Do you know that in cruise ships with a doctor on board, the responsibility is delegated to him?		
Do you know that despite the above, the captain is still legally responsible?		
Do you know that all transported medicines require an import/export licence?		
Do you know that this licence must be specified in order to be valid?		
Do you know that any variation in the conditions or specifications of this licence constitutes an offence?		

	YES	NO
IMMIGRATION		
Do you know Article 115 of the State and Merchant Navy Ports law on aspects of illegal immigration?		
Do you know that a stowaway must be kept on board until handed over to the authorities?		
Do you know that refusal to do this constitutes a serious offence?		
Do you know that hiding someone on board also constitutes a serious offence?		
As does the non-fulfilment of the ship clearance regulations?		
As does the non-fulfilment of the regulations on the enrolment of crews and crew lists?		
Do you consider the lighting and control to be sufficient in the entrance areas?		
Do you consider the lighting to be sufficient in the cargo areas?		
Do you consider the lighting to be sufficient along the ship's sides?		
Do you consider the lighting to be sufficient in the standing areas?		
Do you consider the lighting to be sufficient in the working areas?		
Do you consider the barriers to be sufficient for impeding passage?		
Do you consider the control of access to the cabins to be sufficient?		
Do you consider the identity control to be sufficient?		
Is the deck adequately lighted over all its length at night?		
Do you think that small crafts could approach the vessel to load/unload illicit goods?		
Is lighting, radar or other equipment used to prevent this?		
Is surveillance maintained on any small craft seen close to the vessel?		
Is it illuminated at night time?		
Are the deck and the sides of the vessel illuminated at night or in low visibility		
while in port?		
while anchored?		
while on route?		

	YES	NO
APPLICABLE TO THE RESPONSIBILITY OF THE SHIPPING COMPANY		
Do you know if shipping companies should assist the customs officers to make their inspections more effective?		
Do you know if they allow the customs service access to the vessel and its cargo?		
Do you think they ask the customs service for assessment regarding their security personnel, the cargo or the documentation?		
On reaching port, is there a list prepared of the containers to disembark?		
Have you heard of any case where, when unloading containers they have been damaged in some way?		
If so, did the shipping company notify the customs office of the case?		
Do you think that shipping companies examine and check the safety seals properly?		
Do you think the shipping companies exercise sufficient control over the access to the deck and to the cargo deposits?		
Do you know if the company has a list of authorised vehicles and persons in its offices?		
Do you know if the company restricts the parking of the vehicles to a limited area and if this is sufficiently far from the cargo area?		
Have you heard that the company has issued passes to authorised vehicles and persons identifying them as such?		
Does the shipping company have electronic security systems?		
Do you think that only authorised personnel are allowed access to the cargo areas on board?		
Do you think the controls should focus on the ship access, services or the cargo?		
Do you know if the company has communicated the presence of suspicious packages or any unaccounted for cargo?		
Were these packages kept under observation while the incident was communicated?		
Do you know if the company provides information to the customs service on the stevedores and other companies that lend their services to the vessel?		
Do you think the companies take sufficient care when recruiting employees?		
Do you think they allow only authorised personnel to deal with the information on the cargo operations?		
Do you think that this personnel is suitably trained and identified?		
Do you think the companies ask the customs service for assessment in evaluating and reducing your vulnerability?		
Do you know if the company has made plans to reduce this vulnerability?		
Have you received any training from your company in the identification of illicit substances?		
Do all the employees know what to do if they are suspicious of the cargo or of their colleagues?		
Is there an inspection of the vans going in and out of the installations and of their drivers?		
Is there an identity control for the receivers of the cargo?		
Is there a check on the appropriateness and accuracy of the documentation?		
Is there a procedure for weighing the cargo?		
Is there a procedure for checking the correspondence of the cargo and its documentation?		
Do you think that further measures should be taken to counter risks?		

3.4.4 Check list for concessionaires

	YES	NO
APPLICABLE TO THE RESPONSIBILITY OF THE CONCESSIONAIRES		
Do you know if they inform the customs service of changes in the destinations of the vessels?		
Do you think they ask the customs service for assessment regarding their security personnel?		
Do you think that, as the person responsible for security, you have been sufficiently informed?		
Do you know if the concessionaire has a list of authorised vehicles and persons?		
Do you know if the company restricts the parking of vehicles to a limited area?		
Have you heard that the concessionaire issues passes to authorised vehicles and personnel?		
Does the concessionaire dispose of electronic security systems?		
Are these systems placed at the disposition of the customs officers?		
Do you think that only authorised persons are allowed access to the vessel?		
Do you know if the concessionaires test the security of their concession regularly?		
If so, do you know if they notify the port authorities?		
Do you think the controls should focus on the restriction of access to the vessel?		
Do you know if the concessionaire has ever communicated the presence of suspicious packages?		
And the presence of an unaccounted for cargo on the vessel?		
Were these packages kept under observation while the incident was communicated?		
Has the concessionaire informed you of any internal sanctions for drugs-related matters?		
Do you know if the concessionaire provides information to the customs service on stevedores and other companies who lend their services to the vessel?		
Do you think that the concessionaires take sufficient care when recruiting employees?		
Do you know if they have recruited any employee previously convicted of drugs-trafficking?		
Do you think it is appropriate to ban the recruitment of staff previously convicted of drugs-trafficking?		
Do you think that only authorised personnel handle the information on cargo operations?		
Do you think that this personnel is suitably trained and identified?		
Do you know if the concessionaire provides points of contact to the customs service for legal matters?		
Do you think that these points of access are clearly identified and easy to access?		
Does your company communicate the contents of these matters to you?		
Do you think they should do so?		
Do you think the companies ask the customs service for assessment in evaluating and reducing their own vulnerability?		
Do you know if the concessionaire has made plans to reduce this vulnerability?		
Has your concessionaire given you any training in the identification of illicit substances?		
Do all employees with authorised access wear authorisation badges?		
Do all the employees know what to do if they are suspicious of the load or of their colleagues?		
Do you know if any of them show signs of being associated with drugs matters?		
Do you think that stevedores and container-loaders may also be involved?		

	YES	NO
ON SECURITY MEASURES		
Do you think that continuous training would complement security?		
Do you also consider that the personnel are trained in:		
methods for conducting security inspections		
techniques adopted to escape security measures		
functioning of the technical security aids, if these are used		
characteristics and behaviour of suspicious persons		
detection and recognition of illicit substances		
methods for the physical search of persons and luggage		
Do you think that the coordination between the police, the customs service and the port authorities for determining a threat is good?		
Do you think that the personnel on land are informed of the risks and the fight against drug-trafficking?		
Do you think that security should be revised in collaboration with the customs service and the port authorities?		
Do you think that the security precautions on board are effective?		
Do you think that the greatest deterrent is for the personnel to be aware of the threat?		
Do you think that criteria such as consignees, origin, ports of call, etc, should be analysed?		
Do you think that the presence of security on land can determine the security of the vessel and of the haulage contractor?		
Do you think that the control of access to the cargo zones prevents the use of the vessel for illicit purposes?		
Do you think that the haulage contractors have an influence on security by communicating with land?		
Do you consider the lighting and control to be sufficient in the entrance areas?		
Do you consider the lighting to be sufficient in the cargo areas?		
Do you consider the lighting to be sufficient along the ship's sides?		
Do you consider the lighting to be sufficient in the standing areas?		
Do you consider the lighting to be sufficient in the working areas?		
Do you consider the identity check to be sufficient?		
Are there security checks?		
Is there an inspection of the vans that go in and out of the installations and of their drivers?		
Is there an identity check for the receivers of the cargo?		
Is there a check on the appropriateness and accuracy of the documentation?		
Is there a procedure for weighing the cargo?		
Is there a procedure for checking the correspondence of the cargo and its documentation?		
Do you think further measures should be taken to counter risks?		
Do you think the personnel are always vigilant?		
Are the security guards complemented with alarms and other security devices?		
Are all the spare parts taken on board examined?		
And the provisions?		
Are full unannounced inspections made of the items taken on board?		
Do you know that drugs can be hidden in apparently innocent packages?		
Are the boxes and packages which have already been inspected marked with coloured tape?		
Are the boxes and packages which have already been inspected strapped together?		

	YES	NO
PROCEDURES FOR CONDUCTING INSPECTIONS		
Do you consider that a regular program of inspections reassures the personnel?		
Are inspections made with a certain regularity?		
Do you think that any of the employees might be a drug addict?		
Are the inspection plans drawn up with the collaboration of the person responsible?		
Are these plans modified with experience?		
Do you consider the inspection plan to be sufficiently detailed?		
Does the inspection plan detail the routes to be taken by the inspectors?		
Is there a place designated for the inspection team to send their reports?		
Does the inspection team have sufficient equipment?		
Are identification cards provided to each inspector with the itinerary to be followed?		
Do you know that during an inspection, one's own living quarters cannot be inspected?		
Do you know that the inspection should be conducted following a specific plan?		
Do you know that it is preferable to conduct the inspection in pairs?		
Do you know that there should be a system for marking the "clean" areas"?		
Do you know that you should be informed on the measures to be adopted if a suspicious package is found?		
Do you know that the person responsible for the inspection must make a list of the reports sent?		
Do you know that the discovery of a package does not mean the end of the inspection?		
Do you think that locked rooms should be examined?		
And open spaces?		
And the lifts?		
And the rubbish dumps?		
Do you think that on some occasions, all visitors should be subjected to an inspection?		
Do you consider that passengers and equipment should be examined on land?		
Do you think the method of inspection depends on the danger of each situation?		
Do you consider that the physical inspection is still the best method?		
Do you think that the passengers and visitors should be subjected to a physical inspection?		
Do you think these should be conducted in private areas?		
Do you consider it important that the methods of inspection are not observed?		
Do you think that, in order to be effective, a physical inspection of the packages should be made?		
Do you know the smell of glue in suitcases may indicate the existence of double bottoms?		
Do you know that an apparent imbalance of weights can justify a new inspection?		
Do you know that special attention should be paid to any patch, grease stain or hole on the outside of the package?		
Do you know that special attention should be paid to electrical appliances?		
Do you know passengers should be questioned about the origin of their luggage?		
And about the possibility of them being handled by someone else?		
Do you know that an excess of weight should also be searched for?		
And loose objects inside the luggage?		
Do you know that drugs can be hidden in other recipients and in hand luggage?		
Do you know that the x-ray check is less effective for identifying drugs?		
Do you know that the efficiency of the inspection staff diminishes after a short time, especially during periods of maximum activity?		
Do you know that ionic exploration can be used for the detection of drugs and explosives?		
Do you think it might be necessary to examine the cargo without prior warning?		
Do you know that the inspection of some cargoes presents difficulties because of their nature?		
Do you think it might be impossible to inspect a cargo?		
Do you know that one possible channel for drugs is through the provisions?		

Do you consider it necessary to examine the storage rooms and spaces?		
Do you know that the unexpected package is the one that requires the most attention?		
Do you know that drugs traffickers can use innocent-looking persons?		
Do you know these may be persons that make regular deliveries?		
Do you think that the identification of the personnel helps to counter the risk?		

	YES	NO
POSSIBLE INDICATIONS OF IRREGULARITIESS		
Do you consider the following circumstances suspicious?		
Unknown persons found in unfrequented places		
Unknown persons with packages who want to access the vessel or the installations		
Teams working without supervision on something unnecessary, at strange times and without any justification		
Unplanned work, especially on structures		
Crew members showing undue interest during inspections		
Passengers outside the public or passenger areas		
Unexpected events (e.g. full ballast tanks when these should be empty)		
Things out of place		
Evidence that some package has been opened		
Closed spaces		
Missing keys		
Unexplained faults in mechanical or electrical parts		
Do you think the habits of the crew members should be known?		
Do you think that any deviation form the normal routine should be examined?		
Do you think that periodical inspections should be made?		
Do you think these should vary according to their nature, place and duration?		
Do you think that any unknown person found in the installations should be questioned?		
Do you think any object which is out of place should be examined?		
And any object with no apparent justification?		
Do you think that evidence of undue handling of luggage on board should be searched for?		
Do you think that all accesses and spaces should be locked?		
Do you think that access to keys should be controlled?		
Do you think that the behaviour patterns of the passengers should be observed?		
And that lists should be available with names, dates and places?		
Or with references to money, weight and other factors?		
And the possession of unusual tools?		
Is it taken into account whether the person carrying out the cargo registration is known?		
Is it noted whether the costs are paid for in advance and in cash?		
Have you heard of any case where someone tried to hide the name or address of the payee?		
Have you considered whether the cargo has its origins in a drugs-producing country?		
Is it ensured that the cargo is adequately described in the documentation?		
Do you take pains to ensure that weight/measurements is in harmony with the item?		
Do the staff handling the cargo look for broken safety seals?		
Have you ever found yourself in this situation?		
Did you notify the port authorities?		
If suspicious packages or substances are found,		
Do you try not to damage or open them?		
Is handling them without skin protection and a mask avoided?		
Is it ensured that nobody inhales dust, smoke of fumes?		
Smoking is forbidden near the substance?		

	YES	NO
Is it ensured that nobody tries the substance under any circumstance?		
Hands are always washed after handling to avoid any contamination?		
Clothes are brushed to avoid any contamination?		
The suspicious substances are wrapped in sheets or plastic bags?		
They are put in a safe place or in a safe?		
Are all persons showing an excessive interest in the incident watched?		
Did you know that all of these precautions are essential?		
On finding a suspicious package:		
Should you ask for a witness to confirm its position?		
Should you take photos of the package just as it was found?		
Do you know that fingerprints might be found on the package?		
Should you handle it as little as possible?		
Do you know that you should not announce the discovery, but rather you should inform only the person responsible?		
Do you know that you should stop the crew members from disembarking before being questioned by the police?		
On finding a suspicious package, would you consider checking other similar spaces?		
Do you know that you must write a report signed by witnesses immediately after the event?		

3.4.5 Check list for commercial ports

	YES	NO
Applicable to the responsibility of the Port Authority		
Do you know if the concessionaires assist the customs service to make their inspections effective?		
Do you know if they provide the customs service with access to the information on the vessel and its cargo?		
Do you think they ask the customs service for assessment regarding their security personnel, handling etc?		
On reaching port, is there a list prepared of the containers to disembark?		
Have you heard of any case where, on unloading containers, they have been damaged in some way?		
If so, did the concessionaire notify the customs service?		
Do you think that the concessionaires examine and check the sealed-off containers properly?		
Do you know if the concessionaire has a list of authorised vehicles and persons?		
Do you know if the company restricts the parking of vehicles to a limited area, sufficiently distant from the cargo areas?		
Have you heard that the concessionaire issues passes to authorised vehicles and personnel?		
Does the concessionaire dispose of electronic security systems?		
Are these systems placed at the disposition of the customs officers?		
Do you think that only authorised persons are allowed access to the vessel?		
Do you know if the concessionaires test the security of their concession regularly?		
If so, do you know if they notify the port authorities?		
Do you think the controls should focus on the restriction of access to the vessel?		
Do you know if the concessionaire has ever communicated the presence of suspicious packages?		
And the presence of an unaccounted for cargo on the vessel?		
Were these packages kept under observation while the incident was communicated?		
Has the concessionaire informed you of any internal sanctions for drugs-related matters?		

Question	YES	NO
Do you know if the concessionaire provides information to the customs service on stevedores and other companies who lend their services to the vessel?		
Do you think that the concessionaires take sufficient care when recruiting employees?		
Do you know if they have recruited any employee previously convicted of drugs-trafficking?		
Do you think it is appropriate to ban the recruitment of staff previously convicted of drugs-trafficking?		
Do you think that only authorised personnel handle the information on cargo operations?		
Do you think that this personnel is suitably trained and identified?		
Do you know if the concessionaire provides points of contact to the customs service for legal matters?		
Do you think that these points of access are clearly identified and easy to access?		
Do you think the companies ask the customs service for assessment in evaluating and reducing their own vulnerability?		
Do you know if the concessionaire has made plans to reduce this vulnerability?		
Has your concessionaire given you any training in the identification of illicit substances?		
Are the employees' criminal records verified?		
Do you consider that there is any type of anti-drug policy on the part of the administration?		
Do you think the staff have any knowledge of it?		
Is the staff encouraged to cooperate with these programmes?		
Do all employees with authorised access wear authorisation badges?		
Do all the employees know what to do if they are suspicious of the load or of their colleagues?		
Do you know if any of them show signs of being associated with drugs matters?		

	YES	NO
ON SECURITY MEASURES		
Do you think that continuous training would complement security?		
Do you also consider that the personnel are trained in:		
methods for conducting security inspections		
techniques adopted to escape security measures		
functioning of the technical security aids, if these are used		
characteristics and behaviour of suspicious persons		
detection and recognition of illicit substances		
Methods for the physical search of persons and luggage		
Do you think that the coordination between the police, the customs service and the port authorities for determining a threat is good?		
Do you think that the personnel on land are informed of the risks and the fight against drugs-trafficking?		
Do you think that security should be revised in collaboration with the customs service and the port authorities?		
Do you think that the security precautions on board are effective?		
Do you think that the greatest deterrent is for the personnel to be aware of the threat?		
Do you think that criteria such as consignees, origin, ports of call, etc, should be analysed?		
Do you think that the presence of security on land can determine the security of the vessel and the haulage contractor?		
Do you think that the control of access to the cargo zones prevents the use of the vessel for illicit purposes?		
Do you think that the haulage contractors have an influence on security by communicating with land?		
Do you consider the lighting and control to be sufficient in the entrance areas?		

3 Human factors involved

Do you consider the lighting to be sufficient in the cargo areas?		
Do you consider the lighting to be sufficient along the ship's sides?		
Do you consider the lighting to be sufficient in the standing areas?		
Do you consider the lighting to be sufficient in the working areas?		
Do you consider the identity check to be sufficient?		
Are there security checks?		
Are you able to communicate with the authorities?		
Is there a procedure for sealing off empty containers and containers marked by the customs service?		
Is there a procedure for registering the number of sealed items?		
Is there a procedure for notifying of broken or torn seals?		
Is there a procedure for the issuing of seals?		
Is there a procedure for preventing unauthorised access to the containers?		
Is there any control over the filling of the containers?		
Is there an inspection of the vans that go in and out of the installations and of their drivers?		
Is there an in identity check for the receivers of the cargo?		
Is there a check on the appropriateness and accuracy of the documentation?		
Is there a procedure for weighing the cargo?		
Is there a procedure for checking the correspondence of the cargo and its documentation?		
Do you think that further measures should be implemented to counter risk?		
Do you think the personnel remain vigilant at all times?		
Are the guards complemented with alarms and other security devices?		
Are all the spare parts taken on board examined?		
And the provisions?		
Do you know that drugs can be hidden in apparently innocent packages?		
Are the boxes and packages which have already been inspected marked with coloured tape?		
Are the boxes and packages which have already been inspected strapped together?		

	YES	NO
PROCEDURES FOR CONDUCTING THE INSPECTIONS		
Do you consider that a regular program of inspections reassures the personnel?		
Are inspections made with a certain regularity?		
Are you aware of the risk of violence associated to drugs trafficking?		
Do you think that some of the employees might be drug addicts?		
Do you think any of them are?		
Are the inspection plans drawn up with the collaboration of the Harbour Master?		
Are these plans modified with experience?		
Do you consider the inspection plan to be sufficiently detailed?		
Does the inspection plan detail the routes to be taken by the inspectors?		
Is the layout of the installation taken into account to ensure that all the areas are included in the inspection?		
Is there a place designated for the inspection team to send their reports?		
Does the inspection team have sufficient equipment?		
Are identification cards provided to each inspector with the itinerary to be followed?		
Do you know that during an inspection, one's own living quarters cannot be inspected?		
Do you know that the inspection should be conducted following a specific plan?		
Do you know that it is preferable to conduct the inspection in pairs?		
Do you know that there should be a system for marking the "clean" areas?		
Do you know that you should be informed on the measures to be adopted if a suspicious package is found?		

Do you know that the person responsible for the inspection must make a list of the reports sent?		
Do you know that the discovery of a package does not mean the end of the inspection?		
Do you think that locked rooms should be examined?		
And the open spaces?		
And the lifts?		
And the rubbish dumps?		
Do you think that on some occasions, all visitors should be subjected to an inspection?		
Do you consider that passengers and equipment should be examined on land?		
Do you think that all areas to which the passengers have had access should be examined?		
Do you think the method of inspection depends on the danger of each situation?		
Do you consider that the physical inspection is still the best method?		
Do you think that the passengers and visitors should be subjected to a physical inspection?		
Do you think these should be conducted in private areas?		
Do you consider it important that the methods of inspection are not observed?		
Do you think that, in order to be effective, a physical inspection of the packages should be made?		
Do you know the smell of glue in suitcases may indicate the existence of double bottoms?		
Do you know that an apparent imbalance of weights can justify a new inspection?		
Do you know passengers should be questioned about the origin of their luggage?		
And about the possibility of them being handled by someone else?		
Do you know that an excess of weight should also be searched for?		
And loose objects inside the luggage?		
Do you know that drugs can be hidden in other recipients and in hand luggage?		
Do you know that the x-ray check is less effective for identifying drugs?		
Do you know that the efficiency of the inspection staff diminishes after a short time, especially during periods of maximum activity?		
Do you know about ionic exploration?		
Do you know what high sensitivity is?		
Do you know that this can be used for the detection of drugs and explosives?		
Do you think it might be necessary to examine the cargo without prior warning?		
Do you know that the inspection of some cargoes presents difficulties because of their nature?		
Do you think this inspection might at times be impossible?		
Do you know that one possible channel for drugs is the provisions?		
Do you think the holds should be examined?		
And all the items found there?		
Do you know that the unexpected package is the one that requires the most attention?		
Do you know that drugs traffickers can use innocent-looking persons?		
Do you know that these persons may make routine deliveries?		
Do you think the identification of the personnel helps to counter risk?		
Do you know that the cargo offers opportunities for hiding things?		

	YES	NO
POSSIBLE INDICATORS OF IRREGULARITIES		
Do you consider the following circumstances suspicious?		
Unknown persons found in unfrequented places		
Unknown persons with packages who want to access the vessel or the installations		
Teams working without supervision on something unnecessary, at strange times and without any justification		
Unplanned work, especially on structures		
Crew members showing undue interest during inspections		
Passengers outside the public or passenger areas		

Unexpected events (e.g. full ballast tanks when these should be empty)		
Things out of place		
Evidence that some package has been opened		
Disordered stocks		
Closed spaces		
Pipelines leading nowhere		
Missing keys		
Unexplained faults in mechanical or electrical parts		
Signs of manipulation or forcing of the tank lids		
Do you think the habits of the crew members should be known?		
Do you think that any deviation form the normal routine should be examined?		
Do you think that periodical inspections should be made?		
Do you think these should vary according to their nature, place and duration?		
Do you think that any unknown person found in the installations should be questioned?		
Do you think any object which is out of place should be examined?		
And any object with no apparent justification?		
Do you think that evidence of undue handling of luggage on board should be searched for?		
Do you think that the work teams on land should be supervised?		
Do you think that all accesses and spaces should be locked?		
Do you think that access to keys should be controlled?		
Is it taken into account whether the person carrying out the cargo registration is known?		
Is it taken into account whether the issuer/consignee is a regular client?		
Is it verified that the article corresponds to the client's activities?		
Is it verified that the addresses of the issuer/consignee are full?		
Is it noted whether the costs are paid for in advance and in cash?		
Have you heard of any case where someone tried to hide the name or address of the payee?		
Have you considered whether the cargo has its origins in a drugs-producing country?		
Do you consider whether the load looks normal in terms of the origin, route, destination and the value of the goods?		
Is it ensured that the cargo is adequately described in the documentation?		
If suspicious packages or substances are found,		
Do you try not to damage or open them?		
Is handling them without skin protection and a mask avoided?		
Is it ensured that nobody inhales dust, smoke of fumes?		
Is smoking is forbidden near the substance?		
Is it ensured that nobody tries the substance under any circumstance?		
Are hands are always washed after handling to avoid any contamination?		
Are clothes are brushed to avoid any contamination?		
Is it ensured that there is sufficient ventilation and lighting in confined spaces?		
Are suspicious substances wrapped in sheets or plastic bags?		
Are they put in a safe place or in a safe?		
Are all persons showing an excessive interest in the incident watched?		
On finding a suspicious package:		
Should you ask for a witness to confirm its position?		
Should you take photos of the package just as it was found?		
Do you know that fingerprints might be found on the package?		
Should you handle it as little as possible?		
Do you know that you should not announce the discovery, but rather you should inform only the person responsible?		
Do you know that you should stop the crew members from disembarking before being questioned by the police?		

On finding a suspicious package, would you consider checking other similar spaces?		
Do you know that you must write a report signed by witnesses immediately after the event?		
Do you know that you must include yourself in this report for it to be of use?		
Do you know Article 115 of the State and Merchant Navy Ports Law on aspects of illegal immigration?		

	YES	NO
HIGH-SPEED CRAFT		
Do you know that there are regulations governing the sailing of small crafts?		
Do you think that high-speed crafts (HSC) are a danger to third parties?		
Do you think they are prone to be used for illicit activities?		
Do you know what the conditions are for classifying a craft as a high-speed craft?		
Do you know that these requirements are regulated by the IMO?		
Do you know that, if the Port Captain so requires it, HSC may be obliged to carry identification?		
Do you know that this consists of a number determined by the Ministry of Transport?		
Do you know that this identification must be inscribed on the hull?		
Do you know that if HSC spend more than 30 days a year on Spanish territory, they must request this identification?		
Do you know that if they spend less time, they must request a provisional identification?		
Do you know that this can be requested in any Harbour Master's Office?		
Do you know that all HSC must moor where the Harbour Master says?		
Do you know that they must request authorisation to leave?		
Do you know that when they do this, they must attach a list of crew members and passengers?		
Is this regulation normally fulfilled?		
Do you know they must communicate their return one hour before they arrive?		
Do you know that the documentation must be prepared leaving documented proof?		
Do you think that HSC are aware of these regulations?		
Do you know that HSC must have an insurance policy covering civil liability?		
Do you know that this policy must be for a sum of at least 50 million pesetas?		
Do you know that the Harbour Captain can deny the HSC permission to leave port?		
Do you know on this denial of permission may be indicated the date and time of permission to leave?		
Do you know that the itinerary to be followed by the HSC may be expressly defined?		
Do you know that speed limits may be indicated, in accordance with the sailing areas?		
Do you know that HSC may be required to present international certificates?		
Do you know that they may be required to present their security equipment and measures?		
Do you know that these may condition the permission to leave?		
Do you know that accreditation of the corresponding pilot's certificate may be requested?		
Do you know that sailing a HSC with a modified propeller may be forbidden?		
Have you heard of these restrictions being applied?		
Do you know that the collaboration of Maritime and Aerial Authorities and organisms may be requested in the surveillance of these measures?		
Have you heard of this collaboration being requested?		
Do you know that these regulations will not be applied to HSC destined for use in rescue operations?		

3.4.6 Check list for fishing ports

	YES	NO
APPLICABLE TO THE RESPONSIBILITY OF THE GUILDS		
Do you know if the guilds assist the customs service to make their inspections effective?		
Do you know if they provide the customs service with access to the information on the vessel and its cargo?		
Do you think they ask the customs service for assessment regarding their security personnel?		
Do you think you have received sufficient training as a person responsible for security?		
Do you know if the guild has a list of authorised vehicles and persons?		
Do you know if the company restricts the parking of vehicles to a limited area, sufficiently distant from the cargo areas?		
Have you heard that the guild issues passes to authorised vehicles and personnel?		
Does the guild dispose of electronic security systems?		
Are these systems placed at the disposition of the customs officers?		
Do you know if the guilds examine port security periodically?		
If so, do you know if they notify the port authorities?		
Do you think the security checks should focus on the restriction of access or services?		
Do you know if the guild has ever communicated the presence of suspicious packages?		
And the presence of an unaccounted for cargo on the vessel?		
Were these packages kept under observation while the incident was communicated?		
Do you know if the guild provides the customs service with information on the companies that lend their services to the vessel?		
Do you think that the guilds take sufficient care when recruiting employees?		
Do you think that only authorised personnel handle the information on fishing operations?		
Do you think that this personnel is suitably trained and identified?		
Do you know if the guild provides points of contact to the customs service for legal matters?		
Do you think that these points are clearly identified and easily accessible?		
Do you think the guilds ask the customs service for assessment in evaluating and reducing their own vulnerability?		
Do you know if the guild has made plans to reduce this vulnerability?		
Has your guild given you any training in the identification of illicit substances?		
Are the employees' criminal records verified?		
Do all employees with authorised access wear authorisation badges?		
Do all the employees know what to do if they are suspicious of the load or of their colleagues?		
Do you know if any of them show signs of being associated with drugs matters?		

	YES	NO
ON SECURITY MEASURES		
Do you think that continuous training would complement security?		
Do you also consider that the personnel are trained in:		
methods for conducting security inspections		
he techniques adopted to escape security measures		
he functioning of the technical security aids, if these are used		
he characteristics and behaviour of suspicious persons		
he detection and recognition of illicit substances		
methods for the physical search of persons and luggage		
Do you think that the coordination between the police, the customs service and the port authorities for determining a threat is good?		

Do you think that the personnel on land are informed of the risks and the fight against drug-trafficking?		
Do you think that security should be revised in collaboration with the customs service and the port authorities?		
Do you think that the security precautions on board are effective?		
Do you think that the greatest deterrent is for the personnel to be aware of the threat?		
Do you think that criteria such as consignees, origin, ports of call, etc, should be analysed?		
Do you think that the presence of security on land can determine the security of the vessel and the haulage contractor?		
Do you think that control of access to the mooring areas prevents the use of the vessel for illicit purposes?		
Do you consider the lighting and controls to be sufficient in the entrance areas?		
Do you consider the lighting to be sufficient in the mooring areas?		
Do you consider the lighting to be sufficient along the barriers?		
Do you consider the lighting to be sufficient in the parking areas?		
Do you consider the identity control to be sufficient?		
Is there a security patrol?		
Are you able to communicate with the authorities?		
Is there an inspection of the vans that go in and out of the installations and of their drivers?		
Is there an in identity check for the receivers of the cargo?		
Is there a check on the appropriateness and accuracy of the documentation?		
Is there a procedure for weighing the cargo?		
Is there a procedure for checking the correspondence of the cargo and its documentation?		
Do you think that further measures should be implemented to counter risk?		
Do you think the personnel remain vigilant at all times?		
Are the guards complemented with alarms and other security devices?		
Are all the spare parts taken on board examined?		
And the provisions?		
Are full, unannounced inspections of articles taken on board made?		
Do you know that drugs can be hidden in apparently innocent packages?		
Are the boxes and packages which have already been inspected marked with coloured tape?		
Are the boxes and packages which have already been inspected strapped together?		

	YES	NO
PROCEDURES FOR CONDUCTING INSPECTIONS		
Do you consider that a regular program of inspections reassures the personnel?		
Are inspections made with a certain regularity?		
Are you aware of the risk of violence associated to drug trafficking?		
Do you think that some of the employees might be drug addicts?		
Are the inspection plans modified with experience?		
Do you consider the inspection plan to be sufficiently detailed?		
Does the inspection plan detail the routes to be taken by the inspectors?		
Is the layout of the installation taken into account to ensure that all the areas are included I the inspection?		
Is there a place designated for the inspection team to send their reports?		
Does the inspection team have sufficient equipment?		
Are identification cards provided to each inspector with the itinerary to be followed?		
Do you know that during an inspection, one's own living quarters cannot be inspected?		
Do you know that the inspection should be conducted following a specific plan?		

Do you know that it is preferable to conduct the inspection in pairs?		
Do you know that there should be a system for marking the "clean" areas?		
Do you know that you should be informed on the measures to be adopted if a suspicious package is found?		
Do you know that the person responsible for the inspection must make a list of the reports sent?		
Do you know that the discovery of a package does not mean the end of the inspection?		
Do you think that locked rooms should be examined?		
And the open spaces?		
And rubbish dumps?		
Do you think that on some occasions, all visitors should be subjected to a inspection?		
Do you think the method of inspection depends on the danger of each situation?		
Do you consider that the physical inspection is still the best method?		
Do you consider it important that the methods of inspection are not observed?		
Do you think that, in order to be effective, a physical inspection of the packages should be made?		
Do you know the smell of glue in suitcases may indicate the existence of double bottoms?		
Do you know that an apparent imbalance of weights can justify a new inspection?		
Do you know that special attention should be paid to any patch, grease stain or hole on the outside of the package?		
Do you know that special attention should be paid to electrical appliances?		
Do you know that an excess of weight should also be searched for?		
And loose objects inside the luggage?		
Do you know that the efficiency of the inspection staff diminishes after a short time, especially during periods of maximum activity?		
Do you think it might be necessary to examine the cargo without prior warning?		
Do you know that the inspection of some cargoes presents difficulties because of their nature?		
Do you know that a possible channel for drugs is the provisions?		
Do you consider it necessary to examine the holds?		
Do you know that the unexpected package is the one that requires the most attention?		
Do you know that drugs traffickers can use innocent-looking persons?		
Do you know that these persons may make routine deliveries?		
Do you think the identification of the personnel helps to counter risk?		
Do you know that the cargo offers opportunities for hiding things?		

	YES	NO
POSSIBLE INDICATORS OF IRREGULARITIES		
Do you consider the following circumstances suspicious?		
Unknown persons found in unfrequented places		
Unknown persons with packages who want to access the vessel or the installations		
Teams working without supervision on something unnecessary, at strange times and without any justification		
Unplanned work, especially on structures		
Crew members showing undue interest during inspections		
Things out of place		
Evidence that some package has been opened		
Disordered stocks		
Missing keys		
Unexplained faults in mechanical or electrical parts		
Signs of manipulation or forcing of the tank lids		
Do you think the habits of the crew members should be known?		
Do you think that any deviation from the normal routine should be examined?		

	YES	NO
Do you think that any unknown person found in the installations should be questioned?		
Do you think any object which is out of place should be examined?		
And any object with no apparent justification?		
Do you think that evidence of undue handling of luggage on board should be searched for?		
Do you think that the work teams on land should be supervised?		
Do you think that all accesses and spaces should be locked?		
Do you think that access to keys should be controlled?		
And the possession of unusual tools?		
Is it taken into account whether the person carrying out the cargo registration is known?		
Is it ensured that the cargo is adequately described in the documentation?		
If suspicious packages or substances are found,		
Do you try not to damage or open them?		
Is handling them without skin protection and a mask avoided?		
Is it ensured that nobody inhales dust, smoke of fumes?		
Is smoking is forbidden near the substance?		
Is it ensured that nobody tries the substance under any circumstance?		
Are hands are always washed after handling to avoid any contamination?		
Are clothes are brushed to avoid any contamination?		
Is it ensured that there is sufficient ventilation and lighting in confined spaces?		
Are the suspicious substances wrapped in sheets or plastic bags?		
Are they put in a safe place or in a safe?		
Are all persons showing an excessive interest in the incident watched?		
Did you know that all of these precautions are essential?		
On finding a suspicious package, should you ask for a witness to confirm its position?		
Should you take photos of the package just as it was found?		
Do you know that fingerprints can be found on the package?		
Should you handle it as little as possible?		
Do you know that you should not announce the discovery, but rather you should inform only the person responsible?		
On finding a suspicious package, would you consider checking other similar spaces?		
Do you know that you must write a report signed by witnesses immediately after the event?		
Do you know that you must include yourself in this report for it to be of use?		

3.4.7 Check list for leisure ports

	YES	NO
ON SECURITY MEASURES		
Do you think that continuous training would complement security?		
Do you also consider that the personnel are trained in:		
methods for conducting security inspections		
techniques adopted to escape security measures		
functioning of the technical security aids, if these are used		
characteristics and behaviour of suspicious persons		
detection and recognition of illicit substances		
methods for the physical search of persons and luggage		
Do you think that the coordination between the police, the customs service and the port authorities for determining a threat is good?		
Do you think that the personnel on land are informed of the risks and the fight against drugs-trafficking?		
Do you think that security should be revised in collaboration with the customs service?		

Do you think that the security precautions on board are effective?		
Do you think that the greatest deterrent is for the personnel to be aware of the threat?		
Do you think that criteria such as consignees, origin, ports of call, etc, should be analysed?		
Do you think that the presence of security on land can determine the security of the vessel and the haulage contractor?		
Do you think that the control of access to the mooring areas prevents the use of the vessel for illicit purposes?		
Do you consider the lighting and control to be sufficient in the entrance areas?		
Do you consider the lighting to be sufficient in the cargo areas?		
Do you consider the lighting to be sufficient along the ship's sides?		
Do you consider the lighting to be sufficient in the standing areas?		
Do you consider the lighting to be sufficient in the working areas?		
Do you consider the identity check to be sufficient?		
Are you able to communicate with the authorities?		
Is there an inspection of the vans that go in and out of the installations and of their drivers?		
Is there an identity check for the maintenance operators?		
Is there a check on the appropriateness and accuracy of the documentation?		
Is there a procedure for checking the correspondence of the cargo and its documentation?		
Do you think that further measures should be implemented to counter risk?		
Do you think that further measures should be implemented to counter risk?		
Are the guards complemented with alarms and other security devices?		
Are all the spare parts taken on board examined?		
And the provisions?		
Are full, unannounced inspections made of items taken on board?		
Do you know that drugs can be hidden in apparently innocent packages?		
Are the boxes and packages which have already been inspected marked with coloured tape?		
Are the boxes and packages which have already been inspected strapped together?		
Do you know Article 115 of the State and Merchant Navy Ports Law on aspects of illegal immigration?		

3.4.8 High-speed craft

	YES	NO
HIGH-SPEED CRAFT		
Do you know that there are regulations governing the sailing of small crafts?		
Do you think that high-speed crafts (HSC) are a danger to third parties?		
Do you think they are prone to be used for illicit activities?		
Do you know what the conditions are for classifying a craft as a high-speed craft?		
Do you know that these requirements are regulated by the IMO?		
Do you know that, if the Port Captain so requires it, HSC may be obliged to carry identification?		
Do you know that this consists of a number determined by the Ministry of Transport?		
Do you know that this identification must be inscribed on the hull?		
Do you know that if HSC spend more than 30 days a year on Spanish territory, they must request this identification?		
Do you know that if they spend less time, they must request a provisional identification?		
Do you know that this can be requested in any Harbour Master's Office?		
Do you know that all HSC must moor where the Harbour Master says?		
Do you know that they must request authorisation to leave?		
Do you know that when they do this, they must attach a list of crew members and passengers?		

Is this regulation normally fulfilled?		
Do you know they must communicate their return one hour before they arrive?		
Do you know that the documentation must be prepared leaving documented proof?		
Do you think that HSC are aware of these regulations?		
Do you know that HSC must have an insurance policy covering civil liability?		
Do you know that this policy must be for a sum of at least 50 million pesetas?		
Do you know that the Harbour Captain can deny the HSC permission to leave port?		
Do you know on this denial of permission may be indicated the date and time of permission to leave?		
Do you know that the itinerary to be followed by the HSC may be expressly defined?		
Do you know that speed limits may be indicated, in accordance with the sailing areas?		
Do you know that HSC may be required to present international certificates?		
Do you know that they may be required to present their security equipment and measures?		
Do you know that these may condition the permission to leave?		
Do you know that accreditation of the corresponding pilot's certificate may be requested?		
Do you know that sailing a HSC with a modified propeller may be forbidden?		
Have you heard of these restrictions being applied?		
Do you know that the collaboration of Maritime and Aerial Authorities and organisms may be requested in the surveillance of these measures?		
Have you heard of this collaboration being requested?		
Do you know that these regulations will not be applied to HSC destined for use in rescue operations?		

3.4.9 Survey Results

The overall response to the survey from the various parties responsible for vessels was well below the number expected, at least as regards the surveys completed in writing. This circumstance recurred both in the Spanish and the Italian ports. However, the unrecorded verbal response largely coincides with the written answers, confirming the existence of a low level of knowledge regarding the problems related with the offences under study.

Those surveyed express a deep-rooted sense of awe towards the maritime venture and its commerce, but they deceive themselves and misunderstand the purpose and objectives of the survey by considering that these circumstances cannot happen to them, even though they do not exclude them from happening to others. There is, then, a false sense of security which blocks out reality, a typical situation which makes them more vulnerable to risk.

The first question in the survey, regarding awareness of the IMO Resolution IMO A.872 (20), though mainly answered in the affirmative, shows little knowledge of its content, recommendations or specific aspects, as the rest of the questions show an erratic pattern, typical of a superficial and unfounded knowledge.

The summary of the survey underlines the direct relation with the business philosophy exercised by the shipping companies in matters of organised crime. If a clearly preventive policy is not implemented, the persons responsible on board will get this message and the matter will not be given its due importance, with the result that these innocent persons will end up involved in criminal offences (they do not imagine that this could happen to them).

There is also an overall unawareness on board of the procedures for communicating incidents in the ports, and of the official organisms which should be the receivers of this information. This lack of knowledge may lead to a delay in the report, or in the worst cases, postponement of permission to leave port or general delays caused by the bureaucratic processes they might get involved in

While in the face of the unawareness of the vulnerability of the vessel and its crew an adequate training programme might be insufficient, in the case of the procedure for notifying the authorities on land there is no other solution than the establishment of extensive training programmes, clarifying how to take the first steps and specifying the process to be followed and the advantages these offer, even when it is only a question of a suspicion.

At an internal level, in the shipping company-vessel relation, there is clearly a lack of information regarding the philosophy and the external image to be conveyed, and of any preventive procedures which constitute the first security measures before boarding the ship. Should this be applied, the crews would form part of a dynamic business policy aimed at efficiency and with chances of success, or at least the delinquent would encounter an attitude clearly removed from that of 'laissez-faire'.

Survey result for merchant ships

After grouping together the main points of all the answers selected by blocks, the final result of the survey paints the following picture:

Applicable to the parties responsible for the vessel

- 64.7% of the parties responsible for the vessels knew of the IMO Resolution a.872 (20) which constituted the reference framework for the survey itself.
- The crew generally accepts the role of the customs services, collaborating to a large extent and providing all the means required for the vessel inspection, although they consider that the Customs Service should not have access to all of the cargo on board.
- The majority of them also claim to know about the functions and faculties of the Customs Officers, although the percentage of positive answers drops to 60% when asked about their role in providing information on the crew members.
- With respect to knowledge of the points of contact that Customs may make available in the ports for informing about drug-related incidents and the efficiency of these, there is a widely expressed uncertainty of around 50%.

Applicable to the responsibility of the shipping company:

After consulting about the responsibility of the shipping companies and their direct implication in specific policies in keeping with the OMI Resolution A.872 (20), the following conclusions are established:

- It is considered that the shipping company does not hinder the intervention of the Customs Officers but there is little relation with this official organism as can be seen in the fact that they do not request their assessment in coordinating and improving the security personnel, especially as regards evaluating suspicious cases.
- Regarding the treatment of the cargo containers, the state of the seals and their vulnerability, opinion is divided at 50%, showing that there is great concern over the current measures and their efficiency.

- Similarly, around 65% consider that there is no efficient control of the accesses both of persons and vehicles to the cargo storage areas on land, with no clear separation between parking areas and cargo areas, or any rigour in the passes, registration of pass numbers, etc.
- They do not think that the shipping companies have electronic security systems installed and thus they do not consider either that these can be placed at the disposition of the Customs Service.
- They do not know if the shipping company communicates to the Customs Service incidents concerning suspicious, unaccounted for packages on board, or whether security procedures have been followed with respect to these.
- They do not know about the policies regarding stevedore companies or any other services (companies) and their knowledge of the shipping company's recruitment of employees is scarce, referring in both cases to questions concerning drug trafficking.
- They mostly think that the shipping company does not have a close enough relation with the Customs Service, and thus cannot offer adequate training to their personnel; nor do they dispose of the appropriate channels to provide this. Similarly, neither the level of collaboration with the Customs Service, nor the measures adopted to reduce vulnerability nor any preventive action plans are communicated on board.
- They also mostly consider that, as crew members, they do not receive training courses in the fight against drug trafficking, or any encouragement or sensitisation on the problem, and are not told how to respond to criminal acts, etc.

On analysing the results of this block, it can be observed that the policies of the shipping companies on drugs matters are not thorough and do not constitute a priority for them; nor do they show any interest in training their personnel (on land and crew). Meanwhile, in contrast with the companies' apathy, the answers themselves reveal the great interest of the crew members in receiving this specific training.

On concealment on board:

A percentage of 65 to 85 % is recorded for matters related with concealment, considering that the vessel is an ideal place for hiding drugs, showing that the crew is aware of the vulnerability of the vessel.

On security measures:

- 75% of the crew considers that continuous training would complement security on board, while 55% believe that the anti-drug security of the vessel would improve if the risks were explained, as this would allow a more vigilant and committed attitude to be adopted.
- They openly admit to receiving no training at all as regards the procedures, behaviours and methods used by drug traffickers, nor regarding inspections of persons and luggage.
- The information they consider that on land employees have is acceptable, but they also believe that these cannot fight drug trafficking either.
- They consider the security precautions applied on board inefficient, as regards controls of access to both the cabins and the loading areas, expressing an awareness of an insufficient lighting in high-risk areas which facilitates the undertaking of offences.

- As regards the inspection procedures for the containers and the seals, they do not consider these to be sufficient, and the same applies to the inspection of lorries coming in and out of the premises and their drivers.
- The security measures on board in port are scarce along the hull and especially on the sea side of the ship, being of particular relevance the lack of lighting and the minimal use of break-in detection equipment.
- Although there is some control of access on board as regards the identification of visitors and their access to restricted areas of the vessel, no check or inspection is made of hand luggage either on entering or leaving ship, nor is there any monitoring of the spare parts and provisions. As a result, no procedures are implemented for the identification or immobilisation of suspicious packages.
- There are no security measures on entering cabins, internal accesses on board, nor are there any complementary security personnel, or use of alarms and security devices.

The ships' officers have a good knowledge of the security plans related with the risks of sailing (fire, abandoning ship, etc.) and of the layout of the vessel, while the same cannot be said of their knowledge of crime.

During navigation:

In general, crafts that attract attention are a cause for suspicion, although the obligation to provide help when necessary presides over any question of illicit acts. Most also attempt to identify the craft by communicating the incident to the coastal authorities.

However, except for this customary attitude of sailors, no other precautions or prevention is implemented against possible assaults or in order to reduce the vulnerability of the sides of the vessel.

If it is suspected that there is a situation of risk, the vessel does not have persons qualified to perform selective searches below the float line. The unawareness of procedures against the external actions of delinquents and drugs traffickers is significant.

Procedure for carrying out inspections:

- The negative answers are mostly related to the crew's preparation in carrying out efficient inspections.
- They do not believe that any of their mates might be drug addicts.
- They are convinced that there is no coordination between Customs and the Captain to perform the inspections.
- They consider the inspection plans to be insufficient and that the itineraries to be followed on board do not cover all the options.
- Opinion is divided at 50% each with regard to the equipment available for making an efficient inspection.
- They believe that the passengers and their luggage must be inspected on land and not on board.
- They do not consider the personal inspection to be efficient.
- They are unaware of the technology on the market for detecting indications of crime on board, such as X-rays and surveillance cameras.

- They do not consider the inspection of vehicles and drivers to be efficient.
- The loading of provisions on board is not widely considered as a channel for introducing drugs.
- Anywhere may be a hiding place to a lesser or greater degree, although this is uncommon in the captain's office, pilot's cabin and crew quarters, that is, in spaces occupied by the crew itself.

Possible indicators of irregularities:

- Suspicions are not generally of persons, nor are they due to external signs. 50% of the suspicions are of disordered stocks, things out of place, open packages, alterations in lifeboats and little else.
- No cause-effect relation is established in the prior payment of cargos, or the value of the goods consigned.
- There is a clear lack of attention in the search for indications in containers, or in alterations in their infrastructure.
- There is a lack of knowledge or information about drawing up a full report if a drug trafficking act is detected.

Control of fist-aid kits on board:

There is some knowledge of their contents, control and supervision. Doubts are expressed over the specific documentation, but this would not seem to constitute a point of risk, except for the aspect of the import/export administrative procedure.

Essential substances for preparing drugs:

They do not know about these and they do not think that drug producing countries control them.

Immigration:

It should be remembered that the discovery of a stowaway on board is one of the biggest problems a ship's captain might face. It leads to damage, expenses and problems with the immigration authorities in the port of arrival. There is a good level of knowledge of this matter as far as the physical space of the vessel itself is concerned.

The solution of this type of situation on land is of no concern to the crew, as is expressed in the IMO Resolution A. 872 (20), which limits itself to the consideration of internal aspects of the vessel as is appropriate, this being an eminently maritime resolution.

The problem takes on another human and social dimension when it goes to jurisdiction on land, but this is beyond the scope of this survey, and it is referred to in another part of the study.

Survey result for commercial ports

Applicable to the responsibility of the concessionaires:

Overall, the survey shows a clear lack of positive relations with police institutions or for the coordination of actions against delinquency.

In general terms, in answers equal to or over 60%:

- No request is made to Customs to improve the security personnel, who, furthermore, have not received sufficient training.
- There are no administrative procedures for providing the customs authorities with lists of the containers to disembark. Around 50% know of some damage to the containers which has not been reported to the authorities. The seals are rarely checked.
- There is not sufficient control of the access of vehicles and persons to the cargo areas, with a lack of registration numbers, identification of persons and parking limits. There are no electronic security systems in the cargo areas.
- There is very little communication between the concessionaire personnel on any preventive and control measures that might be in use, confirming that they do not turn to Customs for assessment in drawing up security plans or for verifying the vulnerability of the facilities.

On security measures:

- The personnel do not have sufficient training in making inspections, nor on evasive techniques, technical aids, identification of suspicious persons or of methods of inspection. They do not know about anti-drugs techniques.
- They do not think there is a good coordination with Customs or that the current security precautions are effective, such as the physical barriers at the cargo area accesses, the checks, examination of containers, seals, ways of communicating breakages, control of lorries, spare parts, provisions, hand luggage or equipment sent to land for repair.

Procedures for conducting inspections:

- The administration does not draw up inspection plans.
- There is no methodology in the identification of the inspectors or in the itineraries.
- They do not consider the physical inspection to be a good procedure.
- They consider the documentation check both of the cargo and the drivers to be insufficient.
- They do not have clear ideas on the steps to take in an inspection, nor any of the related aspects.

Indicators of irregularities:

- There is a great unawareness of suspicious circumstances, most of it due to the complete lack of specific instructions for such cases.
- They are not suspicious of persons who show signs of belonging to a higher level than that which they occupy, which indicates disinterest and a lack of concern for specific aspects of their workmates.
- No special effort is made to examine the state of the seals in the containers, or suspicious irregularities. When these did exist, they do not know if they were reported to the authorities.

Illegal substances for making drugs:

The answers, mainly with 50% yes, indicate a great ignorance of such substances, so that they are of little relevance.

High-speed craft (HSC)

- There is little knowledge of what these crafts might represent in the chain of criminal acts.
- Nor do they have any clear knowledge of the laws that regulate and control these.

Survey result on leisure ports

On security measures:

- The personnel have no training in anti-crime security.
- They do not think there is a good coordination with the Customs and Police authorities.
- They do not consider the access control, inspection of lorries, weighing of cargoes to be sufficient.
- They do not think that the personnel is vigilant in these matters, and they do not have any additional alarms or security devices.
- There is no check on the entry or exit of articles for repair or others.

Substances for preparing drugs:

They do not have a good knowledge of what these are, nor of how they are presented. These circumstances are underlined by the answers divided by 50%.

High-speed crafts (HSC):

80% of those surveyed did not know of the existence of a law on this matter. In these conditions, negative answers coincide with ignorance.

Survey result for fishing ports

Applicable to the responsibility of the concessionaires:

A high number of negative answers is given to the questions presented, pointing to a lack of awareness of the matter.

On security measures:

- They point out again and again that they do not receive any type of training or information.
- They do not dispose of any security plans, nor are they aware of the vulnerability of the installations.
- They consider insufficient the measures of control of access and identification, entry of vehicles, their loads and persons.
- They do not have alarms or any other security devices.

Procedures for conducting inspections:

- They do not know the usual procedures that guarantee the reliability of inspections.
- They do not consider the physical inspection to be an efficient method.
- No methods are applied with respect to weight, appearance and no advanced technological means are used.
- They do not consider the checks on vehicles, loads and drivers to be sufficient.
- Little attention is paid to the inspection of provisions.

Indications of irregularities:

- The large number of negative answers in matters relating to the detection of indications shows a lack of knowledge of these matters.
- They do not consider any external manifestations beyond their possibilities to be relevant.
- They do not look for, and therefore do not detect, any strange signs in packages, wrappings etc.

Substances for preparing drugs:

The disparity in the answers indicates that they have little knowledge of this matter.

High-speed craft (HSC):

Although they know that the resolution exists, they do not know of its contents and demands. This question is of little relevance to fishing ports.

Interview with experienced captains

Below are presented the conclusions obtained by the workgroup from interviews with captains with many years of experience at sea. For the obvious reasons of security and confidentiality, no data is given which would allow them to be identified. The information provides some further aspects which are not reflected on the survey forms, which should be accepted as subjective criteria.

- To the question of who the most demanding police in the world are:
    England
    Holland
    Saudi Arabia
- The least demanding:
    Canada
    Australia
    The USA
    New Zealand
- On the highest degree of corruption in the police worldwide:
    Third world (North African Arab)
    South America
    Thailand
    Rumania

- Where the least corruption is found:
    Western Europe
    Canada
    The USA
    Australia
    Japan

It was suggested that in future surveys, models should be added corresponding to types of:

- Vessels, shipping companies, flag countries
- Cargoes
- Nationality, officers and crew
- Collaboration between suppliers and certain authorities on land
- Ports of origin and destination
- Routes and passageways

In general terms, they consider that:

- The inspections are minimal and inefficient, even more so in leisure ports where the different police groups each with different competences, thanks to a lack of resources, do little more than gather in the documents handed to them by the sailing clubs, documents which are not even standardised.

- At present, there is a paradox by which if foreign leisure boats, especially sailing-boats, do not moor in port but anchor offshore, something which is quite common, they are unlikely to receive any kind of inspection. A failure to communicate entry in port for delivery or for a visit by a foreign craft, even one from outside the EU, is not sanctioned by Customs or the Police. A sailing-boat or another leisure craft can remain in our country for several months without receiving one single visit from any police force. Our leisure ports have received no legal instructions or regulations on actions to be taken in the case of arrival of foreign vessels, which are given the same treatment as national vessels.

- The inspections are based more on personal impulses and the spontaneity of certain collaborations than on the actual regulations.

- The EU should unify the computerised data bases on leisure craft, which forms an impressive fleet. In Spain there are more than 150,000 on the 7th list. The following should be unified:

    Documents
    Computerised data-bases
    Shared regulations
    Agile channels of information and communication
    Serious studies on coastal surveillance

- On cruiser-type passenger transport vessels, the inspection of passengers is sufficient, while it is deficient in the case of ferry-type vessels boarded by all types of vehicles.

- There is a lack of knowledge among ships' captains of the IMO Resolution A.872 of 1997 on guidelines for the prevention and suppression of drugs smuggling. It is largely unfulfilled.

- A refusal to cooperate is detected among the crew and the personnel concerned.

- The ships' captains consider their responsibility for security to be indirect from this perspective, although they claim to control all situations on board.

- Knowledge of the basic security procedures by the crews is very scarce.

- Neither captains, officials or crew-members have been trained in this area of security.

- The shipping companies and concessionaires do not identify their responsibilities either, seeing them at most as indirect.

3.5 Human behaviour under pressure

Although this is relevant for all persons and vessel types, passenger vessels should be given special consideration as these perform a quite different function from that of other vessel types. There is a concentration of persons on them who need to be attended to and who, to a large extent, do not know the medium. At eh same time, the crew is affected by the need to add, on top of all the responsibilities that go with sailing a vessel, those related to the services required by the passengers. To the behaviour of the crew and passengers should also be added that of possible aggressors, special assault teams and the relatives of all the persons involved in a possible crisis on board.

This is a matter of human behaviour, not just under pressure, but also routine behaviour.

The underlying cause of many of the critical situations arising on board lies in a lack of prevention by ignoring the fact that the persons involved are subjected to high levels of stress. Consideration of this fact facilitates the detection of the aggressors and makes it possible to prevent actions by the crew members that may have negative consequences.

The complexity of human behaviour demands a great rigour in the exposition of the multiple difficulties concerning the basic aspects of both individual and collective behaviour, considering that *behaviour* is any action of a person that has consequences both for himself or for other persons in his physical environment. The basis of this action has many conditions or factors of many types: psychological, environmental, social, biological, learning, perceptive, cognitive nature, etc.; that is, it is one phenomenon with multiple causes.

3.5.1 Individual behaviour

Knowledge of how people behave individually will provide an insight into the mechanisms governing the behaviour of the masses in crisis situations. Spontaneous behaviour does not exist, since each of our actions has a consequence which in some way requires the next person to respond, thus establishing a chain of action-reaction. And it is this chain and its consequences that modifies the behaviour of persons in their relations and in their environment. In the case of an emergency situation, different people behave in different ways. This behaviour may have a result which is well-suited to the situation or one which is totally erroneous.

Experience has shown that in most critical events, a number of individual reactions took place which saved the situation when all the other intervention systems failed. What do the persons who have survived crisis situations have in common?

In the face of any situation in which a person is under threat, whatever type of threat this may be, if he does not react adequately he will find himself in a pressure situation; that is, a situation which produces a certain level of stress.

Many factors intervene in the result when fighting against the stress produced by the crisis situation and moreover this will vary greatly from one person to another. But there is a series of parameters that are common to all persons.

These parameters make up a graph which serves to evaluate critical situations and the behaviour of the persons involved.

One parameter is the time that passes second by second and which may be a precursor of stress if the required task is not completed in the established time limit.

There are situations in which time is not an important factor, while in others it is decisive.

Another factor which marks the scale in relation to time is the level of activity of the person subjected to the critical event. This level of activity consists of various zones which show the level of stress suffered, as well as the normal levels of activity and the disaster line. (Fig. 3.1)

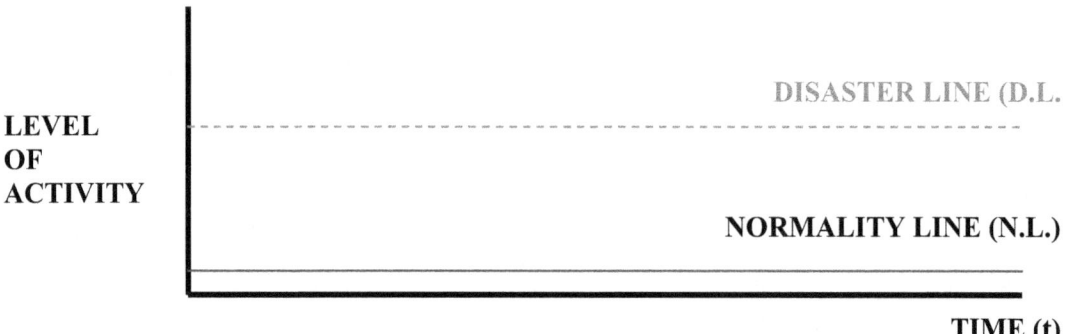

Figure 3.1

The disaster level is reached every day in all walks of life. Extraordinary things happen that have no logical explanation, but an analysis with the benefit of hindsight makes it possible to rationalise the event.

The situations that generate pressure vary greatly from one to another and, as described above, make up quite different graphs.

For example:

a) **Time pressure**
Time establishes a priority in the resolution of the crisis. This breaks the equilibrium raising stress levels due to the requirements of the task to be performed and the impossibility of completing these in the established times: the more time loss suffered, the greater the loss of equilibrium. There are many types of pressure but these are the most common.

b) **Social pressure (success-fear of failure)**
Time does not play an important role in the resolution of this crisis. The pressure level is determined by the environment and the loss of social and family support, etc. The pressure level is accumulative and the disaster line is reached when the person collapses, mainly due to conflicts of role.

c) **Accumulated internal pressure (frustration)**
The stress generated by frustration is accumulative and requires a more or less long time to saturate a person's problem-solving skills and precipitate him towards the disaster line.

d) **Pressure through physical fear**
Pressure through physical fear establishes a need to resolve the situation in the shortest possible time. This, together with the fact that what is threatened is one's physical integrity, generates a high level of stress sending the person towards the disaster line and often beyond it.

3.5.2 Shock and panic reactions

Pressure through physical fear is the most useful for controlling public order and for the subsequent examination of group and mass actions.

The possible reactions of all persons are the same. There is no human being who does not comply with this principle; rather, there are differences between one and another in the intensity of their reactions. Under pressure, reactions range between shock and panic (Fig. 3.2).

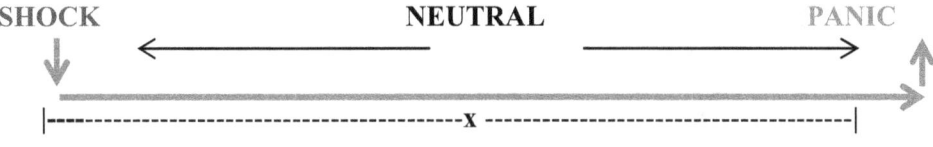

Figure 3.2

Shock is characterised by a slowness of movements or the absence of these, cold sweat, lividity, silence, closed barrier and protective postures, even foetal ones. The output communication channel is closed, but not the input.

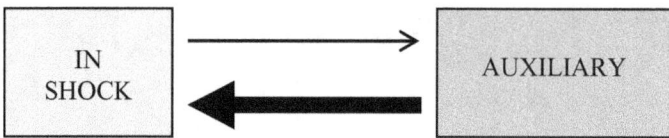

Panic is the opposite of shock; the person shows hyperactivity, hot sweat, redness in the face, screaming and a high tone of voice, open postures. The output communication channel is open, but it is so saturated that it blocks out the input channel.

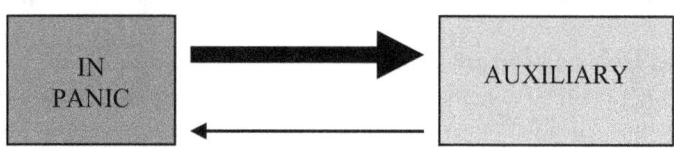

Thus, it cannot be determined whether everybody goes through a period of shock, be this short or long, to then enter a period of more or less profound panic.

LEVEL OF ACTIVITY

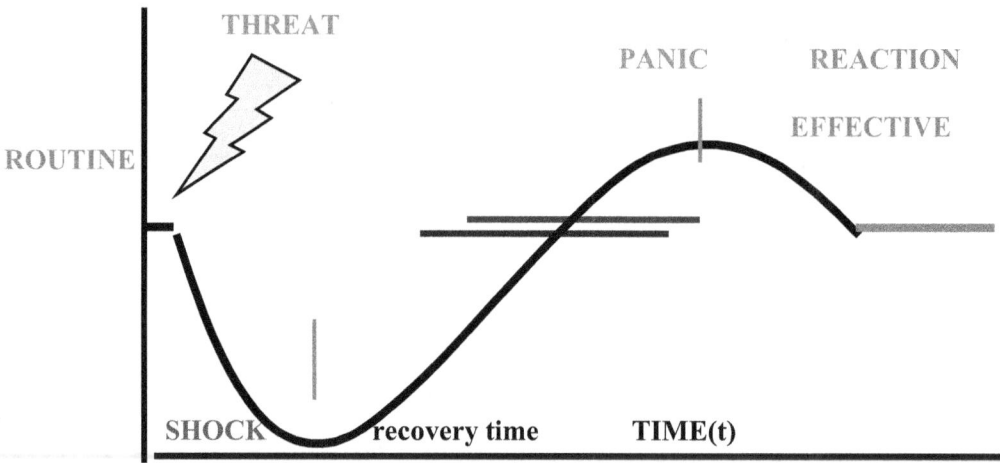

Figure 3.3

Later the effective reaction is reached, which is the objective since this is the only phase which can generate the action which will solve the crisis (Fig. 3.3).

The time that passes from the threat to the reaction is called recovery time. This is the time that we must shorten in order to increase our chances of survival. Among the methods used to achieve this objective are simulation exercises which are intended to generate the experience and knowledge required to overcome the extreme situations we have to face in a crisis.

In the effective reaction, which is given so much importance, the actions which will avoid the threat and make the extent of the damage acceptable are created, these actions needing to be executed in the appropriate time, intensity and place.

All effective reactions involve an ordered decision-making process which will have specific characteristics according to the thought system used by each person:

- *Conscious*: with slow, reflective, easily controllable responses. Good decisions are adopted.
- *Subconscious:* rapid responses, unreflective, learnt by repetition. Good use of protection equipment (hoses, extinguishers, artificial respiration and heart massage).
- *Non-conscious*: very fast, unreflective, involuntary. Hands protecting face, blinking.

It will also contribute to a better, more adequate response to the mental state of persons with respect to the interaction with personal feelings. The clearest example is when an order of priorities has to be selected for abandoning ship, where those with the best chance of survival must prevail over those with less chance.

Finally, in the effective reaction there must be a substantial element of the conservational, fighting, altruist and human instinct present in each one of us.

3.6 Drills

In a well directed drill, for example a fire drill, each person will develop a system of self-protection which will change his manner of acting in real cases of similar characteristics. This will favour the onset of the effective reaction, shortening recovery time. What will the beneficial effects provided by drills be for dealing with a similar event?

- The person will have previous experience of a fire, thus reducing the surprise factor.
- He has subsequently read and informed himself about situations of this type. He has sensitised himself to this matter, becoming aware of the reality.
- The more real the drill, the greater the level of perception acquired for the detection of possible critical signs or indications.
- He will relive mentally the stages of this type of situations, taking into account the errors he made and those he saw being made the first time.
- He will think of or will inform himself about the most efficient actions to be taken, increasing the quality of his consideration of the options.
- Psychologically, he will not have the same predisposition, this now being far more realistic.
- The psychological aspects are not necessarily the same and these can be either positive or negative, without the drill affecting them substantially.
- He will reach the effective reaction more quickly in each critical event.

3.6.1 Psychological aspects of stress situations

The intensity of the changes brought about by this emergency situation varies greatly from one person to another and depends on:

- Subjective perception of the intensity of the threat
- Proximity of danger
- Previous experience (in similar situations)
- Type of personality
- Awareness of one's capacity to overcome the danger successfully

Stages of effective reaction

The effective reaction to a threat depends on many factors which influence in many different ways each of the stages outlined below.

a. **Analysis stage**

The tendency is to react without analysing the situation and the information, coming largely from the eyes that see the main threat, does not take in the importance of secondary threats. The analysis should take place in the brain and not in the eyes. An incorrect analysis will lead to an inefficient reaction to the risk.

To engage in a correct analysis, we must take into account that a great deal of information is stored in our subconscious. This information will come to our help, though not always with satisfactory results, since the required knowledge may not emerge with the appropriate accuracy or may even lead us to believe that certain reactions are the right ones when they are not.

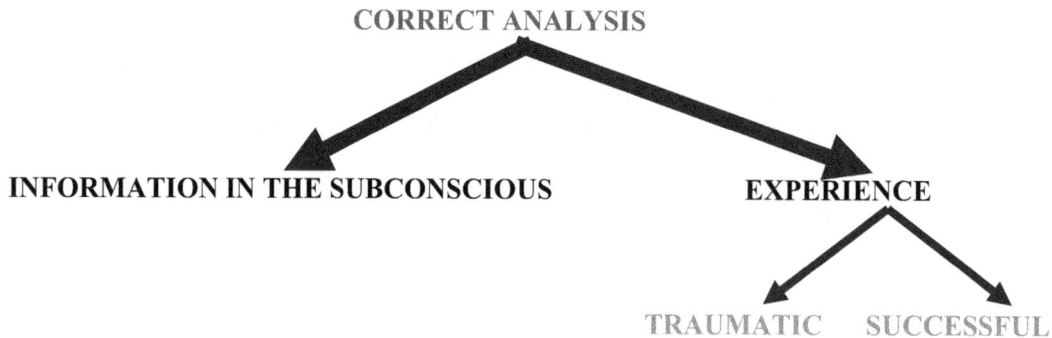

The existence of a prior experience will change the result of the analysis and of the recovery time. It may be wrong to consider that an action taken in the past which solved the crisis then will solve the current situation, while an untreated post-traumatic shock derived from a similar situation may generate a lack of analysis.

The objectives of the analysis stage are:

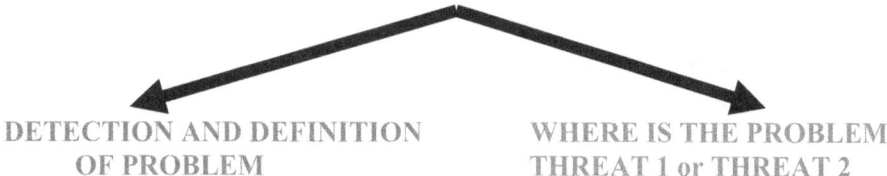

b. **Consideration of options**

According to the analysis made, the options for countering the effects of the crisis are considered. There are only two possible reactions: to gather oneself and head towards the danger to fight it or to escape and flee from the threat.

   A. Towards the threat to fight it
   B. Away from the threat

3.7 Factors interfering in the consideration of the options

Lack of control of affective messages

Anger, honour, fear, hatred, love etc, may lead to serious interferences in the analysis and even more in the consideration of the options. A lack of control over one's feelings leads to a lack of discipline, impatience and self-confidence.

Lack of experience/practice

- Doubt over one's own capacity, even when one has it.
- Unawareness of the keys to the critical event, such as where it is taking place, technical questions.

Over-confidence and previous success

- Do not guarantee success in the current situation.
- Underestimation of the situation.

3.8 Decision

After the analysis and consideration stage, the best option must be selected and approached with all one's attention and energy. Indecision must be avoided at all costs. Achieving this depends on:

- An ordered and conscious process of analysis and consideration of the options
- Operative capacity, previous practice

- Availability of objective data
- Intensity of threat
- Physical information
- Existence and good state of aid devices

3.9 Reaction stage

Although it is not very common to reach this stage and not act, there are cases of mental block when it comes to performing the actions selected in the consideration of options. The problems in this stage are:

- Rapid and erroneous analysis
- Reaction without considering options
- Decision without operative capacity

It is important to activate a reaction system which examines the results, in order to be able to assess again the quality of the decision-consideration of the options-analysis.

All of these stages obviously take up precious time which is not available in some cases. If one accepts that our judgement and reflection are altered under pressure, it is clear that decisions should be taken in routine circumstances. All of this confirms that work with drills, the assault plans implemented and realism in the training of the crew will lead to ever shorter recovery times, and this, in turn will increase the chances of overcoming crisis situations on board.

3.10 Assault forces in Spain

3.10.1 Background

Terrorism, and particularly radical Islamic terrorism, is the great challenge of our days. The analysts consider it the "war of the future". In the face of this new dimension, police groups are reconstructing and adapting their strategies and the armies are collaborating to fight this growing threat.

One of the foundations on which the most fanatical and radical Islamism bases the justification for its massacres, mass killings and the projection of a permanent and unpredictable terror is the distortion of the theory of jihad (holy war). This old idea now has a new dimension which requires different responses since a large number of the most ideologised and fanatical elements are willing to go as far as immolation, by means of suicide, in order to achieve their aims. This occurred with the S 11 assassins, who did not hesitate to crash into the twin towers in scheduled flight airplanes, transformed into a mortal cargo, or those of M 11, blowing up the flat where they had taken shelter when they were about to be arrested in Madrid.

The extreme fanaticism makes any police intervention extremely dangerous. The terrorists' determination in pursuit of the idea that they sustain and that sustains them is unrelenting. This is a terrorism that has hardened and has passed its test of fire over the last decades in numerous conflicts all over the world and which embraces religious, social and cultural ideas to recruit followers in a world full of inequalities. It possesses the human and material resources of a big organisation. Its elements are highly ideologised and have the infrastructure to attack the "faithless" who are their "enemies" anywhere. They show no concern over the methods or consequences of their acts, which are based on the principle that the more victims they produce and the greater the damage, the better, as their repercussions in the media, and thus their impact, will then be even greater.

In these conditions, the democratic governments must direct the efforts of their police forces towards prevention. They must also address the existing inequalities in their social policies, as these form the seeds from which fanaticism springs.

As regards the repression of this terrorism, the work of investigation, analysis and elaboration of information carried out by both the police and the military intelligence services are beginning to overlap, causing a certain degree of confusion. It can be detected that this moment is one of reflection, transition and adaptation of the organisations and responses to the potential aggressions. For military intelligence, terrorism is now a primary objective. For the police forces, this has always been the case, though in another dimension, thus requiring a reformulation of structures and objectives.

When prevention fails, all that is left is to be ready to face the crisis at its height, when the responses follow on from the events and cannot be delayed. It is then that the assault forces come into action and become the centre of attention. The taking of hostages to make demands; hijacking of airplanes or ships and occupation of buildings; assault on the flats where the terrorists take refuge or use as their operations centre; all of these can incur a police intervention requiring highly trained and coordinated forces. In short, they require specialists who can guarantee success or mitigate the consequences of a large-scale criminal act with enormous repercussions.

3.10.2 Spanish special forces

Given the complex organisation of public security, the special forces in Spain have certain special characteristics which are a consequence of our heterogeneous police organisation model. At the present moment, it can be stated that these forces are police forces and are integrated in the security forces and bodies. Included in these security forces, though only as a possible resource and depending on the occurrence of certain specific aggressions in the future, are certain army units. This reflects the fact that, at this moment in history, the situation worldwide is at a turning point which will lead to a greater involvement of the armed forces in the fight against terrorism, at least in some of its dimensions and facets.

In fact, this tendency has already begun, particularly at sea where intervention takes place far from the coast, the navy now playing a prominent role providing "capacities" to any police intervention. "Capacities" should be interpreted as the means of support required to provide the optimum conditions in which the police intervention should take place, such as support in communications, or the detection and pursuit of suspect vessels. Also their vessels can be used as a base of operations from which the intervention or assault takes place. Even underwater surveillance can be of great help.

At present in Spain in matters of terrorism, a great effort is being made to unite forces and avoid duplication. All police and intelligence services were previously focused on the terrorism of ETA and other minor terrorisms. The shockwave of March 11, 2003, after the initial surprise, forced the first decisions to be taken. The threat is now quite different. It is far more widespread, has greater capacity and is more unpredictable. Steps are now being taken. The National Centre for Anti-terrorist Coordination was recently created. This Centre will be a professional, non-political body which will depend organically on the Secretary of State of the Home Office and functionally on the Executive Committee for The Unified Command. It is made up of the Civil Guard and the National Police Corps[2].

The phenomena of terrorism are not something new. Since the sixties, internal terrorism has required answers of the National Security Forces and Corps, particularly the National Police Corps and the Civil Guard, which have led them to create their own units of intervention:

- The Civil Guard created its Special Intervention Unit (**UEI**), which is currently regulated by General Act nº 33/97, of August 4, on "Organisation and missions of the Special Intervention Unit". It currently has its headquarters in Valdemoro (Madrid).

In 1978, the Immediate Intervention Group (GII) of the Civil Guard was created in the image and likeness of the Intervention Group of the National French Gendarmerie (**GIGN**). Various terrorist incidents, among them the Munich Olympics of 1972, had highlighted the shortcomings of the special forces in countering or neutralising extreme situations and highly organised criminal actions with great repercussions in terms of victims and damage. The various governments began to develop initiatives in this sense. In 1982, the Special Intervention Unit was set up, dependent on the Director of the Civil Guard.

- The National Police Corps has the Special Operations Group (In Spanish '**Grupo Especial de Operaciones (GEOS)**'), created on April 1, 1978 upon the decision of the then Interior Minister, Rodolfo Martín Villa. This group has similar functions to the Special Intervention Unit and can undertake the same missions within its area of responsibility or as the culmination of its own investigations and actions.

This unit is prepared to tackle and intervene in crisis situations or in the detention of members of terrorist groups and in other situations involving serious danger and requiring specially qualified and trained components.

This duplicity of units with similar functions is a constant characteristic of our model of organisation revolving mainly around these two police corps which, with few exceptions, undertake a similar set of functions. In fact, in matters of terrorism and on land, the two fulfil identical functions.

---

[2] It was created by *Act INT/1251/2004*, depends directly on the Home Office, is formed by:
- President:
  - The Secretary of State for Security
- Members:
  - The Director General of Police
  - The Director General of the Civil Guard
  - The Director General of Infrastructures and Security Matters
  - The Director of the Home Office Cabinet
  - Secretary

The law refers to an overall assessor designated by the president, but it would seem that this position will be occupied by the Director of the Cabinet of Coordination of the Secretary of State for Security. The case may also arise where persons required to provide assessment on different matters might be called to the committee. The decisions taken by this committee will be of compulsory compliance by the Security Forces.

The question that might be asked is when does one or the other corps intervene. Normally, it is the group that has carried out the previous investigation that performs the service, since they then dispose of more information, and usually under the direction of judges and prosecutors. That is, in general, it could be stated that the intervention is carried out by the police group with the greatest chance of success according to the information available. They are very similar in structure, methods and procedures.

Obviously, this duplicity in questions of operative investigation leads to friction and a certain lack of coordination when parallel actions are prepared. Thus, the recently created joint organs must strive to find solutions by ordering a joint effort to be made on some occasions and on others, adjudicating the execution of the services to one or other of these corps, transmitting to them all of the available information. In this case, "ordering" should be understood in both its meanings, that of establishing an order and that of commanding.

Whenever one of the police groups is involved in an investigation, it will be its own intervention force that will engage in the executive stages of the assault. The target may be a means of transport, for our purposes a certain vessel which has been overtaken by a terrorist group and which represents a threat to the persons on board. The vessel itself may be hijacked to be used as an instrument of aggression, or, in other words, the target of an attack.

When it is stated that either intervention force could take on the mission of resolving the crisis, it is understood that this is valid on land. But on board a ship with problems or one which is immersed in a crisis involving terrorist elements, the assault should be carried out by the Special Intervention Unit (UEI) of the Civil Guard, for the following reasons:

- The Civil Guard is responsible for the surveillance of the waters under Spanish jurisdiction in view of Order LO 2/86, of March 13, of the Security forces and corps. The Civil Guard is the integral police force for the territorial seas.
- The Civil Guard has patrol boats of up to 30 metres ready to provide the required support in the territorial seas. In international waters, the capacity of the Spanish Navy can be relied upon.
- The Civil Guard has been preparing for this kind of contingency for a long time, aware that they must be able to respond appropriately.

It is true that until now the Spanish special intervention groups have not had the opportunity to be involved in serious crisis situations on board vessels or involving vessels. However, they have intervened and now have great experience in ship boarding at high sea through operations against drugs-trafficking at sea.

Any situation such as the one considered here, which is after all a theoretical model, presents other facets and complications in reality. The following aspects will often play a major role:

- Ship's flag country
- Country of origin of crew and passengers
- Country of shipping company and of this company's capital.
- Country in whose territorial waters the vessel is overtaken and countries in whose territorial waters the navigation takes place after being overtaken
- Country in whose port the vessel is or port to which the vessel is bound
- Countries along the route of the hijacked vessel

Means

The means of these groups are sophisticated and each of their components is a specialist in a certain stage or mission of the process of resolution of the crisis. Some are expert marksmen who use highly sophisticated, high-precision weapons. Others exceed in the handling of explosives. They are aware of and trained in all types of theoretical suppositions and they are coordinated, indeed almost synchronised, to work as a team. They work with encoded language and transmissions with formula translators.

Command

The command of these groups is no different from that of the rest of the security forces and corps; thus, depending on his entity, it will either be an officer of the Civil Guard or an inspector of the National Police Force who is in charge of these groups.

3.10.3 Interventions at sea

The guidelines on conducting a boarding are based on the experience of the US troops in the first Gulf War and in the subsequent maritime embargos. Boarding without collaboration from inside the vessel is an extremely delicate operation involving great risk. The American troops, who have performed all types of interventions and are deployed all over the world, have developed protection procedures for their fleet and are highly trained in the boarding of suspect vessels or vessels which represent a threat to their interests. Another field of training is the various maritime embargos they have imposed or been involved in.

It is difficult to foresee that any intervention at sea against an organised terrorist group on board a vessel will not have a high cost, given the complexity inherent in all operations of this kind.

A cruise ship or petrol tanker sailing is an iron fortress, without any feasible access, that can be transformed in a matter of seconds into a ball of fire or sink, to name but two of the most dangerous hypotheses. Moreover, once on board, the assault team has to manoeuvre through the narrow passages and inner accesses until they can control the situation and neutralise the crisis, which means assuming a high cost in risks and lives in the face of a well-armed criminal group carrying explosives and willing to do anything. The operation would involve the maximum risk on a cruise ship with three or four thousand persons on board between the crew and the passengers. If we consider that the crisis might last for days, it is easy to imagine the pressure that any government would be subjected to.

In any case, in the extreme event of the overtaking of a vessel by a large group of terrorists, the intervention would have to be coordinated with naval means, both afloat and underwater, and aerial means at the service of the assault team which would move in and address the resolution of the crisis.

It is difficult to control these extreme situations, even on land, as highlighted by recent events perpetrated by Chechen terrorists in Russian hospitals and schools, which ended with a high cost in victims. At sea, the conditioning factors and the risks are multiplied several times.

It should be taken into account that in times of war responses are urgent and that terrorism in The USA is now a military question, while it is still basically a police matter in Spain, although the Armed Forces are being called more and more to collaborate in these missions, as the current terrorist threat requires. Moreover, the use of arms in Spain as regards the legality of their use and justifying circumstances is quite restrictive, as is logical in a democratic country where the laws are enacted for normal situations.

The government, under pressure from the various demands, will have to decide whether to intervene and to what extent and at the expense of what risks. The decision will not be easy, nor will it guarantee success.

In any case, on the basis of experience and a logical analysis, in the lack of any pre-established procedures, if the action takes place outside Spanish territorial waters only the Ministry of Defence, through the Navy, disposes of the adequate means for guaranteeing an intervention, although the vessel boarding and the final assault, should this be the decision taken, should correspond to the Special Intervention Group (UEI) of the Civil Guard, in keeping with the above considerations.

Moreover, in the face of any crisis of this type and until it is resolved, all of the available forces will be directly or indirectly involved. Some will be in the surroundings to provide support to the action and to the possible victims or for sea rescue operations. The Spanish Navy will contribute all its experience, having normal "visit and register" boarding procedures performed by the fleet escort ships. This knowledge and experience will be of great use. In any case, if the terrorists have already used planes and trains so brutally as means or targets of their criminal actions, an action against maritime traffic cannot be disregarded. The forces called upon to intervene in this hypothetical threat must be on the alert already, as they surely are, and train by practising actions in theoretical suppositions to familiarise themselves with the marine environment.

Given the various hypotheses for the taking of vessels and hostages and the different ends pursued by the perpetrators, and bearing in mind that they will probably make demands, this will ensure that there is some time to reflect on the procedures and means to be used if the crisis is not resolved through negotiation or other means. In the best of cases, this will be a difficult time to prepare the adequate responses to a real threat.

3.10.4 Boarding procedures

The boarding procedures used by the police throughout the world are those obtained from experience in other kinds of criminal activities which form part of the organised crime network via the maritime channel: drugs trafficking, smuggling and illegal immigration. These criminal phenomena have all necessitated boarding procedures, all of these full of difficulties, given the intrinsic complexity of the medium in which they take place.

In the United Nations programme for the international fiscalisation of drugs a Guide for combating drugs at sea was created.[3] It is, in short, an operative document based on the accumulated experience of the police all over the world, particularly with respect to ship-boarding.

It offers some points of interest that can be applied for undertaking a boarding in terrorism situations. Although it has not been followed literally, some of its technical proposals have been taken into account here.

---

[3] This is a reference guide for the application of Article 17 of the United Nations Convention on the illicit trafficking of drugs and psychotropic substances of 1988.

Normally terrorists will at first try to establish and maintain an open communication in order to convey their demands and threats to the government in question. A good negotiator can obtain priceless data in this stage.

To board a vessel, it is important for the military or police patrol boat to put the auxiliary boat in the water, assuming that there is only one target vessel. It is assumed that control of the target vessel by the crew has been lost and that the terrorists on board are in total control of the situation.

It is easier to make the first approach with an auxiliary boat while the vessel remains outside radar detection, around 20 miles away. This first contact is supported by aerial vigilance.

All of these positions should in theory guarantee:

- Good, safe communications between the vessels involved in the boarding
- Visual coverage
- Good position with respect tot the foreseeable headings

The above will provide good information on the structure of the target vessel in order to determine the possible boarding points. It is also of interest to know the number of terrorists on board and the means of response that they have available.

The boarding must guarantee the security of the crew and passengers as well as that of the assault team conducting the boarding. The exact moment of carrying out the action must be carefully chosen and many factors must be considered, particularly: weather conditions, sea-state, size and layout of the target vessel, number of terrorists on board and their positions, arms and explosives they dispose of, safety of the crafts involved in the boarding. It is essential not to overlook the terrorists on deck or the possible positioning of the rest.

The moment chosen for the boarding should be one when the vessel is not moving, if possible, though this is difficult. If the vessel has to be stopped by force, a zone should be selected with little traffic where the evacuation of the crew and passengers is facilitated, this being the major problem.

The possibility of there being arms and explosives on board and their being used against the boarded vessel, its crew and passengers is very high.

On board, the most important matter is the control of the terrorists and the preservation of the safety of the crew and passengers, with aerial support if the assault team has been discovered. Re-establishing control of the vessel is essential. Returning command of the vessel to the Captain and controlling the radio and communications room as soon as possible will be the main guarantee of success.

The case may arise where those who command the vessel are casualties or cannot assume command, so that a crew must be ready at hand who know how to run the vessel. This crew will be provided by the shipping company that manages the vessel.

Once the assault team's presence on board is assured, the arrival of other elements of the boarding team should be facilitated to take the main decks.

One must not rule out the possibility that the terrorists might try to sink the vessel. Hence, a sufficient number of rescue boats and aerial evacuation means must be positioned close by and the nearby hospitals must be alerted. This is essential for saving lives.

The next step will be to put the terrorists under custody and to confiscate their arms and explosives. The bomb-disposal teams will go through and inspect the vessel with the Captain or with the Ship Security Officer (SSO) to locate any explosive devices. This can be extremely complicated, as dogs specially trained in searching for explosives do not work well on board and find it difficult to move around in a medium which moves a lot and has strong smells.

The action on board consists in controlling the terrorist group and managing the situation of the crew members and the passengers, who will be terrified. If possible and if the circumstances allow it, a group of doctors and psychologists should be placed at the disposition of the persons affected. If they are on board the vessel, they will be able to help to recover emotional stability and avoid situations of stress.

If necessary, the affected persons can be registered and taken to a neutral point where they can feel safe and according to the circumstances it can be decided whether they need to be evacuated from the vessel or not.

Once the situation is returned to normal, the state of the ship can be studied with the Captain, verifying whether or not the sailing capacity is affected and the potential risks in order to take the most adequate decisions. A meeting will be held with the Captain, the Vessel Protection Officer, the head machinist and the accountant. After a first inspection of the vessel in search of explosives carried out by the bomb-disposal teams, the vessel will be inspected with the persons in charge by departments.

The rescue boats and the evacuation unit will take position alongside the vessel ready to intervene immediately.

4. Prior preventive measures

4.1 Comparison of equipment and procedures

Until now, no preventive measures aimed at improving security conditions have been incorporated into the building of vessels; now, however, the implementation of the ISPS code will soon make it compulsory to consider new approaches to the building and equipping of ships in response to the needs imposed in today's world.

When analysing other activities which are prone to suffering the consequences of all types of criminal activity, it can be observed that they all have rules and norms which regulate them and establish criteria which must be fulfilled, providing a greater level of security (protection) both to the persons (employees and clients) and to the goods and equipment under their direct responsibility.

The robust appearance of vessels, thanks to their construction in metal under water-tightness conditions, would seem to make them immune to any break-in attempt and endow them and the goods they transport with a high level of safeguard. However, the statistics, which truly reflect the reality of the situation, show that vessels are highly vulnerable in any of the aspects to be considered, while they also present certain obstacles to the intervention of the security forces to re-establish the security lost in cases of attacks on vessels.

For this purpose, it is appropriate to quote, from the contributions made outside the area of maritime safety which fulfil the objectives of improving the safety of persons and goods, those parts which are relevant and significant and which can be related to the topic under study. They are numbered simply to establish an order, and do not coincide with or follow the enumeration of the source of origin.

4.2 Legislative Background

4.2.1 RD 1338/1984, of July 4th, on safety measures in public and private entities and establishments

1. In order to guarantee the physical integrity of persons and the safety of goods in the face of the risks derived from the commission of criminal deeds, public and private entities and establishments must adopt the measures which, for each specific group, or for all groups together, are established in the present Royal Decree.

2. The resolutions of the present Royal Decree will be applied in addition to the special safety norms to which the public and private companies and entities not contemplated specifically in this Decree are subjected.

3. The Director of National Security or the civil governors may demand the implementation in private, industrial, commercial or service entities and establishments, if the nature or importance of the activity, the location of their installations, the concentration of their clients, the volume of their funds or the values they handle, the value of the personal property and objects of value that they possess or any other cause should warrant it, of all or any of the following services or safety measures:

- Department of Security
- Security service
- Alarm and protection measures

4. Companies and entities may contract with duly authorised security companies, the provision of a security guard service, and the installation and maintenance of security systems, the connection of alarm devices, the protection, transport, transfer and handling of funds, assets and goods, of jewels and objects of value and, in general, make arrangements with specialised companies for the assessment and planning of security systems.

5. Alarm devices of any type or model, whether they be optical, photographic, magnetic, electronic and, in general, any technical procedure of use in the identification of possible delinquents and for the prevention of possible break-ins which are to be installed compulsorily, must be certified, in keeping with the provisions of the legislation currently in force.

6. It is compulsory for all establishments or branches of banks, savings banks or any other banking entity, without detriment to any other systems voluntarily adopted by the companies, to install surveillance cameras, of 35mm minimum, capable of retaining the images of any break-in that may occur, and allowing the perpetrators to be identified

7. The appropriate devices should also be installed for the prevention of break-ins outside office hours, capable of immediately detecting any attack on the zones where the funds and values are kept.

8. In all of the affected establishments and offices, the public will be notified, by means of posters (of a large enough size to be easy to read, never less than 18 by 12 centimetres), of the existence of safety measures, with specific reference to the adoption of delayed opening systems.

9. When the value of the goods to be transported is over two million pesetas, the transport must be undertaken in specially equipped vehicles and under the protection of an appropriate number of security guards. The same applies to cases of regular, periodical transport of goods whose value exceeds 1,000,000 pesetas.

10. The transport of samples of jewellery and silverware will be reduced to the absolute minimum, ensuring that the exhibition of this type of valuable objects be made in establishments that fulfil the security requirements.

11. Salespersons shall carry with them only reproductions of the jewels or valuable objects whose sale they are promoting, or the original pieces when their value is under 2,000,000 pesetas.

4.2.2 Order of April 23rd, 1997, determining certain aspects concerning security companies, in fulfilment of the private security law and regulation.

- In the case where there are separating walls shared with adjoining buildings or premises other than those of the company, an inner wall will be built with high-resistance materials and in such a way that its degree of security is Level A, according to UNE standards 108-111 and 108-113, which will be substituted when appropriate by the European standard UNE EN 1143-1.
- Glazing with category A-20 bulletproofing, in accordance with the specifications of the standard UNE 108-131, which will be substituted when appropriate by the European standard UNE EN 1063.
- Bullet proof access double-door, with an airlock system and a remote control opening device, which must be manual and operated from within. The walls that bound or complete the non-glazed zone of the control room will have the same degree of resistance as the glazing of the room.

4.2.3 UNE Standard 108-131, Sections 1 and 2

1. The equipment or systems installed in banking entities dedicated to the recording of images must be positioned in places not visible to the public, and the system of protection against theft of the image devices must have an access delay of at least ten minutes activated during the hours of public opening. This delay may be of the technical type in the case of computer systems and physical or electronic in the case of video recording.

2. The delay system may be substituted by a key to the room in which the equipment is kept, which must be deposited in a container element disposing of the same time delay.

3. The electronic devices installed in banking entities must protect, at least, the elements where the money is deposited, and must meet the requirements established in Section twenty-five of the Order by which certain aspects are specified concerning security companies, in fulfilment of the Law and Regulation on Private Security. Also, the staff of the entity must press the buttons or other means referred to in Article 120.1.c) of the Private Security Regulation, in response to a robbery with intimidation or any other circumstance which, due to its gravity, requires such action to be taken, whenever this action does not involve any risk to the physical integrity of the said staff or third parties.

4. The reinforced cash vaults and the safe deposit box rooms must be bound by a structure of reinforced walls on the walls, ceiling and floor, with access through a door and hatch, both reinforced.

5. The wall will be surrounded on all sides by an aisle with a maximum width of 60 centimetres.

6. The vault's walls, doors and hatches must be built with high-resistance materials and in such a way that its degree of security is at least level C, according to UNE standards 108-111-87 and 108-113-87, which will be substituted when appropriate by the European standard UNE EN 1143-1.

7. The door to the reinforced cash vault will have a blocking device and a delayed opening system with a delay of at least 10 minutes.

8. The vault will be equipped with seismic detectors, microphones or any other devices which enable any break-in through the walls, ceiling or floor to be detected, and will also have volumetric detectors inside. All of the elements connected to the security system must transmit the alarm signal via two separate communication channels, so that the loss of use of one of them will trigger the transmission of the signal by the other.

9. The blocking system of the reinforced vaults must be activated from the closing time of the establishment to the opening time of the next working day.

10. The safes must be made of materials with a degree of security of level D, according to UNE standards 108-110-87 and 108-112-87, which will be substituted when appropriate by the European standard UNE EN 1143-1.

11. The safes must at least dispose of the protection of a seismic detector which will be connected to the security systems of the establishment.

12. The safes will dispose of a blocking system and a delayed opening system with a delay of at least ten minutes.

13. The blocking system of the safes must be activated from the closing time of the establishment to the opening time of the next working day.

14. The public access doors to the cash dispensers and their glazing must have a level of resistance to manual impact of type B, according to the stipulations of UNE standard 108-131, which will be substituted when appropriate by the European standard UNE EN 356.

15. The zone of the cash dispensers where the cash containers are located will have a level of resistance D, according to UNE standards 108-110 and 108-112, which will be substituted when appropriate by the European standard UNE EN 1143-1; and, for the extraction of the containers from then cash dispenser, these will dispose of a delayed opening system with a delay of at least ten minutes, located either in the cash container itself or in the safe in which the container is housed.

16. The seismic detector will be located in the cash container access zone.

17. When the cash dispensers are installed in open spaces and do not form part of the perimeter of a building, the lobby referred to in Article 122.5 of the Private Security Law will be protected by a plate of steel, or an equivalent resistant material, at least three millimetres thick, and the lobby access door will have a level of resistance to manual impact of type B, according to UNE standard 108-131, which will be substituted when appropriate by the European standard UNE EN 356.

4.2.4 Regulations on Equipment

Royal Decree 1338 of 4.07.84 of the Ministry of the Interior on security measures in public and private entities and establishments constitutes the only law applicable to building glass currently in force in our country.

This law exclusively regulates the security levels that must be attained in certain buildings and establishments. Since these establishments handle funds, drugs or medicines, or exhibit valuable articles, these official regulations oblige them to install high-resistance glazing in certain zones. However, a project is under way to develop a European standard, EN 356, which will soon regulate the installation of security glazing against manual attacks.

UNE standard 108-131, parts 1 and 2, "tests for the classification of transparent bullet-proofing materials" also establishes guidelines to be followed by the manufacturers of these products.

MOH glazing fulfils the requirements established by standard MA.02 of the RENAR

RENAR STANDARD MA.02 on ballistic resistant materials for bullet-proofing

IN VIEW OF the stipulations of article 14, clause 8 of the National Law on Firearms and Explosives N° 20,429, articles 4° clause 4, 53° clause 11, 56° clause 5 and other conditions of the regulations, passed by Decree N° 395/75, Law N° 24.492, and Decree N° 252/94, and

CONSIDERING:

That the said article 4°, clause 4 of Annex I to Decree N° 395/75, includes as SPECIAL USES MATERIALS: "... armoured vehicles designed for the protection of valuables or persons, and in general, bullet-proof plates when intended for a specific use of protection";

It is necessary to amplify the gathering of records on special uses materials and, in particular, armoured vehicles and bullet-proof plates, since these are the elements that protect the lives of persons who, due to their activities in connection with the transport of funds, banks, financial entities, etc., are exposed to greater risks than most of society;

That as the above regulations stipulate, the National Firearms Registry is the organism responsible for establishing the norms to lay down the parameters on ballistic resistance for bullet-proofing;

That, to this end, an important study was carried out by the appropriate personnel, both from the National Firearms Registry and from other specialized organisms, undertaking a large number of tests and gathering information on the norms applied on an international level;

That finally the task has culminated in the elaboration of a norm that can be considered to be of the highest level in comparison with those already in existence;

That hence, all material which is imported or manufactured in the national territory must first be technically assessed in order to establish that it complies with the norm, for which purpose the samples required and indispensable for the undertaking of these assessments must be made available to the National Firearms Registry through the Higher Technical College of the Argentine Army or any other body designated by the RENAR;

That once the prototypes have passed the tests, the National Firearms Registry will award on demand of the interested party whenever requested, the certification that guarantees that the material fulfils the requirements of the norm according to the corresponding level of protection;

That similarly, and in order to integrate the National Computer Data Bank in charge of this organism, it is necessary to implement the system allowing the registration of reinforced materials from their origins using the Legal Forms 23,979, indicating their level of protection;

That the necessary steps have been taken by the Office of Operations and Records and the Office of Legal and Institutional Affairs of this National Firearms Register;

That the subscriber is authorised to draw up the present document in accordance with the faculties conferred by the National Law on Arms and Explosives N° 20.429, laws numbers. 23,979 and 24,492, Decrees Numbers 395/75 and 252/94 and other applicable regulations;
hence,

THE DIRECTOR OF THE NATIONAL ARMS REGISTRY RESOLVES TO:

ARTICLE 1: Approve the RENAR MA.02 Norm – Ballistic Resistance Materials for Bullet-proofing, which is incorporated as Annex 1 in the present document and forms an integral part of this Order.

ARTICLE 2: Establish that all bullet-proof material, whether it be manufactured in this country or imported, and in both cases with the due intervention of this National Firearms Registry (RENAR), must fulfil the specifications and requirements of the RENAR MA.02 Norm.

ARTICLE 3: Establish that all material imported or manufactured nationally must be technically assessed in order to determine whether it meets the RENAR MA.02 Norm, for which purpose the required and indispensable prototypes (samples) must be made available to the National Firearms Registry for the undertaking of this assessment through the Higher Technical College of the Argentine Army or any other entity designated by the RENAR

ARTICLE 4: In order to carry out the technical assessment mentioned in the above article, the following procedure will be observed:

- The presentation will be effected to the RENAR through FOUR (4) Legal Forms 23.979 type 22, designed to cover the costs of the technical assessment by make, model or level of protection.

- The RENAR will extend the corresponding order for the undertaking of the technical assessment to the Higher Technical College of the Argentine Army or any other entity technically equipped to perform it.

- With the above order and the required prototypes, the interested party will appear before the authorised entity for the assessment and the latter will then send the result to the National Firearms Registry.

- The RENAR will award the manufacturer or importer an authenticated copy of the results of the technical assessment. If the prototype has passed the test, the manufacturer or importer must assume in writing their commitment to not alter any of the characteristics of the material tested for the level in question.

ARTICLE 5: The Ballistic Resistance Materials for Bullet-proofing that pass the tests referred to in the above article will be awarded by the National Firearms Registry, on demand of the interested parties and whenever they request it, the certification that guarantees that they fulfil the requirements of the norm according to the corresponding level of protection.

ARTICLE 6: The manufacturers and importers who participate in a public or private tender for the provision of reinforced materials must add to their presentation the corresponding "RENAR MA.02 Norm Certification" issued by the National Firearms Registry for the models offered in the tender.

ARTICLE 7: Derogate the RENAR Directive N° 35 of the month of October, 1983, and any other administrative order subscribed by RENAR which goes against the present one.

ARTICLE 8: Notify, register in and join the RENAR National Computerised Data Bank, sign up to the Intellectual Property Register and, once completed, file.

4.3 Protection Equipment Background

4.3.1 New access control systems

There is at present no legislation regulating the equipment that provides security against the threat of criminal activity in the port and maritime areas; such legislation has, however, been incorporated into other areas of transport and commerce, such as air traffic.

There is no European or national law standardising construction with reference to security against possible external threats, other than those concerning climatology and the detailed specifications of how to build a bulkhead or hull, taking into account pressure, high waves, wind etc.

There is absolutely no information available on the type of materials to be used in the construction of the vessel, such as glass, doors, hatches or any other access to the vessel in relation to the properties they might require to withstand possible terrorist attacks, explosions, gunshots, such as resistance, thickness, type of material etc.

Nor do the classification societies (Lloyd's, RINA,) set any guidelines. They make reference to windows, doors, gates and accesses, but only in a very general way, leaving it in the hands of the naval engineers and shipyards to use whatever material they consider appropriate. Thus, the shipyards do not follow any norms or guidelines, installing in their vessels the materials supplied by the specialist companies with which they work.

Contact was made with a company that manufactures a type of glass called STADIP, which is a laminated glass, resistant to strong impacts. This glass fulfils the requirements of RD 1338 of 04.07.84 and UNE 108-131, parts 1-2. All of these norms are applied on land, as stated above, but it is not specified that they should be applied at sea and, if they are used, it is done so voluntarily at the request of the manufacturer or shipbuilder.

4.3.2 New materials

Today's technology provides several devices which could (or should) be applied to vessels, such as materials resistant to different attacks, biometric gauges, bullet-proofing, magnetic cards, glass resistant to the impact of Molotov cocktails, gun and rifle bullets, etc.

Biometric gauges offer a high level of security, especially in access control, as these are based on human biological characteristics, different for each person.

In the same way, cards can be used for access control, but they also allow cargoes to be controlled, since they can store a great deal of information. This device is used on cruisers, as it is easy and fast to handle and provides a detailed control of passengers, crew and movement of goods.

Bullet-proof doors provide a high level of protection in the accesses, even in cases of possible failures in the security system, thus fulfilling a double function.

All of these devices are applied and standardised in the areas of land and air travel, but not sea travel. Although they may be used in some vessels or some port zones, this is always through private initiative.

High-resistance materials, such as security windows or bullet-proof glass, can be used at access points such as metro turnstiles, revolving doors or the air-lock doors of bank branches.

The increasing interest on the part of companies, public bodies, individuals, etc. in security matters makes this an innovative and fruitful market.

Protection against anti-social acts in a building or any other type of scenario is achieved through the implantation of various technical, human and organisational measures.

Of particular importance among the technical measures are the passive protection measures, that is, those whose function is to resist attacks.

In order to ensure that only authorised personnel have access, we have the idea in our heads of those air-lock doors seen in films which assess body weight, heartbeat and other biological factors to allow access. However, these highly sophisticated (and rarely implanted) systems are not very functional or aesthetic.

There are devices on the market today which combine the total reliability of a correct access with a highly refined appearance. Such devices, as shown in the photographs below, are rather more than a simple turnstile or an automatic door.

The philosophy behind the new systems is to combine the efficiency of an agile access control system with the reliability of a high level of security.

To this end, the current market tends towards the insertion of elements that detect and analyse the passage of persons, incorporating in the manufacturing of the equipment high-resistance materials, such as security windows or bullet-proof glazing.

Opaque air-lock   Access Door

Thus, we get devices that can be integrated into any existing reading system (proximity cards, magnetic band cards, biometry, etc.) which, without making it less aesthetic, can efficiently control the existence of any anomalies in the movement of persons.

In this way, we avoid not only unauthorised access (or intrusion), but we can also detect any incorrect behaviour by any authorised person.

4.3.3 Glasses and windows.

There is a wide range of glasses and windows available that can suit any needs and many of the products available today can be applied to the maritime-port installations that require them.

Definition of the SGG STADIP PRODUCT

At a certain pressure and temperature the glass-butyral mass turns solid, forming a compact block which can withstand violent impacts without being perforated, the transparency of the glass being maintained.

In case of fracture, the PVB sheet or sheets hold back the shards of glass preventing their release and thus avoiding any damage that might be caused to any persons or goods that might be close to the glazing.

SGG STADIP can incorporate different types of glass of varying thickness and butyral, giving rise to a truly wide range of compositions to satisfy the current demands of the market in security matters. When two or more butyrals, or glasses of a thickness of over 3 mm, are incorporated, these compositions are gathered, for commercial purposes, under the name SGG STADIP PROTECT.

SGG STADIP Range

A volume of SGG STADIP accepts in its composition:

- Monolithic glass SGG Planilux
- Extra clear glass SGG Diamant
- Thermal insulator SGG Planitherm "S"
- Solar control glass SGG Parsol
- SGG Pink-Rosa
- SGG Reflectasol
- SGG COOL-LITE
- SGG COOL-LITE K

Polyvinyl butyral can be transparent, translucent or coloured.

Depending on the applications for which it is required, the SGG STADIP range can provide:

- · Security and Solar Control: SGG STADIP Solar
- · Security and Acoustic Insulation: SGG STADIP Silence
- · Security and anti-reflection property: SGG Vision Lite

For an adequate thermal protection, any composition of the SGG STADIP range can be perfectly integrated in an insulating volume of SGG Climalit.

Installation and Implementation

For external applications of the SGG STADIP range, that is, closures and facades, the following observations must be taken into account:

- Edges: An adequate treatment of the edges will avoid micro-cracks which could, in turn, lead to thermally induced fractures due to temperature gradients in the glass mass.

- Sealing: It is recommended to require that the glass volume is sealed on both sides, in order to prevent the entry of water in the recessing of the woodwork and thus the possible deterioration of the PVB or the reflector sheets when SGG STADIP incorporates a solar control glass or when these are incorporated on demand.

4 Prior preventive measures 161

QUALIFICATION LEVEL (Ministry of Industry and Energy Order B.O.E. 8-4-86)			TYPE OF ATTACK RESISTED (UNE 108/131)	STAPID CODE	N° HOMOLOGATION OF DEPARTMENT OF INDUSTRY AND ENERGY	THEORETICAL THICKNESS MM.	DIMENSIONS CM.	STAPID
PROTECTION AGAINST MANUAL ATTACK	A		. In free fall from 50 cm.	A/6 A/8 A/10	D.B.T. 2031 D.B.T. 2052 D.B.T. 2012	6 8 10	321 x 252 420 x 252 600 x 321	Security
	B		50 Kg. Ballast bag . Stone 2,65 Kg. Molotov cocktail,1l.	B/13	D.B.T.2004	13	600 x 321	Antiaggression
			Steel ball of 2,26 Kg. from 9m. Boiling 2 hours	B/17 B/19 B/20	D.B.T. 2053 D.B.T. 2002 D.B.T. 2012	17 19 20	600 x 321 600 x 252 600 x 252	Anti-theft
BULLETPROOFING	ARMAS DE GUERRA	A-00	Z-70 B 9 mm	A-00/23	D.B.T. 2006	23	321 x 252	Anti-bullet
		A-00	Z-70 B 9 mm sub-machine gun..	A-00/25	D.B.T. 2022	25	321 x 252	
		A-10	Magnum 357Revolver	A-10/30	D.B.T. 2007	30	321 x 252	
		A-20	Magnum 44 Revolver	A-20/44	D.B.T. 2008	44	250 x 200	
		A-30	Cetme rifle, caliber 7,62	A-30/61	D.B.T. 2009	61	200 x 140	
		A-40	Coruña rifle,caliber 7,62	A-40/65	D.B.T. 2022	65	200 x 140	
	ARMAS DE CAZA	B-00	Shotgun 12/70, scattered shot	B-00/61	D.B.T. 2006	61	200 x 140	
		B-10	Shotgun 12/70 ,concentrated shot	B-10/61	D.B.T. 2006	61	200 x 140	
		B-20	Shotgun 12/70, Brenneke cartridge	B-20/61	D.B.T. 2006	61	200 x 140	
		B-30	Shotgun 12/70, solid steel bullet	B-30/65	D.B.T. 2022	61	200 x 140	

Drainage: The incorporation of SGG STADIP is recommended in case of a wooden frame with drainage, in order to avoid condensations inside the recessing and, thus, possible deteriorations in the PVB or the sheets mentioned above.

Guaranties and tests to obtain the INCE seal

The INCE seal is a mark of quality awarded by the Ministry of Public Works to each production centre independently. The manufacturer in possession of this seal is obliged to distinguish the approved product by incorporating on the label the INCE seal anagram. This guarantee means that the glazing is subjected to a manufacturing control and supervision by a competent entity other than the manufacturer itself.

The INCE seal guarantees:

- The establishment of some parameters that allow a level of quality to be ensured
- A pre-established self-control system on the part of the manufacturer
- Inspections or controls in the production centre on the part of the Ministry
- Sample tests in homologated laboratories

Self-control tests on components:

- Absorption of water vapour of the dehydrating product contained in the spacing intercalation profile
- Control of homogeneity of the mixture
- Measurement of the proportion of base/sealing accelerator of the second barrier
- Initial Hardness of second sealant
- Resistance of second sealant to shearing
- Continuity of fist sealant (butyl string)

Self-control tests on intercalation profile:

- Verification of perfect symmetry of profile
- Verification of degreasing

Self-control tests on the vitreous component:

- Optical quality of glass
- Dimensional controls on glass
- Control of sides and edges
- Control of cleaning water hardness and internal cleanness of vitreous elements

Self-control tests on the finished product:

- Angularity and geometry of volume after twenty-four hours
- Initial measurement, after twenty-four hours, of dew which must always be below -55°C
- Penetration of intercalation profile
- Shift between glasses (sliding)
- Planimetry control

It can be deduced then, considering all of the tests to be performed before the product reaches the market that those products that obtain the certiifcation of the INCE seal are of a high quality and reliability, and that they provide us with the security required by each circumstance

4.3.4 M.O.H. Security Glasses

All bullet-proof glasses have an anti-splintering coating. MOH security glasses are made up of different thicknesses of glass and polymer of very high resistance and total transparency, low weight, UV protection and thermal insulation, making them suitable for any level of security required (anti-vandalism, antitheft, bullet-proof, etc.).

MOH Glass range

- MOH anti-vandalism glass

Total thickness: 10 mm
Total weight per square metre: 21 Kg

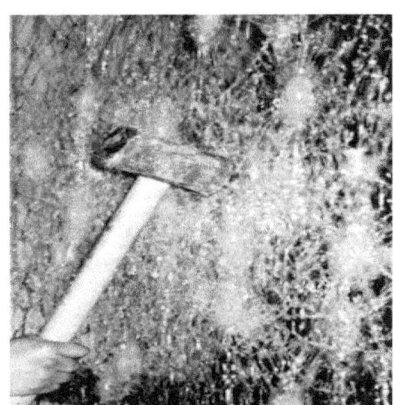

- MOH RB1 Glass

Anti 9 mm and 3.57 Magnum integration (Luger ammunition).
Total thickness: 21 mm
Total weight per square metre: 50 Kg

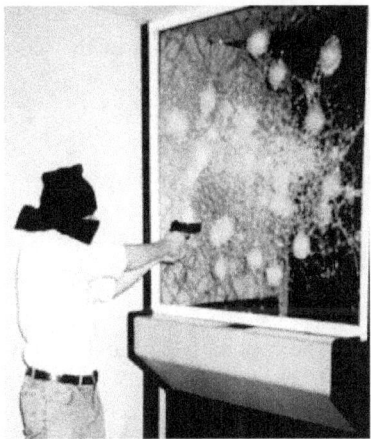

- MOH RB2 Glass

Anti 3,57 Magnum Integration (special high-speed ammunition)
Total thickness: 27 mm
Total weight per square metre: 67 Kg

- MOH RB3 Glass

Anti 44 Magnum Integration
Total thickness: 32 mm
Total weight per square metre: 75 Kg

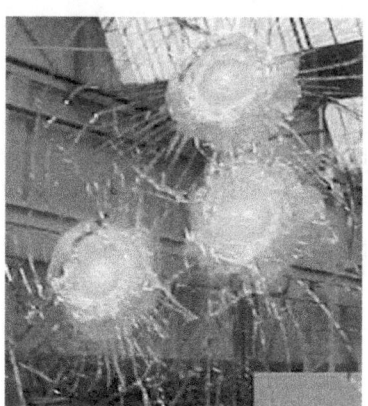

- MOH RB4 glass

Antifal integration
Total thickness: 50 mm
Total weight per square metre

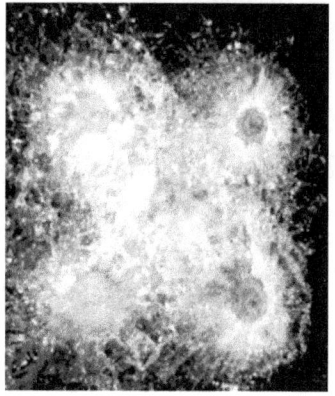

4.3.5 Doors

Doors are normally the first barrier or security protection we find, since they separate the outside (possible threats, adverse situations) from the inside, providing a certain security.

This security can be divided, at this primary level, into three elements:

- The door itself
- The doorframe
- The security lock

Reinforced Doors

Reinforced Doors are the most widely used as the main entrance of offices and businesses, although they are also becoming more commonplace in private homes. The layers that they are composed of (sheets that are used to open and close the doors) can be made of wood, alloys and metal. They are coated with a steel sheet of two millimetres thickness on both sides.

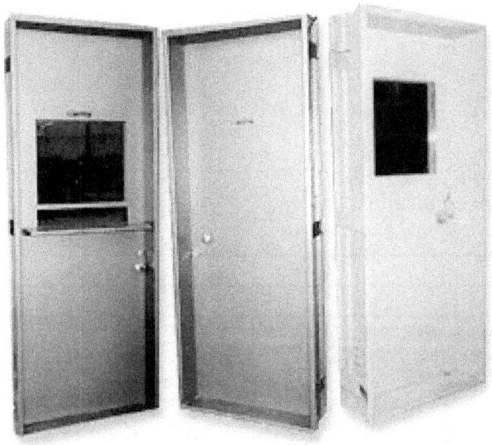

Main characteristics:

- Lock: They normally have a cylinder that prevents extraction by means of picklocks or drills, and withstand a pressure of up to 500 kilograms, although this depends on the model selected and the size of the door. Experts recommend the installation of a lock with a double security shield.
- Keys: are normally custom-made, that is, manufactured specially for a specific door. It is extremely difficult to make copies of these keys. Thus, once the door is installed, the owner of the building is handed five sets of keys to distribute as he wishes. It is recommended to leave one set outside the building, in the hands of a person of trust. Otherwise, if the key is forgotten or lost, the makers of the door would take on average between four and five hours to open it. Moreover, it can only be opened if the lock and part of the steel plate is broken.
- Profiles: Steel plates on the inside of the door. Prevent the use of levers to force them open.
- Peephole or eyehole of 180 degrees.
- Fireproof materials: Manufactured with materials that prevent the passage of fire, smoke, gases and heat. Also constitutes an acoustic insulator.
- Blockage on four sides: Once the key is turned, the door is blocked on all sides. This means that the steel bars move in unison. One bar moves towards the top frame, another to the bottom, the third to the side of the hinges and the fourth towards the side of the lock. There are also reinforced doors on the market that do not have this property of blocking on all sides. The difference is that they have screwed rods with a lead cap at the end. However, the experts recommend the first type.

Drawbacks:

Despite having steel bars, the wood on the inside means that levers can be introduced in the parts composed of wood.

Level of reinforcement

These doors can withstand attacks by conventional arms depending on the arms and ammunition used and taking into account the speed of impact.

LEVEL		ARMS	AMMUNITION	SPEED (m/s)
UNE	CEN			
A-00	B-2	Sub-machine gun 270B	9mm Parabellum Spanish NATO	380/400
A-10	B-3	357 Revolver	Magnum high-speed without reinforcement	410/430
A-20	B-4	44 Revolver	44 Magnum high-speed without reinforcement	410/440
A-30	B-5	Cetme 7,62 - 5,56	5,56 X 51 Spanish NATO	920
	B-6		7,62 X 51 Spanish NATO	780/830
A-40	B-7	Short Carbine	7,62 X 51 Spanish NATO	820/830

Armoured Doors

At present, in view of the increase in use and lowering of the price of reinforced doors, armoured doors are found almost exclusively in vaults containing objects of great value such as antique furniture, works of art, etc. Similarly, they are used as systems of protection in museums and conference centres where special events are held. Armoured doors, less vulnerable than reinforced doors, are made up of tubes of steel and special concretes, as well as various alloys and the so-called stiffeners, elements that are inserted on the surface of the door to preserve the solidness of the steel plates placed on the outer and inner faces. On top of these steel plates are placed the chosen boards of wood. The cheapest of these is sapelly; walnut, oak and pine are the most expensive. Their main quality is their high resistance to any attack.

Main characteristics:

- Closing mechanisms. These are encrusted in the structure of the frame. The lock normally installed in this type of door is considered one of the safest on the market. Its success lies in the fact that its latches are usually oblong, rounded or rectangular. Once the door is closed, the front, top, bottom and lateral parts of the lock are activated.
- Lock. Another alternative is the installation of a combination lock. These are locks which are used to block access and can be mechanical, delayed, electronic, digital, etc. The most common are:
    - Disc combination lock, has the advantage of allowing numerous combinations
    - Electronic lock, allows a connection at any given moment and its immediate disconnection, as well as the possibility of blocking or delay by means of a code.
    - Hinges: equipped with reinforcements that resist the actions of saws and levers.
    - Frames and anchors: these are made of solid iron and, since the inside of the door is completely formed of steel, there are no weak points.

Drawback:

The price, which is high, since the security system they offer is superior to that of reinforced doors.

Security Doors

Security doors are the most widely used in private homes. Their installation is not limited to the outer door; they are also used in internal spaces and areas.

Main characteristics:

- They do not need to be composed of steel plates.
- Price: The cost is far lower than that of a reinforced or armoured door.
- The base material, whether it be wood, metal or PVC, is reinforced with horizontal and vertical profiles resistant to fire and gas.
- Lock: It has safety bars that prevent its extraction by use of lock picks.

Drawback:

It is less secure than the other two. Not all have profiles that prevent the use of levers to force them open.

Security framework

The security framework, like the door to which it is adjoined, can be reinforced or armoured and is fixed to the wall by means of three anchors on each side.

4.4 Security systems and access control

4.4.1 Operational security

To design effective security measures, one must first:

- Enumerate and assess potential threats
- Define what degree of security is required
- Analyse the security measures available
- Undertake monitoring, verification of threats and amplification

It is the company contracting the service that establishes the parameters on which the security system implanted is based; they will also determine which personnel can access each previously delimited zone.

All security systems must first have a deterrent effect with respect to possible attempts to violate the security system.

1. Surveillance

Surveillance is related with:

- Verification and checking of the system
- Authentication of users
- Sophisticated user authentication systems are difficult for intruders to break through.

One problem is the possibility of the system rejecting legitimate users:

- A system of voice recognition might reject a legitimate user with a cold.
- A digital fingerprints system might reject a legitimate user with a cut or a burn.

4.4.2 Verification of threats

This is a technique by which users may not have direct access to a resource:

- Only the operational system routines called monitoring programmes have access.
- The user requests access to the operational system.
- The operational system denies or permits access.
- Access is made by a monitoring programme which then passes on the results to the user's programme.

It allows:

Break-in attempts to be detected as and when they occur.
Warning to be made in response.

4.5 Ship to Port communications on arrival/departure (case of Barcelona)

Without interfering with the possibility of using at all times VHF channel 16 or the obligation to listen to it permanently, for all the situations outlined below, communication with the Barcelona CRCS ('Barcelona Traffic') and with the General Ship Information and Instructions Service will also be made through the following channels:

- VHF channel 10, when the vessel is further than two miles from the mooring buoy 'S' (Sierra) or the mooring buoy 'N' (November), (CRCS).
- VHF channel 14, when the vessel is within a circle of radius of two miles from the mooring buoy 'S' (Sierra) or the mooring buoy 'N' (November), in the access channel and any other port waters (Harbour pilots).

Two situations are considered in reference to these communications:

Vessels mooring in the Port of Barcelona

All ships mooring in the Port of Barcelona must make contact with the Barcelona CRCS ('Barcelona Traffic') and with the General Ship Information and Instructions Service at least one hour before arriving at the mooring buoy S' (Sierra) or at the mooring buoy 'N' (November), indicating whether the captain has exemption from the harbour pilot service and providing these centres with the appropriate information.

In addition to the above, high-speed vessels must make contact with the General Vessel Information and Instructions Service four miles from the mooring buoy 'S' (Sierra) or 'N' (November).

While approaching the mooring buoy 'S' (Sierra) or 'N' (November), the vessel will continue listening to VHF channel 10 (as well as channel 16). When it is two miles from the buoy, contact will again be made with the Barcelona CRCS ('Barcelona Traffic') to communicate port traffic and passage to channel 14 with the General Ship Information and Instructions Service.

Once the vessel is within the two mile circle from the 'S' (Sierra) or 'N' (November) buoy and in contact with the General Ship Information and Instructions Service, it should proceed as follows:

Ships that have to anchor

When there is no mooring available or when, for whatever reason, the vessel must remain anchored, the General Ship Information and Instructions Service will notify the captain of this, indicating the anchoring zone and any other relevant information. Once the anchoring manoeuvre is completed, the ship's captain will communicate this circumstance to the General Ship Information and Instructions Service.

Ships that have to enter port with the Harbour Pilot on board

The vessel will proceed to the established Harbour Pilot boarding point, with the instructed engine regime. Once the harbour pilot is on board, the captain of the vessel, directly or through the harbour pilot, will communicate this to the General Ship Information and Instructions Service. During the manoeuvre, the captain of the ship will be permanently listening to this service through VHF channel 14, for a safer navigation through the port and for mooring instructions or any other information of interest for the ships.

Ships whose captains are exempt from the Harbour Pilot Service

The ship's captain will make contact with the General Ship Information and Instructions Service through VHF channel 14 to gather information on the internal traffic in the Port of Barcelona or, if necessary, to head towards the designated anchoring point. He will also notify this service of his passage by buoy 'S' (Sierra) or 'N' (November), and will remain in contact with the service through VHF channel 14 for a safer navigation through the port and for any mooring instructions or any other information of interest for the vessel. Once the mooring manoeuvre is completed, the vessel's captain will communicate this circumstance to the General Ship Information and Instructions Service.

Ships leaving port

The captain of the ship will notify the General Ship Information and Instructions Service of the estimated time of departure through VHF channel 14, one hour before setting sail. When the vessel is ready to set sail, the captain will again notify of this so that the harbour pilot, moorers, etc. can be sent.

If the ship is allowed to set sail without the harbour pilot (exemption from Harbour Piloting Service) or abandon the anchorage point without entering port, the captain will communicate his plans shortly before beginning the manoeuvre to the General Ship Information and Instructions Service through VHF channel 14, for the purpose of coordination and information.

All vessels undertaking the departure manoeuvre will continue to listen to VHF channel 14 until it is two miles from the mooring 'S' (Sierra) or 'N' (November), at which point it will make contact through VHF channel 10 with the Barcelona CRCS ('Barcelona Traffic'), continuing to listen to the radio from this point for at least the first hour of sailing after passing the said mooring buoy. In any case, when passing by the said buoy, contact will be made with the General Ship Information and Instructions Service for the purpose of coordination and information.

The communication and linking devices that the Barcelona CRCS disposes of are:

- VHF Radio
- DSC (Channel 70)
- Short/medium wave radio
- Electronic mail
- Fixed and mobile telephone
- Internal communication with other traffic and rescue coordination centres and with the centre of Madrid.

- Internal communication with the Port Authority of Barcelona Control Centre and the Barcelona Harbour Master's Office
- Coastal Rescue Services
- Fax
- Navtex
- Radar

4.6 Benefits of new technologies in applications in *security*

Maritime transport is a low-margin business demanding a high degree of efficiency. Ports and terminals are also managed on tightly controlled budgets.

For many companies, the imposition of the ISPS codes implies an increase not only in security but also in costs.

Computers, both hardware and software, offer numerous solutions to problems which are difficult to control using traditional methods.

In the field of cards and their readers, one can already find on the market those that can verify in real time the identity, whereabouts and activities of each of the persons on board, which should mean everyone.

This card reader, designed to meet the demanding requirements of a maritime environment, is used, for example, to record who has boarded a lifeboat during a simulation. If a crew member is in the wrong place, the system indicates the number of the place where he should go, which, in terms of control, replaces the old procedures based on paper records.

Previously, security measures normally consisted of an identification card with a photograph and the verification of the employees' data by the guards.

Of course, unauthorised personnel could use falsified or stolen cards to access high-security zones of a vessel or port. Badly trained or idle security guards often contributed to this lack of security.

It is a well-known fact that more locks and more guards is not the answer; for this reason, the electronic personnel identity card was designed, controlling the movement of its carrier in any area of the vessel or port.

It can follow the trail of anyone moving in the accesses or key points of the vessel from the moment they cross the gangway, without making them lose time with retentions and security checks. Two-phase proximity monitors follow all employees using the gangway and know whether they are carrying the card and whether they are boarding or leaving the vessel. One monitor detects the movement and the other perceives whether the person crossing is carrying the card. A crew member without a card will not get very far because an alarm will go off.

Unlike human guards, who have to stop all employees to check their passes, the IR system does not interrupt work. The crew members can carry their cards in any garment and proceed with their duties.

While the vessel is at sea, the monitoring of personnel is relatively simple. However, when the vessel interacts with other vessels, both in port and at sea, hundreds of persons can cross the gangway connecting them.

The system has a remote control element, by which the company directors can connect to it by Internet form any point and without any risk of interferences. Moreover, this system records the level of training, certification and even the blood type of each crew member. In case of emergency, it can also determine whether the employees are in the lifeboats or whether they are somewhere else on the vessel, in a simulation.

The information is kept in one place only and can be accessed easily, on board or on land, without piles of filed papers or outdated card systems.

New security systems are being created which withstand the meteorological situations encountered at high sea and adapt to the type of vessel and its needs, fulfilling at the same time its main function – to prevent the entrance of any unauthorised person.

Until now, it had been believed that the norms could be fulfilled simply by incorporating new staff to boost security, which also facilitated activities on board without any great burden to the company's economy.

The incorporation of new technologies has shown that investing in a computerised security system is not only more economical, but also simplifies the movement of personnel and cargo on the vessel, optimising time, since nobody needs to verify the identification of the personnel.

The system is automatic and provides a great deal of information in an instant. This information is stored in a data base easily accessed both from the vessel and from land. It allows the ship owner to carry out a real-time control of the vessel. With the system of cards and their associated readers, the exact position of each crew member is known at all times, which is of great help in emergency situations

4.7 Sniper operations in vessel boardings

A.   *General.* The use of snipers in support of vessel boardings is a resource available to the Assault Force Command Unit. The objective of the sniper team used is to establish a degree of safety for the mobility of the assault teams around the vessel during the boarding and after the assault has been carried out.

B.   *Use.* The use of snipers will depend on:

- Number of snipers available
- The terrain
- Obstacles
- Number of targets
- Distance

The sniper team will consist of a team of two, shooter/observer. They must provide security in the 360° surrounding the target, if possible. They should be used in advance of the main assault force. By positioning the sniper teams in their places in advance, information on the target zone can be passed on to the assault force. This information will be transmitted to the Assault Force Command Unit to help plan the operation.

When snipers are used in conditions of reduced visibility, all friendly forces should be marked in order to identify them clearly. The marking procedures will depend on the night vision devices used by the snipers (IR sources active or not).

IR sources active:

(I.R laser designators). All allied forces should wear I.R. tape.
- a. Non active IR sources:
  Night-vision scope. IR chemical lights should be used.
- d. Helo support – One possible method for a sniper team when the use of teams of snipers in the front lines is not feasible.
  (1). Use – Two helos are normally used, one at port and the other at starboard of the vessel which is the target. Two snipers will be used for each helo.
  (2). The vessel is responsible for providing 360° of security on the target while the main assault force is boarding the vessel in question.
  (3). Equipment
  - Night vision equipment
  - I.R. laser designators

5. International Policy of Cooperation in the Fight against Crimes at Sea

Below is presented the recently signed agreement of collaboration between the USA and the Marshall Islands in view of the relevance of its contents and the operating procedures proposed, representing agreed limitations.

Only those paragraphs which are directly related with the present chapter are quoted.

Agreement between the Government of the United States of America and the Government of the Republic of the Marshall Islands Concerning Cooperation to Suppress the Proliferation of Weapons of Mass Destruction, Their Delivery Systems, and Related Materials by Sea, signed on August 13th, 2004, with provisional application from 13.08.2004.

Deeply concerned about the proliferation of weapons of mass destruction (WMD), their delivery systems, and related materials, particularly by sea, as well as the risk that these may fall into the hands of terrorists;

"States or non-state actors of proliferation concern" means those countries or entities that should be subject to interdiction activities because they are or are believed to be engaged in: (1) efforts to develop or acquire WMD or their delivery systems; or (2) trafficking (either selling, receiving, or facilitating) of WMD, their delivery systems, or related materials.

"Security Force" means:

a). for the United States, the United States Coast Guard and the United States Navy; and
b). for the Marshall Islands, the National Police Force of the Marshall Islands.

"Security Force Officials" means:

a). for the United States, uniformed or otherwise clearly identifiable members of the U.S. Security Force, who may be accompanied by uniformed or otherwise clearly identifiable members of the Departments of Homeland Security and Justice, and others duly authorised by the United States and notified to the Competent Authority of the Marshall Islands; and
b). for the Marshall Islands, uniformed or otherwise clearly identifiable members of the law enforcement authorities of the Marshall Islands Security Force.

"Security Force vessels" means warships and other vessels of the Parties, or of third States as may be agreed upon by the Parties, on which Security Force Officials of either or both Parties may be embarked, clearly marked and identifiable as being on government service and authorised to that effect, including any vessel and aircraft embarked on or supporting such vessels.

"Warship" means ships belonging to the armed forces of a State bearing the external marks distinguishing such ships of its nationality, under the command of an officer duly commissioned by the government of the State and whose name appears in the appropriate service list or its equivalent, and manned by a crew that is under regular armed forces discipline.

"Suspect vessel" means a vessel used for commercial or private purposes in respect of which there are reasonable grounds to suspect it is engaged in proliferation by sea.

"International waters" means all parts of the sea not included in the territorial sea, internal waters and archipelagic waters of a State, consistent with international law.

Article 3
Suspect vessels

Operations to suppress proliferation by sea pursuant to this Agreement shall be carried out only against suspect vessels, including suspect vessels without nationality, and suspect vessels assimilated to vessels without nationality, but not against a vessel registered under the law of one of the Parties while bareboat charter registered in another State not party to this Agreement.

Article 4
Operations in International Waters

Authority to Board Suspect Vessels. Whenever the Security Force Officials of one Party ("the requesting Party") encounter a suspect vessel claiming nationality in the other Party ("the requested Party") located seaward of any State's territorial sea, the requesting Party may request through the Competent Authority of the requested Party that it:

    a). confirm the claim of nationality of the suspect vessel; and
    b). if such claim is confirmed:

        i. authorise the boarding and search of the suspect vessel, cargo and the persons found on board by Security Force Officials of the requesting Party; and
        ii. if evidence of proliferation is found, authorise the Security Force Officials of the requesting Party to detain the vessel, as well as items and persons on board, pending instructions conveyed through the Competent Authority of the requested Party as to the actions the requesting Party is permitted to take concerning such items, persons and vessels.

5.1 Contents of Requests

Each request should contain the name of the suspect vessel, the basis for the suspicion, the geographic position of the vessel, the IMO number if available, the homeport, the port of origin and destination, and any other identifying information. If a request is conveyed orally, the requesting Party shall confirm the request in writing by facsimile or e-mail as soon as possible. The requested Party shall acknowledge to the Competent Authority of the requesting Party in writing by e-mail or facsimile its receipt of any written or oral request immediately upon receiving it.

5.2 Responding to Requests

If the nationality is verified, the requested Party may:
- decide to conduct the boarding and search with its own Security Force Officials;
- authorise the boarding and search by the Security Force Officials of the requesting Party;
- decide to conduct the boarding and search together with the requesting Party; or
- deny permission to board and search.

- The requested Party shall answer through its Competent Authority requests made for the verification of nationality within four hours of its acknowledgment of the receipt of such requests. The requesting Party shall acknowledge to the Competent Authority of the requested Party in writing by e-mail or facsimile its receipt of any written or oral response from the Requesting Party immediately upon receiving it.

- If the nationality is not verified within the four hours, the requested Party may, through its Competent Authority:
  - nevertheless authorise the boarding and search by the Security Force Officials of the requesting Party; or
  - refute the claim of the suspect vessel to its nationality.

- If there is no response from the Competent Authority of the requested Party within four hours of its acknowledgment of receipt of the request, the requesting Party will be deemed to have been authorised to board the suspect vessel for the purpose of inspecting the vessel's documents, questioning the persons on board, and searching the vessel to determine if it is engaged in proliferation by sea.

Right of Visit. Notwithstanding the foregoing paragraphs of this Article, the Security Force Officials of one Party ("the first Party") are authorised to board suspect vessels claiming nationality in the other Party that are not flying the flag of the other Party, not displaying any marks of its registration or nationality, and claiming to have no documentation on board the vessel, for the purpose of locating and examining the vessel's documentation. If documentation or other physical evidence of nationality is located, the foregoing paragraphs of this Article apply. If no documentation or other physical evidence of nationality is available, the other Party will not object to the first Party assimilating the vessel to a ship without nationality consistent with international law.

Use of force. The authorisation to board, search and detain includes the authority to use force in accordance with Article 9 of this Agreement.

5.3 Shipboarding Otherwise in Accordance with International Law.

This Agreement does not limit the right of either Party to conduct boardings of vessels or other activities consistent with international law whether based, *inter alia*, on the right of visit, the rendering of assistance to persons, vessels, and property in distress or peril, or an authorisation from the Flag or Coastal State, of any other party, or other appropriate bases in international law.

Article 5
Exercise of Jurisdiction over Detained Vessels, as well as Items and Persons on Board

1. Jurisdiction of the Parties. In all cases covered by Article 4 concerning the vessels of a Party located seaward of any State's territorial sea, that Party shall have the primary right to exercise jurisdiction over a detained vessel, cargo or other items and persons on board (including seizure, forfeiture, arrest, and prosecution), provided, however, that the Party with the right to exercise primary jurisdiction may, subject to its Constitution and laws, waive its primary right to exercise jurisdiction and authorise the enforcement of the other Party's law against the vessel, cargo or other items and persons on board.

2. **Jurisdiction in the contiguous zone of a Party**. In all cases not covered by Article 4 involving the vessel of a Party that arise in the contiguous zone of a Party and in which both parties have authority to board and to exercise jurisdiction to prosecute—

   a). except as provided in paragraph (b), the Party which conducts the boarding shall have the primary right to exercise jurisdiction.

   b). in cases involving suspect vessels fleeing from the territorial sea of a Party in which that Party has the authority to board and to exercise jurisdiction, that Party shall have the primary right to exercise jurisdiction.

3. Disposition Instructions. Consultations as to the exercise of jurisdiction pursuant to paragraphs 1 and 2 of this Article shall be undertaken without delay between the Competent Authorities.

4. Form of waiver. Where permitted by the Constitution and laws of a Party, waiver of jurisdiction may be granted verbally, but as soon as possible it shall be recorded in a written note from the Competent Authority and be processed through the appropriate diplomatic channel, without prejudice to the immediate exercise of jurisdiction over the suspect vessel by the other Party.

Article 6
Exchange of Information and Notification of Results of Actions of the Security Forces

1. Exchange of Operational Information. The Security Forces of both Parties shall endeavour to exchange operational information on the detection and location of suspect vessels and shall maintain communication with each other as necessary to carry out the purpose of this Agreement.

2. Notification of Results. A Party conducting a boarding and search pursuant to this Agreement shall promptly notify the other Party of the results thereof through their Competent Authorities.

3. Status Reports. The relevant Party, in compliance with its laws, shall timely report to the other Party, through their Competent Authorities, on the status of all investigations, prosecutions and judicial proceedings and other actions and processes, arising out of the application of this Agreement.

Article 7
Conduct of Security Force Officials

1. Compliance with Law and Practices. Each Party shall ensure that its Security Force Officials, when conducting boardings and searches pursuant to this Agreement, act in accordance with its applicable national laws and policies and consistent with international law and accepted international practices.

2. Boarding and Search Teams.

a) Boardings and searches pursuant to this Agreement shall be carried out by Security Force Officials from Security Force vessels and vessels and aircraft embarked on or otherwise supporting such Security Force vessels, as well as by vessels and aircraft of third States as agreed between the Parties.

b) The boarding and search teams may operate from Security Force vessels of the Parties and from such vessels of other States, according to arrangements between the Party conducting the operation and the State providing the vessel and notified to the other Party.

c) The boarding and search teams may carry arms.

Article 8
Safeguards

1. Where a Party takes measures against a vessel in accordance with this Agreement, it shall:

- take due account of the need not to endanger the safety of life at sea, including, but not limited to:
  - taking precautions not to hazard unduly the vessel or the vessel's crew while boarding; and
  - taking account of vessel location, *e.g.,* in a traffic separation scheme, to avoid inadvertently endangering other vessels in the vicinity in the course of boarding;
- take due account of the security of the vessel and its cargo;
- not prejudice the commercial or legal interests of the Flag State;
- ensure within available means, that any measure taken with regard to the vessel is environmentally sound under the circumstances;
- ensure that persons on board are afforded the protections, rights and guarantees provided by international law and the boarding State's law and regulations
- ensure that the master of the vessel is, or has been, afforded the opportunity to contact the vessels' owner, manager or Flag State at the earliest opportunity and provided the necessary information to file a claim pursuant to Article 13, paragraph 2.

2. Reasonable efforts shall be taken to avoid a vessel being unduly detained or delayed.

Article 9
Use of Force

- All uses of force pursuant to this Agreement shall be in strict accordance with the applicable laws and policies of the Party conducting the boarding and applicable international law.
- Each party shall avoid the use of force except when and to the degree necessary to ensure the safety of Security Force vessels and officials and where Security Force Officials are obstructed in the execution of their duties.
- Only that force reasonably necessary under the circumstances may be used.
- Boarding and search teams and Security Force vessels have the inherent right to use all available means to apply that force reasonably necessary to defend themselves or others from physical harm.

5.4 Intervention of Spanish Security Forces. Possible Procedures

The intervention procedures for vessel boarding by specialist units of the FCSE are extremely difficult to explain and it may not be wise to do so considering that, as regards the diffusion of this information among the civil ranks of merchant ship crews, the intention is never to cause any harm, but quite the opposite.

It should be taken into account that each unit acts according to certain guidelines in which the security of the group is paramount over any other consideration and that, given the variability of the circumstances, conditions and parameters and the enormous influence of the human factor in each of these units, no action can be resolved by copying previous actions, although certain procedures are common and are widely accepted.

A handbook issued by the SEAL assault force has been used, showing some procedures which may or may not be used alongside others that can be used aboard a merchant ship, in order that the crews can get as clear a picture as possible of the way of thinking and operating of these persons who are experts in the fight against delinquency, but who still also do anything possible to save the lives of those on board the vessel.

The text and the figures have been somewhat modified to make them more easily comprehensible to the ordinary civilian.

5.4.1 Procedures

1. Introduction
   - Below will be presented various tactics of armed assault, including standard procedures such as insertion, infiltration, target actions, integration of forces and their consolidation. The different situations will dictate the application of the general procedures outlined below, while there are also a great number of tactics used to capture specific targets.

2. Pre-boarding
   - The insertion of snipers/observers must be carried out at the earliest opportunity in order to provide early information on the target activity, hostile forces and data on the surrounding environment. From positions close to the target, the information is communicated by satellite to the command zones and to the assault forces that remain in the approach unit. The data must be transferred in real time, so as to give 'eyes' to the mission planners and verify the situation.

3. Insertion/infiltration
   - Insertion inside the area of operations can be performed from the air, the sea or from underwater platforms. The insertion/infiltration of the selected zone is normally managed by the coordinator. This allows the marine assault forces to maintain communications with the first man to dive overboard and facilitates the reconnaissance insertion for the swimmer/climber. The low freeboard and the small signal of the inflatable dinghy make these ideal for infiltrating swimmers in the selected areas.

- The launching of the reconnaissance swimmer/climber must be coordinated with the observers/snipers. Before insertion, a review of the swells and currents must be made. In areas known for their big swells (for example, The Gulf of Mexico and the North Sea) this procedure is of great importance. The platoons of reconnaissance swimmers/climbers must communicate with a coordinator in order to define the spot where the main swimmer is to be released. An extensive communication will be established when a large amount of equipment is transported or when it is necessary to swim long distances. The currents, lighting and environmental factors will determine the distance at which the reconnaissance swimmers and the coordinator will enter the water. In conditions of low lighting, a distance of between 500 and 1000 metres is sufficient.

- Once in the selected zone, the reconnaissance swimmers/climbers set up the platform with whatever means they have available, check out the surroundings of the boarding zone and position the ladders and climbing aids ready for the arrival of the coordinator. The climbers are responsible for safety while the coordinator is climbing and selecting a safe place for the swimmers to get ready for the boarding.

- The main swimmer must be accompanied by an appointed pair of swimmer/shooters. Once the swimmers board, the commandos circle the target downwind, positioning themselves at no more than 1500 m from the target. At the same time as the boarding, the commandos close the objective and are under the orders of the commander in charge.

- Once the target is reached, the boarding team takes off their flippers, securing them to the ladder or structure, and start to climb. The bottom of the ladder should be secured to the structure in order to prevent the flippers and equipment from pushing out the ladder.

- After climbing, the boarding team consolidates their position in the area designated by the climber leaders. Once all the members are safely in the area, the operations for an immediate attack will be conducted. The weapons, lights and communication equipment must be made ready while the climber leaders maintain security.

4. Target actions

- At the first opportunity, communication must be made with the assault forces. When the swimming platoon begins to infiltrate the hostile platform/vessel/place, the forces must be notified and mobilised to the reaction position.
- While a careful approach is being made to the hostile place, the boarding team must be prepared to proceed immediately to the boarding.
- At the same time as the swimming platoon are approaching, the aerial assault forces will be in a 4-5 nautical mile leeward radius from the platform, ready for boarding. This distance keeps the forces far enough from the target so as not to be detected by the noise of the rotor and close enough to get to the scene in 90-120 seconds after the call.
- The swimming platoon continues its approach to the hostile place. If it is detected, the boarding teams will neutralise the opposing forces and proceed immediately towards the hostile place. The careful approach should be continued if the commander in charge thinks that the above conflict has not been detected. The aerial boarding team is called using a predetermined signal. Entry into the room must be carried out once the rotor of the approaching plane's engine is heard.

- The aerial boarding teams either throw down a rope or perform an insertion on land at the designated points. The shooters build passages and towers. The commanders and control elements position themselves in a place where they can control the operation and inform their superiors.
- The specific mission of the boarding teams will be conducted in a specific order. In general terms, the priorities will be as follows:
    1) Rescue and secure the hostages
    2) Neutralise the terrorist threat
    3) Communicate the *Hostages Unknown Terrorist Seals* (HUTS) reports to the appropriate authorities
    4) Safeguard/secure the gear and platform equipment
- Once the operations are completed, the HUTS reports must be communicated to the commander in charge.
- The hostages must be secured and consolidated in a separate zone from that in which the terrorists have been neutralised. The transfer of the hostages from the zone is the responsibility of the tactical commander. The explosive devices and traps and the hostages affected by the traps will be immediately taken and handed over to the EOD staff. The hostages will be evacuated from any place where danger exists.

    - The possibility of snipers, unexpected terrorists and dangers of fire/chemicals/explosives must be considered and detected in advance. Once the hostages are secured, if any terrorists escape, there will continue to be a significant threat to the hostages and friendly troops. If the operations are continued, the following conditions must be adopted:
        - Additional measures must be taken to safeguard the hostages at the consolidation points and in their surroundings.
        - The teams must be sent to capture the terrorists who are still in the zone.
        - Measures must be taken to safeguard the helicopters, friendly troops and the landing spots selected for the mission.
        - Measures must be taken to secure the route along which the hostages will be conducted from the consolidation point to the extraction point.
    - Wounded personnel and hostages are given priority over wounded terrorists for their evacuation and must be stabilised on the spot. After transferring the hostages, the boarding team will be extracted as ordered by the commander in charge.

5. Communications.

a) A communications plan and a contingency signals plan are obligatory. The lights, covered or not, pyrotechnics, and network transmissions are all essential in ensuring the effectiveness of the communications.

b) The communications equipment must be waterproof, secure and must float in order to be used in sea operations. As far as possible, the waterproof material should not interfere in the operations or in the functioning of the equipment. The communications commander and control personnel must be positioned so as to be able to establish satellite communications without delay.

5.4.2 Hostile operations on board

1. Introduction
a) This document provides some basic guidelines in the organisation of tactics and equipment recommended in operations with helicopters against a potentially hostile target

2. Background
b) At present, the foremost SEAL platoons are led by fleet commanders in boarding operations against potential hostile targets or oil platforms. Given the great variety of reasons for conducting this operation in the marine environment, the continuous use of the SEALs in boarding operations is ever more probable.

3. Scope
c) The following standard procedures provide recommended guidelines in the pre-combat training of SEAL platoons outlining tactics, staff and equipment in boarding operations.

5.4.3 Team-planning required

1. Discussion
a) During the course of the latest operations of SEAL platoons based on boarding operations, a large number of movements have been made both on land and by air. In order to perform a good transfer to the operations zone, a prior planning and preparation of the teams must be made.
b) The following factors must be reviewed by the SEAL platoon commander before making any movement from the initial base zone in order to obtain an appropriate logistics plan.
   - Detailed orders for all personnel
   - Per diem advanced requests
   - Full inventory of all personnel and operations team
   - Total weight of all personnel and operations team
   - Cargo manifest of all personnel and operations team
   - Updated sailing list of platoon with security specifications
   - Inspection of commander and all of the platoon of all the operations team
   - Full revision of all hazardous cargo
   - All of the information on the requested traffic in the transport of personnel and equipment. The total weight and volume of the cargo must be included, as well as the type of hazardous cargo, number of passengers, volume of space for pallets, travel itinerary, food for all personnel during flight, mission priority.
   - Identify liaison officers/coordinators for each task during transit.
   - Identify a safe storage of arms, hazardous cargo and equipment at different points of the transit.
   - Positioning of personnel at key points.
   - Identification of cargo elevators at the various selected points
   - Identification of transport of personnel at each chosen point
   - Identification of alimentation facilities at the various chosen points
   - Request for documents required in each hostile country
   - Passports and visas required in each hostile country
   - Identification of requirements and security for radio communication
   - CONFIRM, RECONFIRM and RECONFIRM all the above before departure.

c) The correct placement of the pallets for all of the equipment is essential. All associated equipment must be separated into the following categories:
- Personal bag (with bullets and magazines), security rope bags, spy bags, explosives
- Personal bag
- Arms boxes
- User Manual (ammunition and explosives)
- Operational Bags with departments

d) After categorising the equipment, all personal and operational bags will be placed in a cardboard box (4 foot by 4 foot) and will be covered with plastic protection bags. The cardboard box will be placed on a wooden or metallic elevatable pallet of 4 foot by 4 foot. The cardboard box will be secured to the pallet and marked with a SEAL identification tag.

e) The rest of the operational items will be placed on wooden or metallic elevatable pallet of 4 foot by 4 foot and secured forthwith for transport.

f) The placing of the cardboard box denominated *Triwall* on pallets allows it to be easily transported by the United States Air Force planes. All cargo transport helicopters are prepared to transport metal or wooden pallets. Moreover, *Triwalls* are used by all the *VERTREPS* and *COMREPS* when they transport equipment from vessel to vessel. Also, the *Triwall* can be easily handled by the elevators.

5.4.4 Special equipment

1. Communications earphones for snipers

a) The cranial earphones for snipers must be made in such a way that they allow the air-lifted sniper to have simultaneous communications links with the members of the boarding team (MX-300R UHF) and with the pilot through the plane's internal communications system (ICS).

b) The most common support planes used in boarding operations are the SH-3, CH-46, and SH 60. The air-lifted sniper must be careful in the case of this last plane as it has incompatibles ICS systems. This plane requires some adaptors different from those of the ISC earphones.

2. Radiotelephone earphones for communications

a) Cranial radiotelephone earphones must be made in such a way as to allow the radiotelephone to have simultaneous communications links with the members of the boarding team (MX-300R UHF) and the AFC, OSC, and all of the support plane (HST UHF-SAT).

3. Communication earphones of the boarding team commander

a) It is essential for the boarding team commander to have a clear and direct link with all of the members of his boarding team. During the boarding, there is a great deal of background noise (for example, the noise of the plane or ship). With a standard hand-held communicator or a throat microphone, the background noise makes communications almost impossible.

b) The use of cranial communications earphones helps to filter the background noise without interfering with the capacity of the AFC to monitor all the communications (MX300-R UHF).

4. **Construction of cranial communications earphones**

a) The construction is based on isolating the various systems from one another (for example, Motorola in one ear and ICS in the other). The mouthpiece is just one part of the set of earphones and is used to speak in isolated systems. This is achieved by connecting two micros in one, using cable links (make sure that the search areas are clean in the two micros.) The military Motorola and the ICS system can be the two systems which are interchanged or built separately to fulfil the requirements of the mission. The ICS devices were all acquired by several helicopter squadrons The (CX-4831) adaptor is only used with CH-46 ICS.

5. **Optical Visor 3000**

a) The telescopic visor 3000 is an instrument mainly used by air-lifted snipers for making precision shots (quick death) during daylight hours. The telescopic visor 3000 is an electronic device requiring two photo-cell batteries (size A-76). The sight generates a red point inside the optical tube for aiming. This red point is manually adjusted using two wheels to centre it. The red point must be adjusted to aim and impact at 200 metres. To obtain a better result, the target in question must be sufficiently illuminated without the help of mechanical devices. When the telescopic visor 3000 is mounted, the clasp that holds the visor to the weapon frame must be adjusted. The sight point must be screwed up to 65 inches of weight. Once the sight point is centred, it must remain thus, the weapons being kept in arms cases to prevent them from being loosened.

6. **Instantaneous Dupont dissection torch**
a) The Dupont torch is used by the boarding team for making an opening without explosions in the compartments and spaces on board vessels or oil platforms. The main concern with respect to explosives is the pressurisation of the space or the compartment to be opened. This can prove fatal for anybody who finds himself in these spaces. The type of situation will dictate the method to be used by the boarding team. However, if the ROE prevents the use of explosives, the Dupont torch provides an excellent alternative to the AFC.

7. **TD-100 Laser Target Signaller**

a) The TD-100 is an infrared/red point laser signaller. The use of this optical visor is similar to that of the Aimpoint 3000. The TD-100 is designed to signal hostile targets to the air-lifted sniper during hours of darkness.
b) With the aid of NVG glasses (PVS-5B or ANVIS-4), the TD-100 in infrared mode is better for quick death during hours of darkness and the use of the NVG reduces the confusion of targets. With a view to distinguishing the good man from the bad man, infrared lights must be used to distinguish the members of the boarding team.
c) The TD-100 can be installed in the M-16 rifle. Select the red point mode, put the rifle on your shoulder and search for a good sight by looking through the rear part and centring it at the front part with the target at a distance of 5 metres. As with any precision optics, once mounted, the weapon should be kept in a protected place.

5.5 Preparation of plane and pilot's report

1. Preparation for insertion on plane

a) Insertion by plane used in boarding operations is normally carried out by fleet sections. This fleet consists of the planes SH-3, CH-46, SH-60, and CH-53. The CH-46 is the preferred insertion platform thanks to its capacity for transporting a full cargo of 16 SEAL men of the *Helo assault Force* and two men of the EOD.

b) Disadvantages: without its electronic package, the SH-3 is limited to 8 passengers. The SH-60 is normally limited to 3 passengers due to its electronic package for antisubmarine combat. The CH-53 should not be used, since its rotor may prejudice the personnel at the point of insertion. However, the SH-60 and the SH-3 are suitable as the sniper platform. In many cases, the commander of the boarding team will not have the option of selecting the plane he considers most appropriate.

c) When the CH-46 is used for an insertion, several things have to be performed prior to the mission:

1. Remove the side doors.
2. Install ropes to secure in the SAR arm. The rope must be installed in such a way that it can be quickly released.
3. The mounted *spy* must be placed in such a way that it fits in the hole.
4. The ladder will be positioned so that it will be extended from the front right door.
5. The ICS must be available for the AFC.
6. All communications must be checked in advance by the boarding teams.
7. The mission, the mounted *spy*, the security ropes, the reports made on the crews and commanders before boarding must be checked.

d) Most civil vessels do not have the capacity for helicopters to land on their decks. The extraction of the boarding team from the selected ship's deck requires the use of a structure. Moreover, the main function of this structure is the emergency extraction of the boarding teams if, for any reason, they should have to abandon the vessel a jump into the water.

e) The ladder has the same purpose, allowing the boarding teams to return to the helicopter without the need to land.

2. Preparation of sniper planes

- The sniper plane must have both doors open so that the sniper can shoot freely from both sides. The elimination of doors and windows will be essential on most planes
- Communication between pilot and sniper must be installed and regularly checked.
- *Fastrope* must be installed in the SAR jacket in case the sniper has to insert onto the deck of the vessel in question.
- If the secondary mission of the sniper plane is that of SAR, it should be equipped with a full kit for the rescue of persons.
- A ladder must be installed.
- The mission pilot and crew should be provided with SPIE and *Fastrope* kits before the plane takes off.

5.6 Use of snipers

1. Concept of operations

- The use of snipers during a boarding operation is a highly valuable resource which should be available to the boarding force command. Normally, the SEAL section should consist of two qualified military snipers. The snipers whose task it is to support the boarding operations should be experienced SEAL operators confident enough to be able to work independently without instructions, to take fast and competent decisions concerning the use of "mortal force" as applied in current "rules of engagement".
- During a boarding operation, two snipers will be used. Each sniper will be assigned his own plane. The prime responsibility of the sniper is to provide high-precision support for the duration of the specified mission.

2. Use of snipers

- The sniper plane will join the boarding force insertion plane 5 miles to the stern of the contact of interest. The sniper plane will take position in front of the boarding team insertion plane. All planes will reach the contact of interest at a height of 50 foot AGL.
- Once the stern of the contact of interest is reached, the sniper plane will manoeuvre to port and starboard of the point of insertion of the *fastrope* of the boarding forces. The insertion plane must follow immediately behind the sniper plane and take position to insert the boarding team. The sniper plane will maintain an angle of attack of 45 to 60 degrees while providing security. As well as giving cover, the snipers are required to pass on information regularly to the members of the boarding team on hostile spots, number of enemies, booby-trap bombs, weapons, most direct and accessible routes to the bridge and all movements of unknown personnel and their description.
- Once the boarding team has been inserted and has begun its movement around the bridge, the sniper will sweep in front of the boarding team as they head for the bridge, securing them against any threat.
- Once the boarding team has taken and secured the bridge, the sniper will maintain his position providing security against any further insertion. The sniper will not abandon his position until ordered to do so by the boarding team command.

5.7 Treatment of prisoners

1. Concept

The treatment of prisoners is a prime concern in the concept of the mission. Crews on board a merchant ship normally consist of twenty or more persons. The crews of merchant ships will mostly be non-hostile. This requires a thorough preparation on the part of the boarding teams in prisoner treatment and crowd control tactics and procedures.

2. Treatment of prisoners

- In the treatment of prisoners, the amount of force used to dominate an individual is in direct proportion to the amount of force the prisoner uses to resist. In other words, only the force

required to secure an individual should be used. It is not authorised to use lethal force on an individual who does not represent a threat of physical damage to oneself or to others.
-
- The six basic rules of the treatment of prisoners are:
    - Speed
    - Immobilisation
    - Search
    - Silence
    - Separation
    - Precaution

The two-man rule must always be used: one man to establish security while the other deals with the prisoner.

To better understand the six rules and their application, these are further detailed below:

- **Speed**. The faster a prisoner can be immobilised, the less time he will have to react to the situation.
- **Immobilisation**. The immobilisation of prisoners can be undertaken by any member of the boarding team at any stage of the mission. Each member of the boarding team must have in his possession before beginning the mission enough equipment to hold up to six prisoners either with handcuffs or with collar-chains.
    - During the initial attack, if a prisoner is found while the boarding team is mobilising towards the bridge, the first two men will move to the appropriate side (so that the rest do not have to stop) and will hold the prisoner, while the rest continue towards the bridge. The two men who remain behind holding the prisoner will handcuff him to the vessel and quickly rejoin the group.
    - If a prisoner is found in a confined space during the initial attack and the first two men cannot walk to the side to secure the prisoner, he will be knocked to the floor and the group will proceed forward. The last two members of the group will stop and will hold them, handcuff them to the vessel and will rejoin the group.
    - If there are a large number of prisoners who will hinder the boarding team, leaving them short of units for the final attack on the bridge, the group will ignore them and proceed towards the target.
    - Once the bridge has been taken, all of the prisoners will be secured using handcuffs before any movement or questioning. After securing the bridge, it will no longer be necessary to hold the prisoners at one point of the vessel.
    - During the mobilisation of prisoners, corporal control must be maintained.
    - Always handcuff behind the back.
    - If it can be avoided, do not place blindfolds on the prisoners, as this will make mobility difficult and will make some prisoners lose control in situations in which they would not do so normally.
    - Check the ship's deck; at times it may be so hot that it will burn the prisoner's skin on contact and will make him lose control.

Search

- Place the prisoner face down with arms and legs stretched out. Always approach from behind, placing your feet between his legs. At this point, if he moves, he can be disabled with a kick in the groin. With one foot between his legs, place your knee on his back and one hand on his head, forcing him against the deck. With your free hand, begin a thorough body search.
- When performing the search, begin either from the head or the feet towards the other end of the body. After completing the first half of the search, check under him for possible hidden booby-trap bombs. To do this, turn the prisoner round. Always do this in such a way that, if there is a bomb, his body can be used as a shield against the explosion.
- Once the prisoner is face down, complete the search. The main rule is to have a logical order in the search, otherwise parts of the body may be forgotten.

Silence

- Never allow the prisoners to speak, especially among each other. If they are allowed to talk, they can organise and counter-attack. It is of interest to have the prisoners as disorientated as possible.

Separation

- During a boarding mission, it is difficult to separate the prisoners, since there are a large number of persons in a limited space. The prisoners will normally be consolidated in one or more points.

Precaution

- It is the responsibility of the boarding team to provide security for the prisoners. Before mobilising any prisoner, security must be established all along the route to the second stopping point. If the shortage of personnel does not allow for an adequate security along the route, the prisoner will be moved in a "frog leap" movement. Security will be established as tactically as possible along the route towards the second stopping point. Then the prisoners will be repositioned and security will be established again up to the second stopping point. After this, the prisoners will be mobilised to the second stopping point. This process will be repeated as many times as necessary to complete the movement to the area of processing and searching of the prisoners.

5.8 Follow-on security forces

1. Use of follow-on forces

- The follow-on security forces must be taken on board once the SEAL boarding team has established an initial control of the spaces and before conducting internal clearance operations of the contact of interest.
- Additional follow-on forces should be dispatched to secure communications installations, for engineering, handling at stern, and the establishment of the detainee holding and processing area.

- Surface vessels must be at hand at an optimum speed and ready to serve to provide SAR support, and to act as an emergency evacuation platform and give support as ordered.
- The EOD personnel must be with the initial boarding teams and extracted with the same, if necessary.
- The decision to send the boarding team on board the COI will be taken by the OSC in accordance with the recommendations of AFC and other relevant factors.
- The clearance of the COI by the SEAL boarding team will then begin and will require a significantly longer time. During this clearance, medical care may be required on board. The wounded will be evacuated as required. Regrouping areas will be established and all passengers and crew counted, registered and organised in safe areas in case they need clearing.
- When required, the COI, the crew and the passengers will be transferred to the appropriate authorities; the boarding team will move the COI, unless security is required.

2. Establishment of detainee holding and processing area

- Before determining the detainee holding and processing area, communications must be established between the AFC and the follow-on force command. It is the responsibility of the boarding team command to establish the detainee holding and processing area to consolidate all of the detainees encountered during the undertaking of the evacuations from the internal spaces and compartments of the COI.
- The boarding team and the follow-on team must have a "detainee movement point" at some point along the route towards the "detainee holding and processing". (Normally the "detainee holding and processing area" is located outdoors, usually on the open deck or VERTREP station). Before any mobilisation of prisoners, a safety corridor will be established to safeguard and assist in the control and movement of prisoners. (Schema 23.1, 24.1.)
- The SEAL boarding team must have the capacity to carry out the boarding mission in full without the assistance of a follow-on team.

5.9 Clearance of internal and external spaces

1. Room Clearances by two men

- Normally, in most contacts of interest at sea, the clearance made by two men is the most common procedure. This is due to the limited size of most compartments and spaces found on most vessels and oil platforms. Obviously, there are some exceptions to the rule.
- The standard procedure for conducting the basic clearance by two men is as follows:
    - The assault group (commonly referred to as "train") gathers outside the entrance to the room to be cleared. Security is maintained at the rear by number 5 or the last of the train. Security upfront is maintained by the *pointman* (PT), the security of the door is the task of number 1 and the breaking of the door is the responsibility of the door-breaker. No clearance should be attempted unless there are at least two back-up team members in line prepared and ready to assist the members of the primary clearance team (schema 5.1)

5 *International Policy of Cooperation in the Fight against Crimes at Sea*   **191**

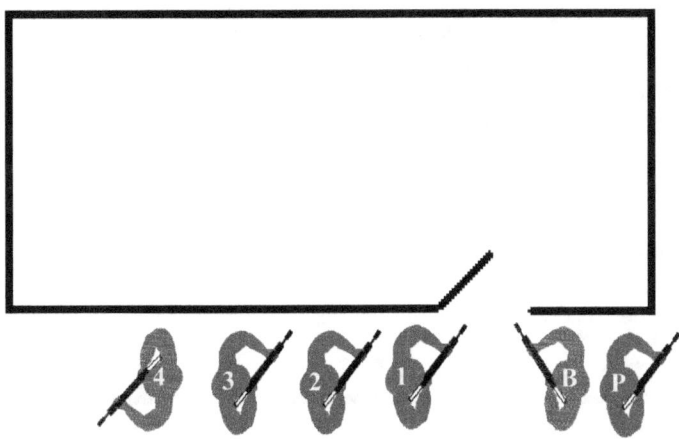

Schema 5.1

- Each member of the line will quickly get ready before entering the room.
- Once each member is ready, beginning from the back of the line each member will give a push to the person in front to signal that he is ready. If he is not ready, he will not pass the signal.
- Once the signal reaches number 1, he knows that all those behind are ready. Then, Number 1 enters into eye contact with the door-breaker, nodding his head three times after which the door is broken and the two men enter and conduct the clearance (Schema 5.2).
- The standard operating procedure for any room clearance is as follows: Number 1 always moves to the left, staying 30 to 45 cm from the wall, penetrating 75% of the way along the bottom of the wall. Number 2 always moves to the right, staying 30 to 45 cm from the wall, penetrating 75% of the way along the bottom of the wall.
- The "field of fire" for the first two men to enter never changes, no matter how many men conduct the clearance. The initial field for Number 1 is always just below the wall; then, he will make a sweep through the room to his right. Number 2 will use just the opposite procedure, sweeping to his left.

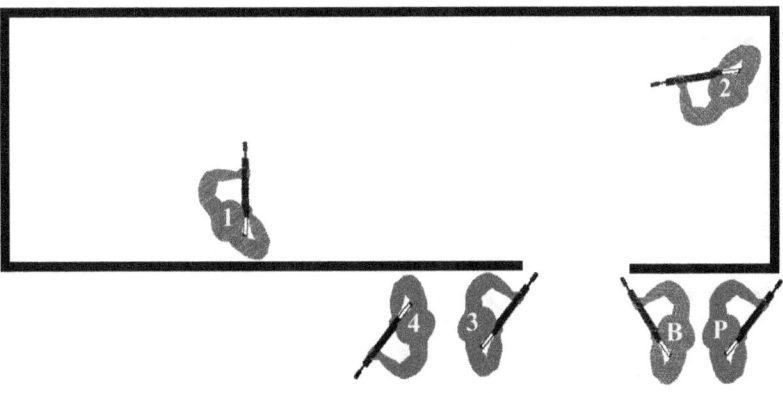

Schema 5.2

- As soon as each man's field is cleared, each man will respond with the verbal signal "Clear".
- As soon as the door is broken, the door-breaker and the *pointman* will walk along the hall to the closest room to reposition themselves as before (Schema 5.2).

The *pointman* will maintain security and the door-breaker will remain at the left or right, depending on the door, and will wait until the line joins them. Numbers 3 and 4 will assume the responsibility of 1 and 2 for the next room. After the first room has been cleared, Numbers 1 and 2 will go to the end of the line and will assume the responsibilities of the former 4 and 5 (Schema 5.3).

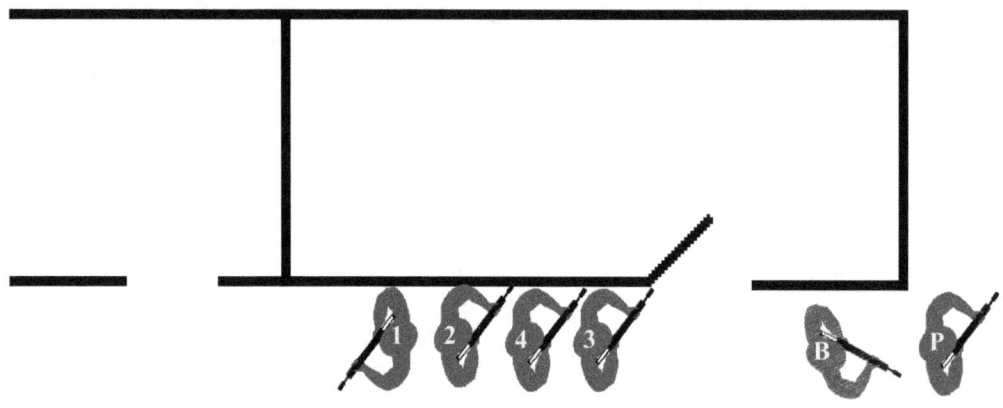

Schema 5.3

2. Clearance by four men

- Room clearances made by four men are conducted in the same way, but two men are added. Clearance by four men is the standard procedure for large rooms.
- The procedure for conducting a clearance by four men is as follows:
- Grouping in the train (schema 5.4)

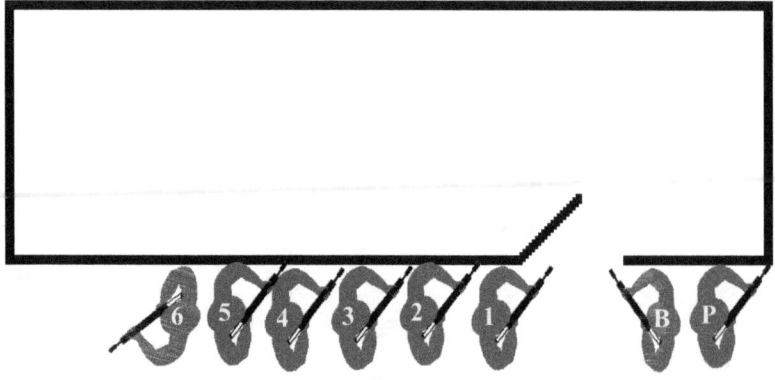

Schema 5.4

- The line is then prepared as described in the above procedure.
- The signal is passed when ready, the door-breaker breaks the door. The *pointman* and the door-breaker move on to the second door. The four-man team enters the room and conducts the clearance.

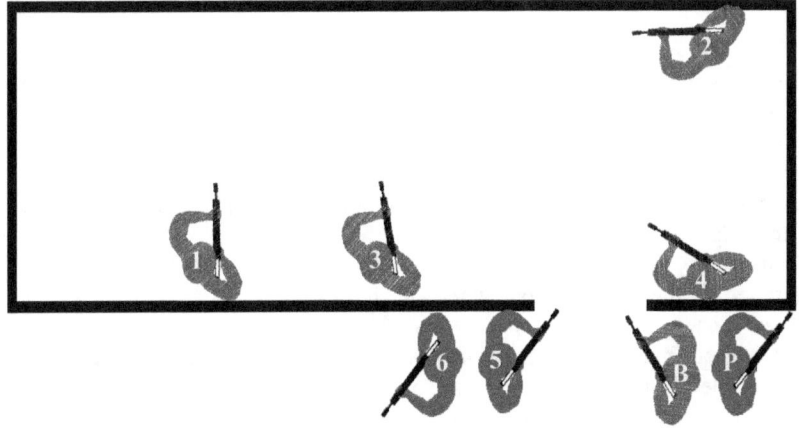

Schema 5.5

- Numbers 1 and 2 conduct the standard clearance. Number 3 enters the room directly behind Number 2, moving to the left along the wall, penetrating halfway along the bottom of the wall. Number 3 must remain between 12 and 18 inches from the wall. The field of fire of Number 3 is in the centre of the room, and he then sweeps towards the left until close to Number 1 (Schema 5.5).

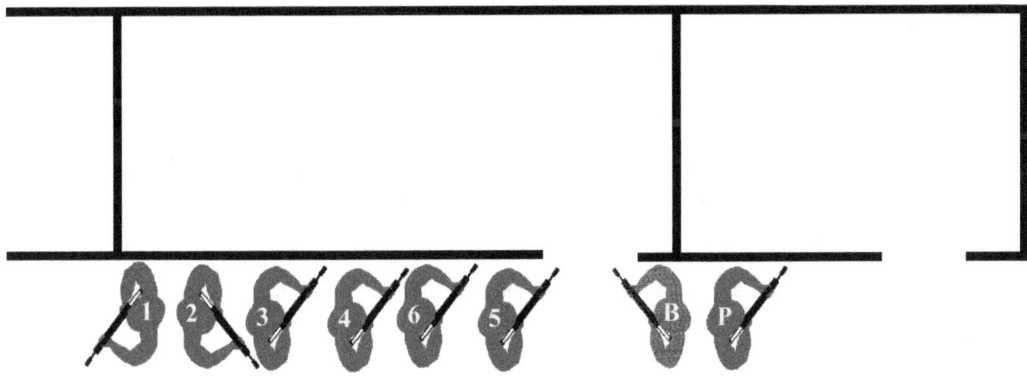

Schema 5.6

- Number 4 enters the room directly behind number 3, moving to the left along the wall, penetrating halfway along the bottom of the wall. Number 4 must remain between 12 and 18 inches from the wall. The field of fire of Number 4 is in the centre of the room, and he then sweeps towards the right until close to Number 2.

- Once the room is cleared, the team withdraws. The first to enter is the last to leave. The order of withdrawal should be 4,3,2,1.
- The four-man team will proceed to the end of the line (Schema 5.6).

3. The train

- The train will continue its procedure until all spaces and compartments are cleared (Schema 5.7).
- During the initial internal clearance, the first room or passage of each level will be designated as the "prisoner holding area". This area will be used as a point of consolidation for the detainees encountered during the level-by-level, room-by-room clearance. Two men will be designated as security for the "prisoner holding area". These are normally the first two men to initially clear the compartment.
- If a detainee is found during the clearance (and does not pose any threat), he will be held and searched in the compartment where he has been found. The train will continue clearing spaces (Schemas 5.8, 5.9).
- If it is a four-man clearance, the last two to enter the compartment (numbers 3 and 4) will be responsible for the security of the prisoner and his transfer to the "prisoner holding area". The last man to enter the compartment (number 4) will be responsible for transferring the prisoner to the holding area during the clearance. If the room does not represent any threat, the rest of the clearance team will abandon the room and proceed to the rear of the train. In a two-man clearance, Number 2 assumes the responsibility for handling the prisoner. Number 1 maintains security in the room. The same rule is applied; the last man to enter mobilises the detainee.

4. Corridor clearance

In "L" shape
The clearance of the "L" shaped corridor must be conducted by one single man. Security at the rear is always the responsibility of the last man in the train (Schema 5.10, 5.11).

In "T" shape
The clearance of the "T" shaped corridor must be conducted by two men. In this type of corridor, the door-breaker must step outside the train during the formation of the grouping prior to the corridor clearance. This gives the door-breaker an easier access to the front of the train. The normal position of the door-breaker in the train is behind the *pointman* (Schema 5.12, 5.13).

Four-directional
This type of corridor must be cleared by three men. Again, the door-breaker steps outside the train (Schema 5.14).

5. Indoor stairs

- Stairs are normally cleared by one single man. The *pointman* will clear the front part of the train. If the train is to enter through a door on a particular level of the COI using the stairs, a two-man clearance will be made. The first train will stop, prepare for the clearance and pass on the signal. Once they are ready, the *pointman* and the breaker will conduct the clearance. The *pointman* moves to the door, taking up a position from which he can cover the rest of the stairs below him. The breaker moves forwards to a position from which he can cover

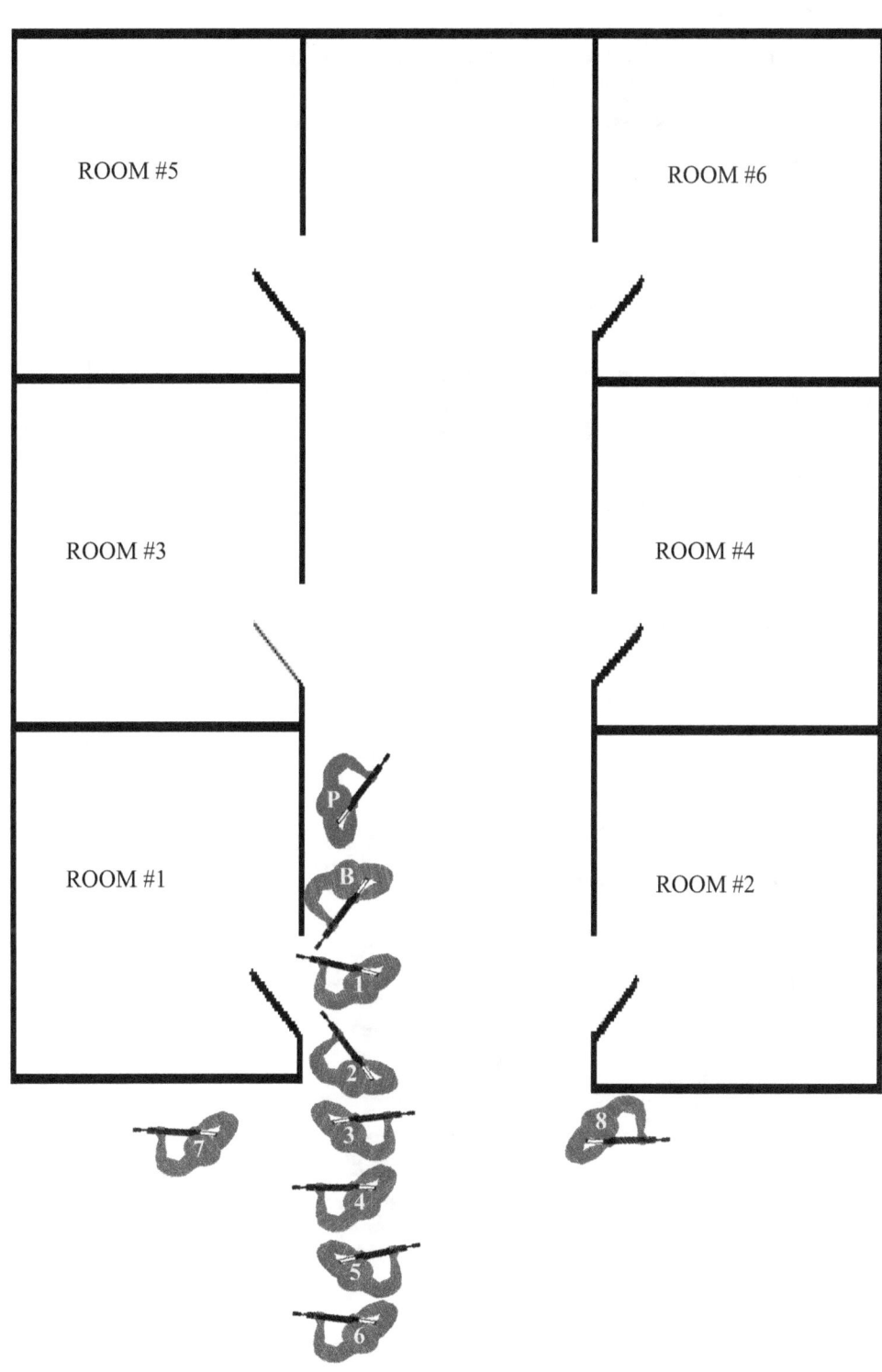

Schema 5.7

the door and, if necessary, break the door without interfering in the capacity of the clearance team to go through the door and clear the corridor on this level.

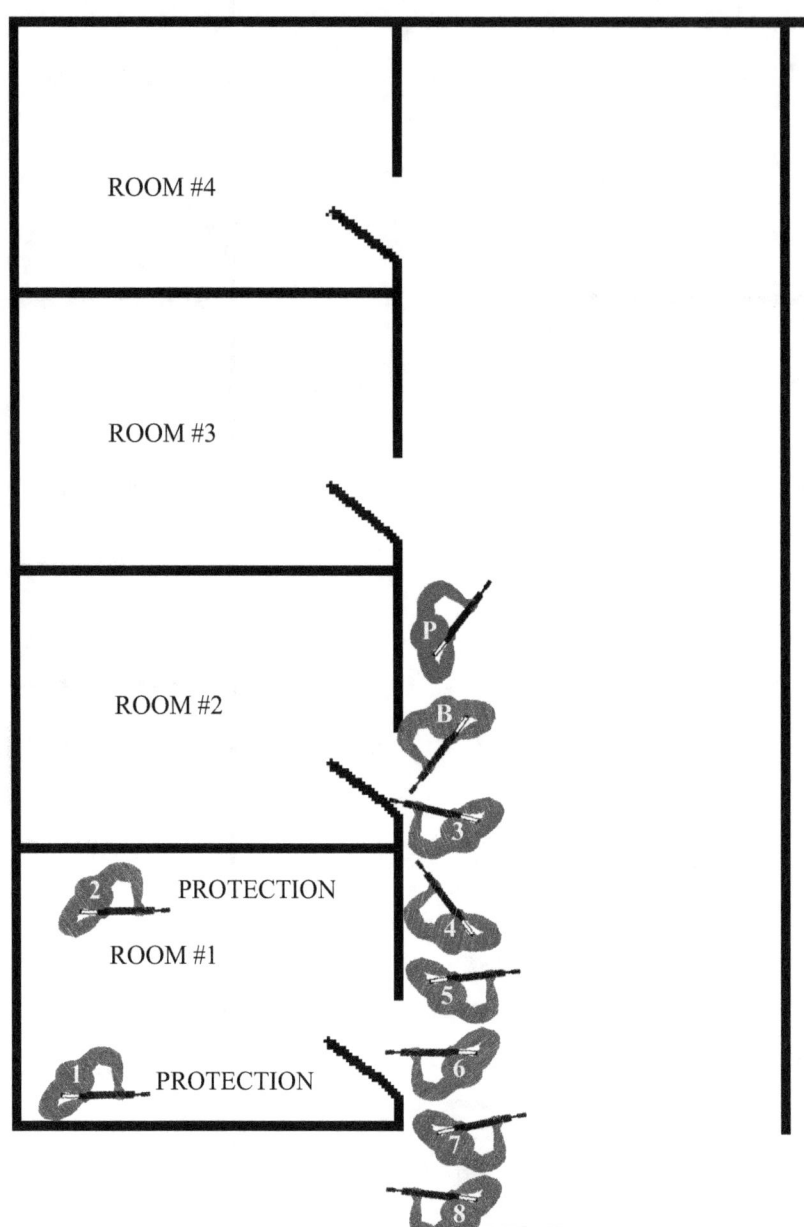

Schema 5.8

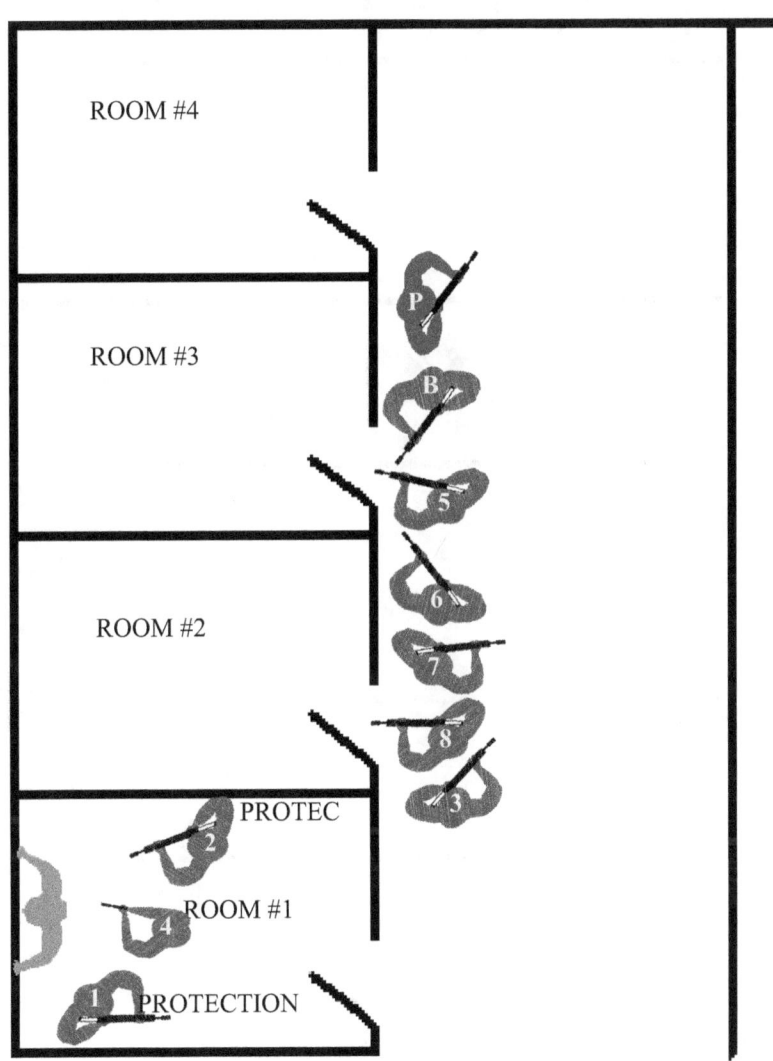

Schema 5.9

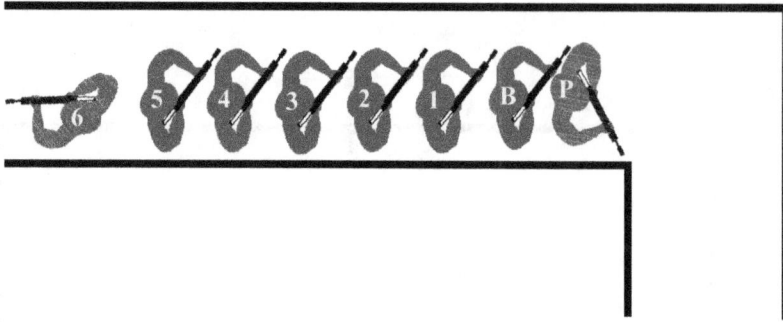

Schema 5.10

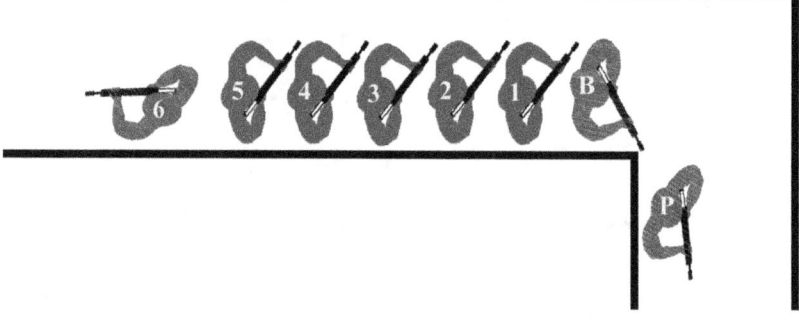

Schema 5.11

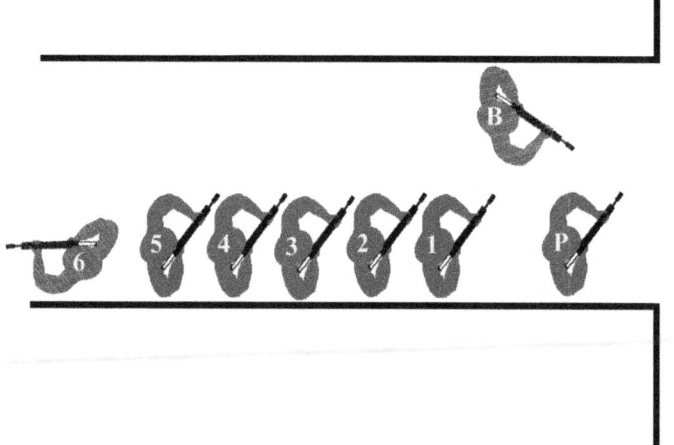

Schema 5.12

5 International Policy of Cooperation in the Fight against Crimes at Sea　　　　　　　　　　**199**

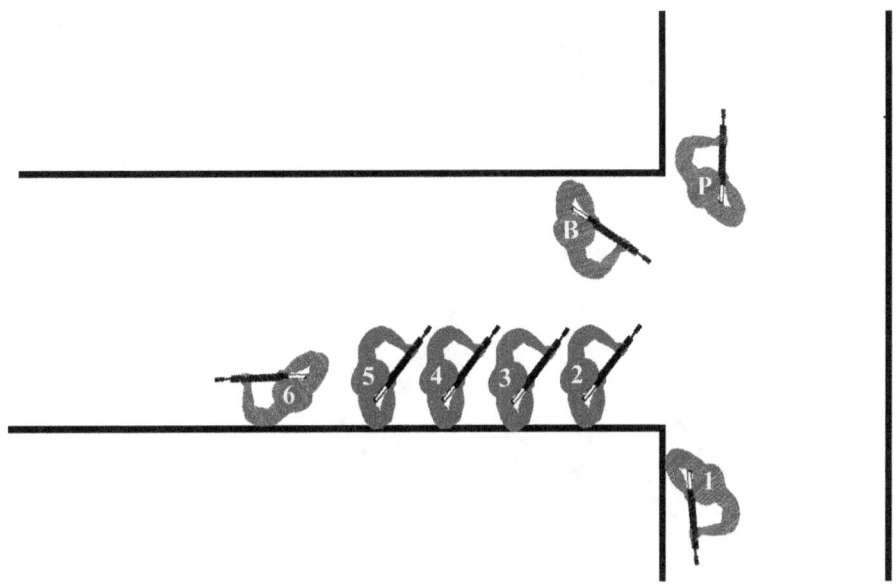

Schema 5.13

6. Outdoor stairs

- Outdoor stairs are mainly located on the main superstructure. The best method for clearing a stretch or stretches of stairs is to use a four-man clearance group.
- The standard operating procedure is as follows: left, right, forwards, backwards. Number 1 always clears to the left, Number 2 to the right, Number 3 to the front and Number 4 to the rear. In this way, 360 degrees of security is maintained.
- The rest of the train takes up positions behind Number 4.
- Number 5 becomes the *pointman* for the rest of the train. Number 5 and the rest of the train will move towards the stairs, but not before the first clearance group moves to the second level.
- Once Number 5 hears the "clear" call, he will lead the rest of the team to the next level of stairs and will stop. The clearance team will maintain its position until the last man in the train has passed. The clearance team will then join the end of the train
- Number 5 now becomes Number 1. As soon as the pointman has four men, the procedure can be repeated.
- This tactic allows the train to establish an "area surveillance" as they advance towards their target. Remember that the remaining member of the team will normally look for his own fields of fire.

7. Open deck

- Normally the transfer to the open deck is associated with the insertion of the boarding team and their transfer to the superstructure of the contact of interest. When an insertion point is planned on the open deck, the shortest and most direct route to the bridge should be prepared, if possible. The transfer to the bridge should be made either from port or starboard, so that one of the fields of fire is suppressed and the team only need to focus on those of the front, rear and one of the sides.

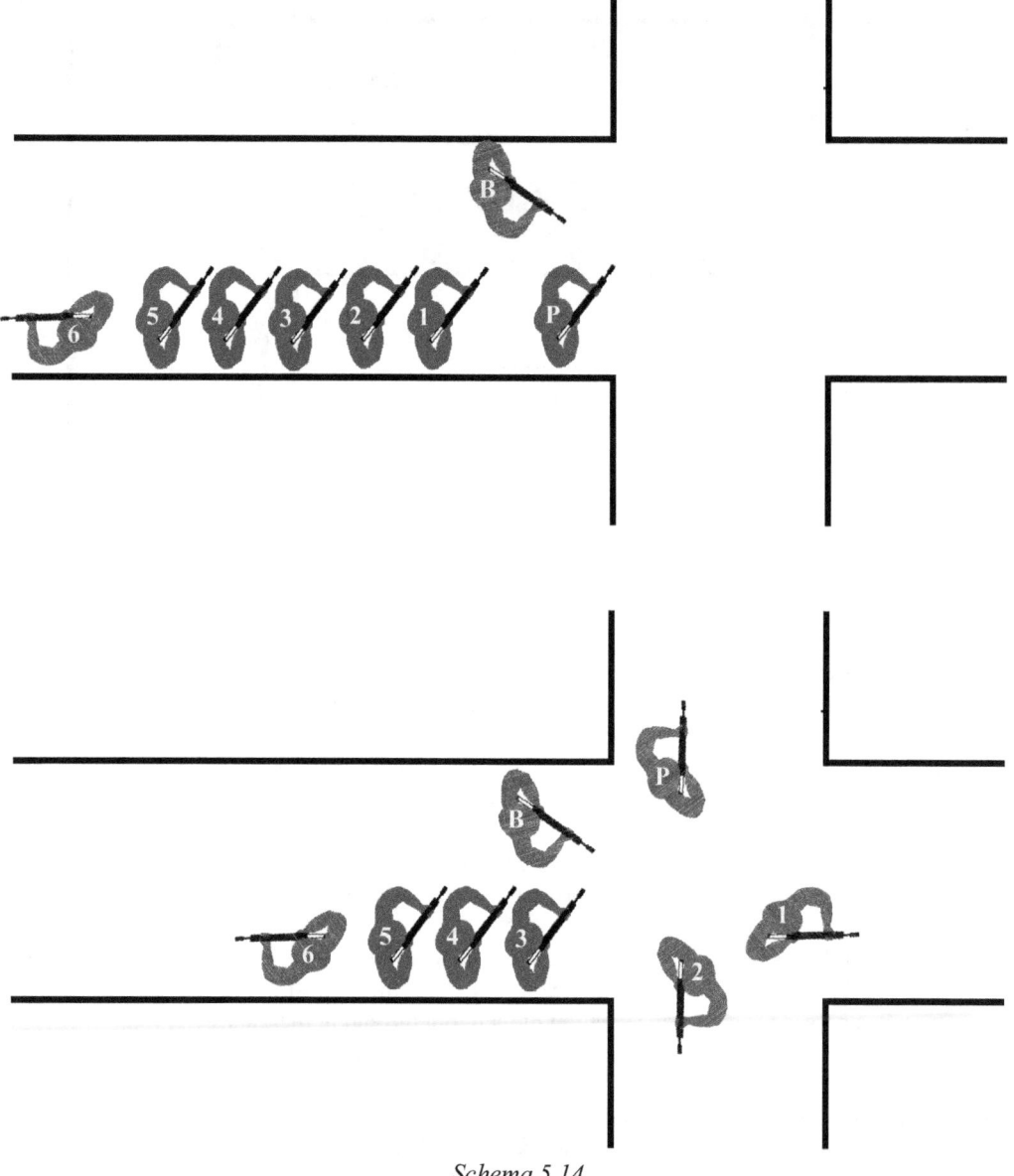

Schema 5.14

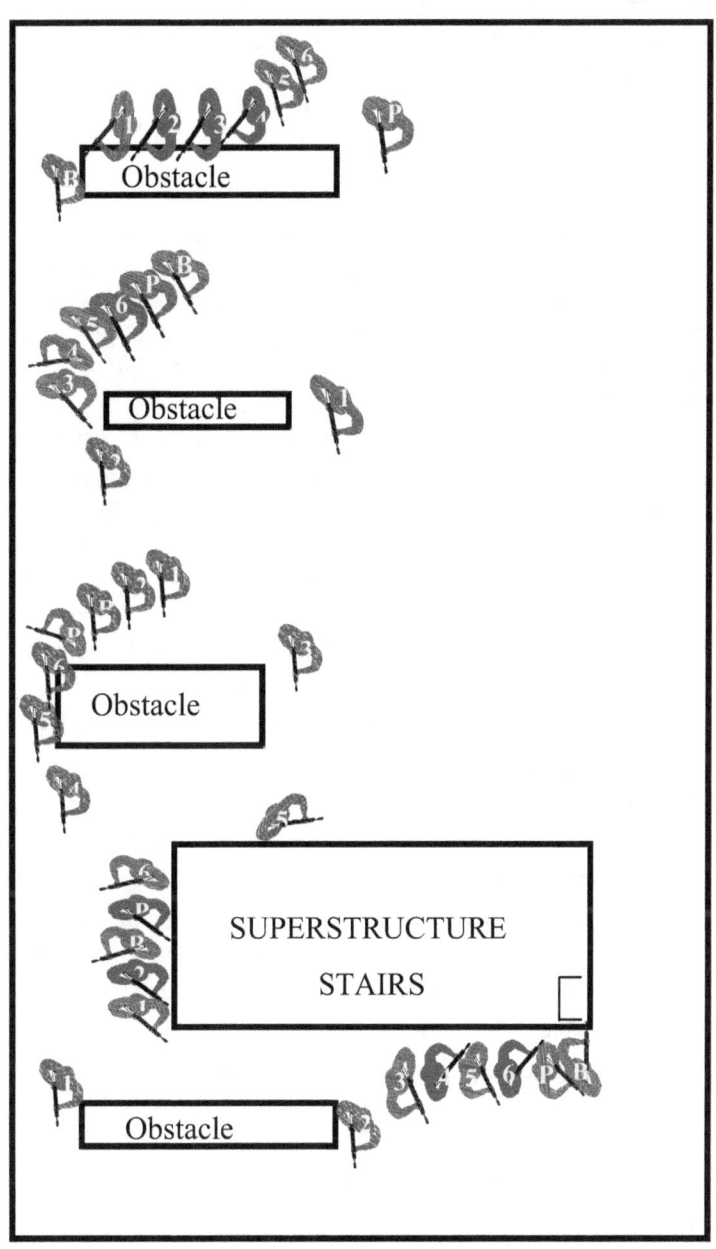

Schema 5.15

- During the boarding, the transfer from the insertion point to the bridge must be carried out in an "area surveillance" type transfer. The clearance of the open deck must be seen, as the boarding team heads towards the bridge, as a clearance of multiple rooms. This means that all the dead spaces and structures encountered along the route must be cleared using basic CQB techniques (Schema 5.15).

8. Bridge

- The prime target in a hostile boarding is the bridge. In most merchant ships, if you control the bridge, you control the vessel. The ship's captain is normally at the bridge next to the vessel's communications area. On most civil vessels, an "emergency stop" can be found in one of the bridge panels. The bridge area must be secured by the boarding team in the shortest possible time, as this reduces the crew's reaction time. Do not prejudice the security of the boarding team because of an inadequate speed.
- The bridge is normally cleared by groups of four with at least two in support.
- There is always a real possibility of having to break the entrance to the bridge mechanically or with explosives. Among others, Flex Liner or Data Sheet explosives or explosive foam can be used. Axes, hammers and other tools are some of the objects that can be taken by the boarding team in their operations. These objects are carried by the breakers. Also, two men must be designated as "torch operators".
- Once the bridge is secured, the following events should take place in the following order:
    - Bridge secured by a four-man clearance team.
    - Communications established with the authorities.
    - All detainees are held on the bridge.
    - The captain is identified and taken to the bridge, instructed to stop the vessel, and presented a full list of the crew and all of the documentation of his cargo.
    - If the captain does not stop the vessel immediately, the boarding team will stop it.
    - The C-2 unit establishes itself in full in the surroundings of the bridge. Normally, the C-2 unit consists of the boarding team commander and his radio communicator.
    - The security force is left on the bridge together with the C2 unit.
    - The follow-on team is inserted and used.
    - A boarding team commander orders his team to begin the internal clearance.
    - The internal clearance is completed. All detainees are counted and an inventory is made of the cargo.
    - The detainees are supervised by the security forces to be searched and processed.
    - The boarding force extracts the persons involved.
- The boarding team must be able to complete any part of the boarding mission without the help of the follow-on force, in case the follow-on force cannot be inserted in the COI for whatever reason.

5.10 Vessel-boarding (surface boarding)

Purpose

To establish certain future guidelines for SEAL personnel concerning advanced maritime training techniques, involving vessel and non-land platform boarding.

Discussion

a) The two-week training period undertaken was the first one ever to be held on vessel and non-land platform boarding. The discussion below outlines the problems concerning the "practical" procedures of these boardings, rather than the problems related with tactics.

The main danger for the diver is getting tangled up in the climbing rope used to connect the diver's UBA to the mooring rope. If this is made firm with ropes under the water in controlled conditions with good visibility, as in training tanks for divers or swimming-pools, this operation does not cause any problems.

Under normal environmental conditions, at night and in open waters, there is the danger, when mooring, that the diver might get tangled up in the mooring rope. The problem is the ascent line or rope. If a diving team encounters some type of current or swell, it is quite possible for some of the divers to get tangled up in while they are ascending to the surface

Once on the surface, the diver proceeds to take off his UBA while still attached to the ascent line or rope (In most cases, the divers do not surface in the same spot). If there is some type of current or swell, if visibility is severely reduced and physical contact with the other members of the diving team is not possible, there is a danger that one UBA device might be pushed against another diver of the team. For example, if a diver gets tangled up after releasing his UBA and the other eight divers have done the same, the weight of the diving apparatus would mean that the diver entangled in the ascent line/rope would be dragged down to the bottom and not be able to rise to the surface.

If this operation is performed next to an oil platform, due to the swells normally found around oil platforms, there is a level 5 possibility of something like this happening, on a scale of 1 to 10.

The second problem is to make a unit float next to a mooring rig. In normal mooring conditions, the procedure does not pose any problem. But it is necessary to train in unfavourable and adverse conditions for a mooring mission on a target. Conditions of reduced visibility, swells and the problem of encountering obstacles such as the rudder of a boat, pipelines, underwater structures etc. will be additional problems in the most difficult boarding operations, increasing confusion when boarding and mooring to a structure with the mooring rig and rope.

In targets with many obstacles, as might be the case with an oil platform with a lot of pipelines and other things, it is better to eliminate the use of a mooring rope by the diving team. All members of the formation should be secured to their team-mates by a rope.

A ladder formation is recommended for the diving team, with one diver leading the formation. The second mission of the attack diver is to maintain the guide rope. Once alongside the target, the mooring rig/line man must search for the first point to secure the mooring rope.

After attaching the mooring rope to the primary fastening point with a carabiner, the mooring rope man places the hand of the second man on the primary fastening point. The mooring rope man takes his fastening rope to his team-mate and hands it to the second man. Then the mooring rope man swims to the second mooring point and attaches the other free end of the mooring rope, to which the divers will fasten themselves. This diver will return to the position occupied by the second man and the rest of the diver team and will give them the signal that the security mooring rope is attached. This method means that the man in charge of securing the mooring rig and searching for primary and secondary fastening points does not have to swim with the other seven divers of the team hooked onto him, thus reducing the confusion factor to a minimum.

After returning to the primary fastening point, the man carrying the mooring rig will hook the second man onto the mooring rig. This process is repeated with all of the divers of the formation and they will than move on to the second fastening point, so that they will all be tied to the mooring rig. After the diving team has moved along the guide rope, the first man to reach the second fastening point places his hand on the guide rope and feels around until he has his hand on the second fastening point. The first man will take the second man's hand and place it on the second fastening point, and will pinch his hand to signal that this is the second fastening point. The second man will attach himself to the guideline with his carabiner and will perform the same procedure on the man behind him. They will proceed thus with all the team. The diving team must not separate.

Signals for the approach of swimmers

1. The diver platoon will enter the water in pairs.

2. The platoon will form a line, and head towards the assault target.

3. Beginning at the end of the diver platoon, the last (8th) man will attach his fastening rope to the team-mate in front of him in the formation (7th). The fact of being attached by the team-mate behind is the signal for each man that the team-mate behind is ready to begin the advance towards the target. Thus, when the first man of the formation, the guide, is attached by the man preceding him, he will know that the group is ready to start the advance.

It is clear that none of the swimmers/divers should attach to the man in front of him unless he is totally prepared and ready to initiate the mission, as this is the signal that indicates to the rest of the group that he is ready.

4. The man guiding the group, once he has attached and decided to initiate the advance, will pull the arm of the OIC (2° hombre) thus signalling that he is ready to initiate the dive.

5. The man controlling the time grasps the hand of the guide and sets in motion the watch chronometer. The guide initiates the dive and the rest of the divers follow in formation.

The average time for a formation of eight men to swim 100 yards is four minutes.

6. Normally when the diving team has reached the target, they will have to move towards their right or left to search for the first securing point. The signal to indicate the attachment of the mooring rig is to raise a closed fist in the direction in which the diving team are to move. This signal will only be

effective in sea conditions with high visibility. When there is no visibility, the first man pushes the second man in the direction in which the diving team is to move. This push will be given by all the team. When the first man finds the fastening point, he will make the team stop by raising his closed fist, or in the case of zero visibility he will simply stop swimming. All of the divers must be well informed and must know exactly how to react in each situation.

7. The first man will be the first swimmer to ensure that the diving team reaches its target. Once alongside the target, it will be his further responsibility to take the group towards the fastening point in a safe and controlled way. After finding the first security point, he will then set about searching for the second one and attach the mooring rig. Obviously, the role of first man should be undertaken by the man with the most experience.

8. Once the first man has located the first fastening point for the mooring rig, he will attach the mooring kit to the fastening point using his carabiner.

9. After securing the mooring rig, the first man will reach for the second man's nearest hand and squeeze it. This will be the signal to the second man that he has reached the fastening point. In zero visibility conditions, this will be the only way for the second man to know where he is. It will also be the signal for the second man that the first man is preparing to attach the mooring rig.

10. When the first man is ready to attach the mooring rig, he will release himself from the safety line and place it in the security point, on the second man's hand, as this man will have his hand on the rig's security point. This indicates to the second man that the first man is about to leave in search of the second security point. The first man will let go the rope from his bag (containing the rope) while searching for the second security point. After finding it, he will attach the end of the mooring rig to the second fastening point. He will immediately return swimming following the rope to the first fastening point, where the second man is.

The man with the rig must always carry an extension for the mooring rig/rope, in case the first one is too short.

The mooring rope must be rolled up in an "S" shape, be tied together with a rubber band and kept in a bag which does not impede swimming and which comes out of the bag without getting tied up or tangled when holding it.

To minimise as much as possible the confusion factor in the case of reduced visibility with swell or current, the mooring rope must not float near the diving team, as this will make it much more difficult to locate the second security point as there would be obstacles, little visibility and swell or current. The operation becomes more complicated when trying to guide a group of seven swimmers, though the confusion factor is reduced when just one of the divers is in charge of securing the mooring rig by himself.

11. Once the first man has attached the mooring rig and returned towards the position of the first fastening point of the mooring rig, he will take the second man's hand and take it away from the first fastening point to place it on the mooring rig rope attached previously when his hand was squeezed. This was the signal to the second man that the mooring rig rope is already attached and that he can begin to move along the rope in the direction of the second security point.

This step is repeated throughout the group so that each of the divers moves along the mooring rig rope. It is the responsibility of each diver to press the hand of the man behind him to signal to him that this is the mooring rig rope. This is the only way of passing on the signal in the case of low visibility.

12. Once the first man has reached the second fastening point, he will place his hand on this and the safety rope. Then, the first man will slide his hand along the mooring rig rope in the direction of the second man and will located the ring of the first fastening point. On reaching the fastening ring, the first man will secure himself to the security ring with his carabiner.

13. After securing the mooring rig, the first man will take the security ring with his hand and slide it along the rope towards the position of the second man until he locates the next fastening point along the mooring rig. Once this point is located, the first man will take the hand of the man nearest to him and place it on this fastening point, and will press his hand against the fastening point. This will be the signal to the swimmer that this is the mooring rig and its designated security point. When the swimmer is sure that this is his security point, he will secure himself to it with his carabiner.

This process is repeated throughout the diving team from front to back until reaching the last diver. It is the responsibility of each diver to situate the man behind him on the security points, as this will be the only way they will be able to work in case of low visibility.

When the last man of the diving team has secured himself to the security point, it will be his responsibility to initiate the process of returning along the rope and ascending to the surface. This will be done by a hand squeeze signal.

14. Once the last man is secured to the security rig rope and ready to return along the rope, he will release himself from his safety rope and inform the next diver by squeezing his hand.

No diver should pass on the hand squeeze signal until he is sure he is ready for the ascent along the rope.

15. This process is repeated throughout the group until the first man receives the hand squeeze signal. This will let the first man and the official responsible that all the divers are ready to ascend.

16. Beginning with the first man of the diving team and after the first man is sure that all the men are ready to ascend, the first man will send two hand squeezes down through all the team.

The two squeezes will be received by each diver and passed on to the next diver before beginning the ascent.

17. Beginning at the rig end and after the last man at the rig is ready for the ascension to the surface, two hand squeezes will be passed on from front to back to the next diver in the team until the last diver is reached.

18. These two hand squeezes have been passed from man to man from the first to the last.

19. After the first man has received the two hand squeezes from the second diver, he will know that everyone is ready to ascend to the surface. The first man will squeeze the second man's hand three times, which will tell him that they are about to rise to the surface. This signal will be repeated throughout the team.

20. When the three squeeze signal reaches the last diver, he will breathe in fresh air from his UBA, close the UBA valve, grip the shoulder of the man in front and push him towards the surface. This is repeated throughout the group until they begin to move towards the surface.

21. The divers will have to ascend and come up as close as possible to the target, taking off their oxygen masks before reaching the surface to avoid making any noise when coming to the surface.

22. Once on the surface, the officer in charge will count the heads and make the group move towards one or another side to search for the point where the boarding will take place.

23. Once the boarding point is reached, the man in charge of the ladder moves forward and maintains position while the rest of the equipment is prepared as close as possible to the side of the target. The rest of the team waits close together.

24. When they are ready, the men in charge of the ladder and the spade, as well as the man in charge of security, will approach the side to get a good angle with respect to the hull of the vessel to place the ladder and the hook with the pulley; each of these will be right next to the side of the target. While the man places the ladder, the first officer and the second man move their flippers and prepare for the ascent by the ladder making as little noise as possible.

25. Once the ladder is in position, the pointman and the officer in charge go up the ladder. The man who positions the ladder then withdraws it and hides it under the side of the vessel.

26. In order to be exposed as little as possible while climbing the ladder, the man will stop just before reaching the top and will take a look to ensure that there is no danger of being seen. If there is no danger, he will continue climbing and position himself on deck to perform a further security reconnaissance on deck.

If all is clear and there is no danger of being discovered, the man who has got on board will make a signal to the officer in charge to continue climbing and will continue the surveillance of the surroundings.

27. Once on board, the officer in charge will place the safety rope and will make a signal to the others in the diving team that they can begin to climb on deck. In low visibility conditions, a red and green light may signal the advance or not of the rest of the group. If there is a security hook for the ladder, the security rope should not be used.

28. The swimmers will wait next to the hull of the vessel at the end of the ladder having taken off their flippers, holding on to the ladder. Depending on the sea state, the divers should either have taken off both flippers or just have one on. In this way, they will be able to climb the ladder more quickly. The flippers should be secured to the ladder to prevent them from rising to the surface.

29. Once the swimmers begin to climb the ladder, the officer in charge must guide the team towards a safe point on the vessel before the assault. The rule is to have all 360 degrees controlled. The officer in charge must guide the team towards a safe point to prepare the assault, the weapons and explosives and revise the assault targets.

30. Once the assault team is prepared, their equipment ready and checked, and the team counted, they will move towards the final point of the assault. The team will move on all fours or crouched down, maintaining constant surveillance.

31. Finally, all the magazines and weapons will be ready to go into action and will move towards the point of entry, where the explosives will be placed. The team will move towards the final point of attack. The officer in charge will coordinate all the operation and the explosives will go off. The assault will thus be completed.

32. After the assault, a report must be made on the situation and the authorities will be informed.

33. It is important to maintain security throughout the operation.

5.11 Possible actions of the crew

In the previous sections of this chapter, criteria and procedures of assault forces in vessel interventions have been presented.

Up to now, the crew-member has been a dummy, suppressed from the beginning, first by the delinquents/terrorists and then by the new assault of the special forces.

His contribution in one or other stage of the event has been null. He is the first actor, playing his role, but has never been given the opportunity to intervene, to do something to help him overcome the negative conditions of the stage on which he finds himself, on the basis of the natural laws of his survival.

The big question is whether the actions he might take on finding himself in such an unfortunate situation will contribute to a successful rescue and the return to normality or will hinder the high-risk actions of the FCSE, endangering the lives of all. Thus, it could be said that since the crew is not a group trained and practised in techniques and tactics of this sort, corresponding only to the special forces, no principle of universal application can be established. Nor can it even be said when and at what moment such tactics and techniques might be valid, since the variability of circumstances surrounding this type of situations means that no degree of precaution will be sufficient.

Since, due to the reasons indicated above, there are no compulsory rules nor even any rules designed for the crew-members of a vessel in situations contemplated in the security handbooks, this section will outline some recommendations that come from various sources and are positive in different situations. They tend to deal with prevention or the aggravation of the consequences, so that they should be interpreted as partial solutions which, if not known previously, are unlikely to occur to the human mind when subjected to the pressure of a situation of immediate danger.

5.11.1 Hijacking

As is the case of some ambushes, some hijacks can be survived with careful planning and foresight. Do not follow the crowd: one should choose from all the different routes to the destination and from all the shipping lines that can be used.

The first priority is to determine whether oneself, or those who accompany you, might be a potential target. More likely than not, the choice is based more on what someone represents than on who he really is: terrorists often attack people because of their nationality. If they simply want Spanish hostages, their requirements are met due to the simple fact that you are in the wrong place at the wrong time.

The second factor to bear in mind before a trip is the booking, route, shipping line and type of place assigned. When it is a case of air flights to high-risk countries, two bookings should be made in different companies to then select one of them.

The ticket should be collected at the airport, so that one's personal movements are known by a small number of people. There are airlines such as Swissair or SAS that have no political implications. Some American companies are clear targets, as are those of the Middle East. Neutral countries should be selected as even those countries with imperial colonies are potential targets.

Avoid Stopovers

Make sure the route is a direct one, without stopovers, a precaution which is particularly important when the trip takes you through the Middle East. Some airports overlook certain security norms so that while one may have to pass through thorough security checks before boarding in the airport of origin, other passengers may board in stopovers where the checks are less exhaustive.

If there is a stopover, a walk through the terminal might avoid finding oneself trapped in a vulnerable airplane, as some terrorists have boarded during stopovers disguised as cleaning staff: thus, a walk might reduce the possibilities of finding oneself involved in a hijacking.

If one has to fly to a particularly problematic point, some airlines stand out for their high level of security; for example the Israeli El Al takes great care over its luggage register, electronic controls and passenger checks. El Al may be a potential target but it is at least a 'hard' target.

The place one occupies on a plane can also reduce the risk: an aisle seat is exposed to the reach of the hijackers. Window seats are safer and those that are near the doors might provide an opportunity to escape when the plane is detained in an airport.

Travel Tourist Class

The "neutral" seats of the tourist class are less prone to attracting attention than those of first class. If the terrorists want to show their determination, they may shoot some hostages and are likely to select among those passengers who are clearly important.

Clothes and manners can also attract attention. In some countries, jeans are considered western clothes and are thus suspicious. Clothes from military sources should be avoided, especially war clothes. Luggage can also attract attention, whether because of its abundance or because of its military precedence, as in the case of a soldier's sleeping bag or a khaki bag.

Luggage labels should only bear one's work address and never that of the hotels one came from (in the end, these precautions also reduce the risk of robbery in the airport). Jewels, a flashy shirt and clothes with strong ethnical connotations can also involve some risk and reduce the possibility of being a "grey person", a "Mr Nobody" who can go unnoticed among the other passengers.

Discrete passport

Finally, a passport and wallet can provide information. The collection of visa stamps from countries with terrorism problems should be avoided: in many countries the entry and exit visas can be sealed on a separate page, when possible.

The description of one's occupation might lead to a greater risk, since government and military staff are considered "targets" by a large number of hijackers, something which can be a great drawback when there is a possibility of execution of hostages.

It is worth always carrying photographs of your family and children in your wallet or passport. This gives the image of being a family person with persons under your charge and thus one might be considered less adequate for execution. In contrast, a photograph of one's wife or girlfriend in a swimming costume might make one a corrupt and decadent westerner in the eyes of some hijackers.

Action

If the worst happens and one is a hostage on a hijacked plane, one must follow the old military maxim: "Keep your eyes open, your mouth shut and do not offer to do anything voluntarily" However, this last part might be modified as long as it affords a chance to escape.

While the hijacking is taking place, the terrorists will be very nervous and any quick or unexpected movements of the passengers might provoke violent reactions. They might attack or signal someone as a future victim of execution or may kill one suspecting that one is an airline security guard.

By means of a thoughtful observation, a picture must be drawn in one's mind of the number of hijackers and their way of operating. In a big plane, it is possible for the hijackers to gather together all the passengers or to situate these at different points to maintain surveillance over all the passengers.

Tiredness and tension

As time passes, everybody will be affected by tiredness and fatigue and the need to perform one's bodily functions. This will increase the tension and the presence of children will aggravate things even more.

The hijackers will probably free the girls, children and old people if the plane lands in the place where the negotiations are being held. These freed passengers will be able to give details on the hijackers to the security forces, assuming that the plane is in a reasonably pro-western country.

If a plane next to the door is occupied, this may represent the last opportunity to escape. However, when travelling with a group, fleeing might make one's fellow passengers potential victims of an execution. Note how the hijacker is armed: if he holds a pistol, there are some chances of survival, and an opportunity may even offer itself to overpower him.

The most dangerous situation is when the hijackers have automatic weapons and explosives. The explosives may be distributed throughout the plane and they may threaten to set them off if a rescue attempt is made. Also, automatic weapons are extremely imprecise in untrained hands and could cause victims if there were a shoot-out with a security guard on board.

If there is a shoot-out, crouch down as low as possible. Window seats offer better protection, although it is more difficult to escape. If there is a security guard on the plane, he will have a low-speed weapon which will not damage the plane's fuselage, but the hijacker might use a high-speed 9 mm weapon, and if the fuselage is perforated, this might cause decompression.

Rushed rescues

In any case, the purpose of the hijacker is to take the plane to a place where negotiations can be initiated. There have been cases recently in which rushed rescue operations have produced more victims than expected after the police or army assaulted the plane.

If there is an operation of this type, it is likely that the assault team will order the passengers to crouch down. In this way, they will be able to identify the hijackers, who will probably be standing in the aisle.

The passengers' attitude should be to crouch down and await the end of the shoot-out – the assault team will react to any violent or unexpected movement. The assault will be preceded by the launching of stun grenades and both the passengers and the hijackers will suffer an immediate feeling of dizziness. Then, the team will set about getting the passengers off the place as fast as possible, so each passenger should simply follow instructions.

Keeping calm

However, if the plane reaches a neutral or "friendly" country where the hijackers can negotiate, the recommended attitude is to assess the situation.

There may be friends of the hijackers in the airport who will take charge of the negotiations with a foreign power and with the most reasonable of the men and women who have hijacked the plane. In these circumstances, a leader might appear from among the passengers: this could be the commander or a mature, experienced passenger.

By then, the plane and the passengers will have become the object of negotiations and its security will be the most important question. This may be the time to wait patiently. If the case arises that one is led off the plane and taken to a hotel or closed space, one should attempt to get some luggage or toiletries: none of these might be available where you are taken.

During a hijack, all comforts on board disappear almost immediately, as the hijackers will prevent the flight staff from moving freely around the plane. It is thus advisable to have in one's hand luggage toiletries and any medicine one might need.

5.11.2 The boarding

In response to the series of hijackings that took place in the late sixties, anti-terrorist units have prepared different methods for intervening in hostage-taking situations. These are not easy missions. The terrorists have everything in their favour: they normally have a clear field of vision and can massacre the passengers in a matter of seconds.

When a rescue attempt is to be made, it must be planned to the last detail and implemented with clinical precision.

Information and planning

In some cases, the hijackers have freed men and women who are sick or old, or children. These persons will be vital, since they can provide information on the number of hijackers and their arms and equipment. They also provide information on their level of preparation and their motivations, although these will be known in part thanks to the conversations held with the control tower.

Undermine the hijackers' resistance

It is essential to verify how close the forces can get without alerting the hijackers. Disguising as ground staff gives good cover, although the ladders, weapons and equipment will be hard to conceal. The night is obviously the time when the hijackers are most tired and will provide reasonable cover.

If the plane's Auxiliary Power Unit (APU) is disconnected due to a lack of fuel, the indoor lights, air-conditioning and other supplies will switch off, leaving the plane in darkness. If the ground staff at the previous airport where the plane stopped can inform about the fuel levels and these indicate that there will soon be a shutdown, then an attack can be planned or the hijackers can be informed that the plane will be left with no energy due to a failure in the APU. The timing must be perfect – it was a lack of coordination that produced several victims in Malta Airport when the Egyptian special forces attacked a hijacked passenger plane.

Talking to the outside

The negotiations team can provoke tiredness in the hijackers if they are capable of keeping them talking, although they must bear in mind the danger the passengers are in, as well as their continuous discomfort. At times, the negotiators can talk to the hijackers outside the plane, without the need to go on board.

Losing patience

Once the hijackers lose their patience with the negotiations team and begin to kill hostages to show that they are serious, the boarding group must be ready to move quickly.

As it is unlikely for the hijackers to have weapons with war ammunition, the assault force should wear bullet-proof vests, which will give them sufficient protection. The new light Kevlar vest can be worn without reducing the mobility of the wearer. The use of bulletproof vests is also important for the assault team's morale.

Assault team weapons

The weapons used for this task may include cutting equipment, stun grenades and automatic weapons. The linear cutting tape is a flexible plastic or metal tube with explosive and a notch down one side which, if correctly positioned, acts as a load to open the way through the plane's fuselage, thus providing a means of access. It can be attached magnetically or with adhesives.

Weapons for the shoot-out

The favourite portable weapons of the anti-terrorist teams vary greatly. The United States Delta Force used the venerable M1919A1 0.45 pistol at first: its great power of impact can knock a man down without perforating the plane's fuselage. Hollow-point ammunition, which crushes when it hits the target, has a devastating effect o, white tissues, but does not rebound or cause damage to the internal controls and devices of the plane.

New ammunition

Some new plastic ammunition loses speed after covering a short distance, but is lethal inside the space in which the action will take place.

Automatic weapons with high-capacity magazines, such as the Browning High Power, provide sufficient ammunition for the short but violent action which will follow the entry onto the plane. However, spare magazines should be taken in case the shoot-out lasts longer than expected.

Entering the plane

If the hijackers are divided, some on the flight deck and others among the passengers, the attack will require two teams and the assault will have to be organised so that one team moves towards the front door and the other towards the back door of the plane. Of course, in these cases the planning must be meticulous in order to prevent the assault groups from shooting at each other. The entry must be preceded by the launching of stun grenades which will momentarily disable the enemy but will not cause serious injuries among the passengers

Effects of a stun grenade

When a stun grenade explodes in a small space such as the inside of a passenger plane, all of those who are near it will be completely deafened: those who are too close to the explosion will suffer a rupture of the eardrums. The flash will leave anyone looking in the direction of the explosion temporarily blinded, the image remaining on his retina for at least 10 minutes.

Speed means success

No matter what your training has taught you, you must be prepared for anything when entering the plane. The hostages may not be where they were expected to be, so the instinct to advance with great caution is very strong. However, the attack will only be successful if it is carried out quickly: the hand-grenades and the suddenness of the assault will disturb the hijackers. It is very important not to give the hijackers time to recover.

Standing targets

All the training undertaken makes sense at that exact moment when life or death depends on your split-second reactions. If the information services have provided photographs of the terrorists, you will at least have some means of identifying them. Otherwise, you will have to go for anyone who is armed and standing.

The passengers can be evacuated from the plane as soon as the hijackers are distanced from one of the main exits.

The members of the assault team will position themselves next to the exits to ensure that no hijacker tries to sneak away by this route and to coordinate the security forces deployed outside the plane. There have been cases where escaping passengers have been shot by accident.

Withdrawal

After overpowering the hijackers and checking that the plane is "safe", the assault team must disappear from the place. It is essential to maintain the maximum anonymity, as it is undesirable for their arrival at a future crisis to be uncovered by the press and announced on radio and television. The special forces must therefore maintain total secrecy as regards their men. This can help to save lives in the future, and not just those of the passengers

5.11.3 Recommendations for persons caught in hijacking

Family man

If you are held in an enclosed space, talk about your family. Act like a normal person and you will be treated better. Do not talk about politics.

Non-provocative luggage

Do not carry religious or any other type of symbols: the hijackers may not share your views. Nor should you wear tee-shirts with political slogans.

Comfortable clothing

Travel with comfortable clothing: if hijacked, you have to keep cool, clean and healthy for some time. Play mind games to keep your concentration.

Illness

If you pretend to have symptoms of illness and can keep up the farce, you may be released earlier.

Decompression

Most modern guns can perforate the fuselage of a plane, which will cause a loss of pressure. For a fanatical or nervous hijacker, this may not be too important, but it could make the plane fall and kill everyone.

Delicate documents

Do not carry with you compromising documents; keep them in your luggage. If a hijacker discovers that you are connected with some official or government organism, you will be dealt with more harshly.

"Grey man"

If your airplane is hijacked, the best way to survive is to keep quiet and not attract attention. Disturbed by the situation itself, the hijackers normally act without asking too many questions against anyone who might seem to be offering resistance.

Avoiding or overcoming a hijacking

1. Travel with an airline that has few or no political enemies.
2. Do not wear clothes with military symbols, new or old.
3. Do not carry your belongings in military bags.
4. If the plane is hijacked, keep quiet and do not attract attention.
5. Observe closely the terrorists' activity; if you manage to escape, you will be able to help the security forces.

Assault

Surprise is a key factor in the success of an assault on a hijacked passenger plane: the assault team has to climb on board and secure the plane in a matter of seconds. The security forces have to deal with the terrorists immediately or they will start to massacre the passengers.

Friendly posture

Do not take any weapon when leaving the plane or you may be shot on the presumption of being a terrorist. When you get out, throw yourself on the ground, even if you are wounded, with arms stretched out, and stay there until evacuated by the security forces.

Cutting charge

One of the best ways of entering a plane is by using a cutting charge: this is a flexible tube with a groove down one side, and can be used to penetrate the fuselage wall.

Bullet-proof jackets

The members of the assault team will probably be wearing bullet-proof jackets.

Obey all orders

Obey the assault team's orders without questioning or protesting. They will consider everyone as potential threats, so they will act ruthlessly until everything is under control.

Movements

When involved in combat in the small space of the inside of an airplane, it is important to wear clothes that cannot get caught or make you trip over.

Supervise the grenades

When passing through the airplane, anyone with a weapon in his hand is an obvious target, but do not ignore the danger of hand-grenades. An apparently inoffensive passenger began to roll out grenades along the aisle when the German antiterrorist group GSG9 assaulted a passenger plane in Mogadiscio.

Soft-point ammunition

If soft or hollow point bullets are used, the bullets that miss the target will not rebound on the plane. They have another clear advantage: no hijacker hit by a bullet of this type will be in any condition to continue fighting.

Use of tear gas

If tear gas is used, you should protect your face against the seat cushions.

Distraction

During the assault, there will be lots of noise and lights that will distract you. Most of these will be to divert attention: the real assault will take place somewhere else.

Stun grenades

These will be used once the entry is made. They will cause temporary blindness, burst the eardrums of those in the vicinity and create confusion and panic.

Crouching

As soon as the action begins, crouch down on the floor under your seat and stay there. Do not drag yourself out into the aisle; you may be stood on by a member of the assault team attempting to take control of the plane.

6. Ship Intervention simulations

The purpose of this chapter is to show a preparatory work procedure of the exercises to be carried out in compliance with the philosophy imposed by the ISPS Code, according to which the crew should be prepared to take on the responsibilities that must now be assumed in situations involved in the term security.

As each security situation is unforeseeable the way it will start and in how it will evolve and taking into account the knowledge provided in the previous chapters, and as these are the only ways of action known in part by the special force that might intervene in the event, the cases presented only refer to the assault forces, while each SSO should update them in accordance with:

- the type of ship
- its construction in superstructures
- the distribution of special spaces
- its degree of vulnerability
- the number and composition of crew members
- the relationship with the ship's traffic
- the degree of the threat suffered by the ports it frequents
- and any other configuration of circumstances and conditions that make the active participation of all the members of the ship possible

6.1 Moored ship, ship taken over by terrorists and placing explosive artefacts

In this type of drill the procedure is followed to put on the location of the start of the security situation on the ship deck, the progressive evolution both in the positions and attackers and the crew and the responses and actions that are necessary for the complete control of the situation.

Case:

- They access the ship using the anchor chain. They hide in the forecastle, behind the starboard turnstile and make sure they have not been seen.
- They enter the emergency group premises to place the explosives (Fig. 6.1).
- Walking along the side of the deck they easily reach the forecastle. The paint shed is locked but the emergency group door is easily opened. This would be a discreet place to place the explosives.
- They leave the emergency group premises and make their way to the stairs on starboard (Fig. 6.2).
- They make their way along the starboard side and walk discreetly along the deck until they reach the compartment (Fig. 6.3).
- Access inside the compartment can be through 3 numbered entrances indicated in red. They use access no. 1

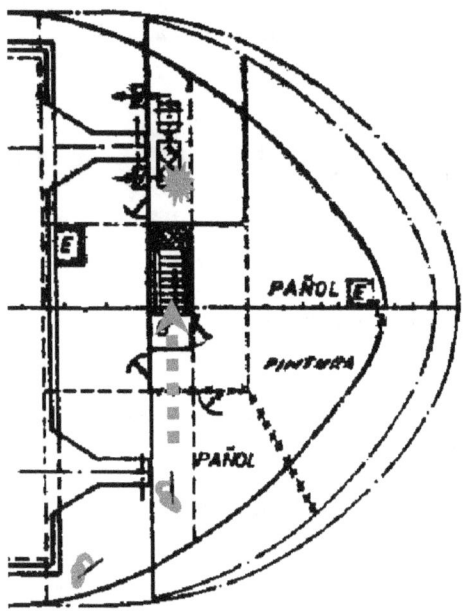

Fig. 6.1

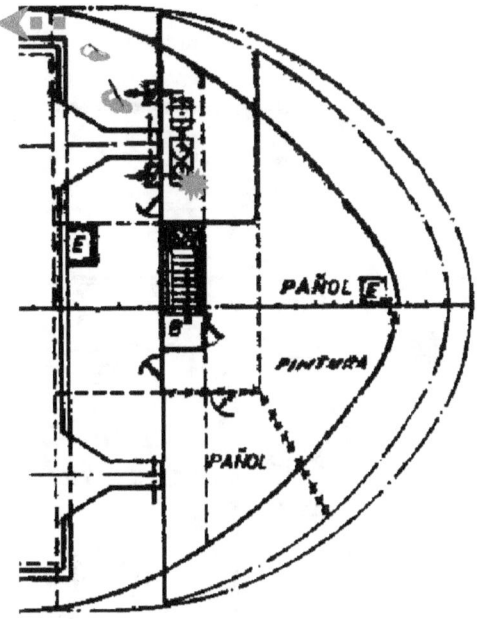

Fig. 6.2

- They reach the ship's compartment. They find the port side entrance to the main deck and enter the kitchen.
- They go right along the deck and when they reach the compartment they enter the main deck on port side: They find the kitchen, in silence, and enter. They have to be quick to place the explosives before the crew wakes up.
- At a given moment they are discovered and a hostage taking situation commences. They do this at various points of the ship, especially on the bridge (Fig. 6.4).
- As the ship is anchored, the bridge guard officer alerts of the situation and manages to raise the alarm in the port control tower.
- A process of negotiation is initiated which does not produce good results in the first hours and the authorities, in accordance with the forces of intervention of the state security corps, decide to intervene.
- The attack considers all the possibilities that the ship offers and which are shown in Fig. 6.5 and 6 6.

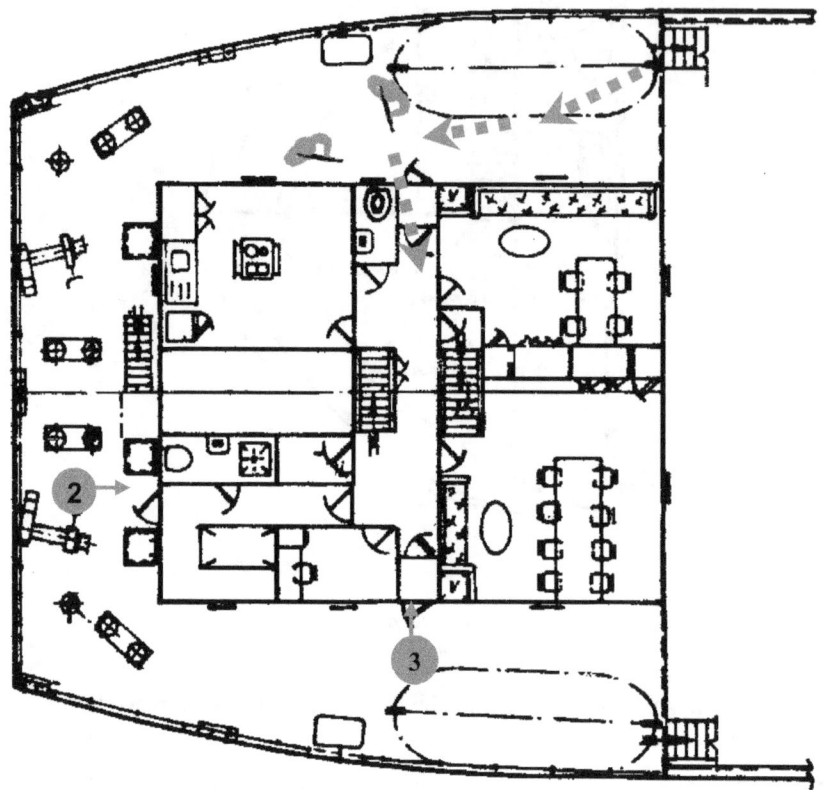

Fig. 6.3

The route of the terrorists (in red) inside the compartment is shown with the broken red lines and the crew members that were discovered and taken as hostages (in green).

6 Ship Intervention simulations 221

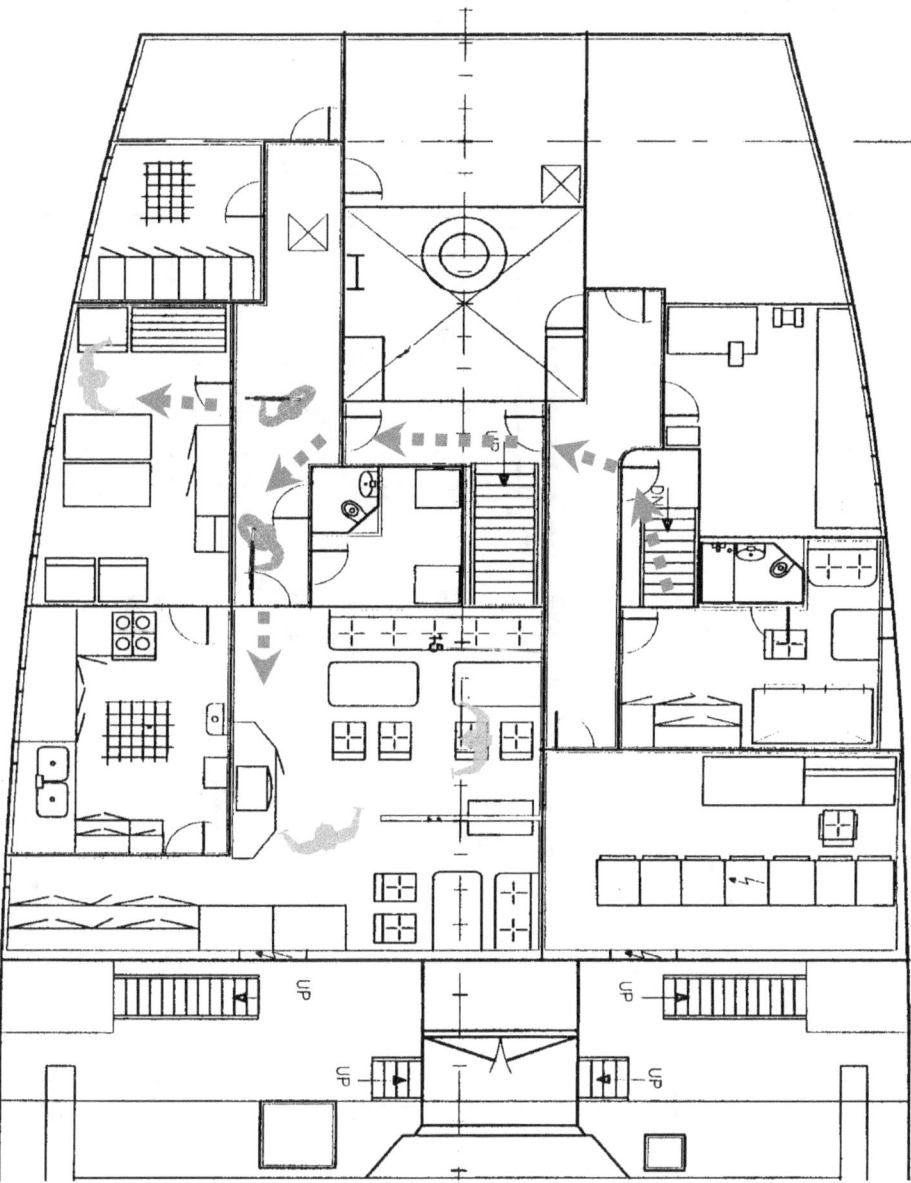

Fig. 6.4

From this moment on, once the terrorists have been discovered and the alarm raised all over the ship as well as out to the port authorities, they start the complete taking of the ship, leaving aside the main objective of sabotaging the activity of the ship with bombs; they move on directly to taking the ship, which they did not intend to carry out, but had kept it only as an alternative solution, as has become the case.

Attack by divers /frogmen

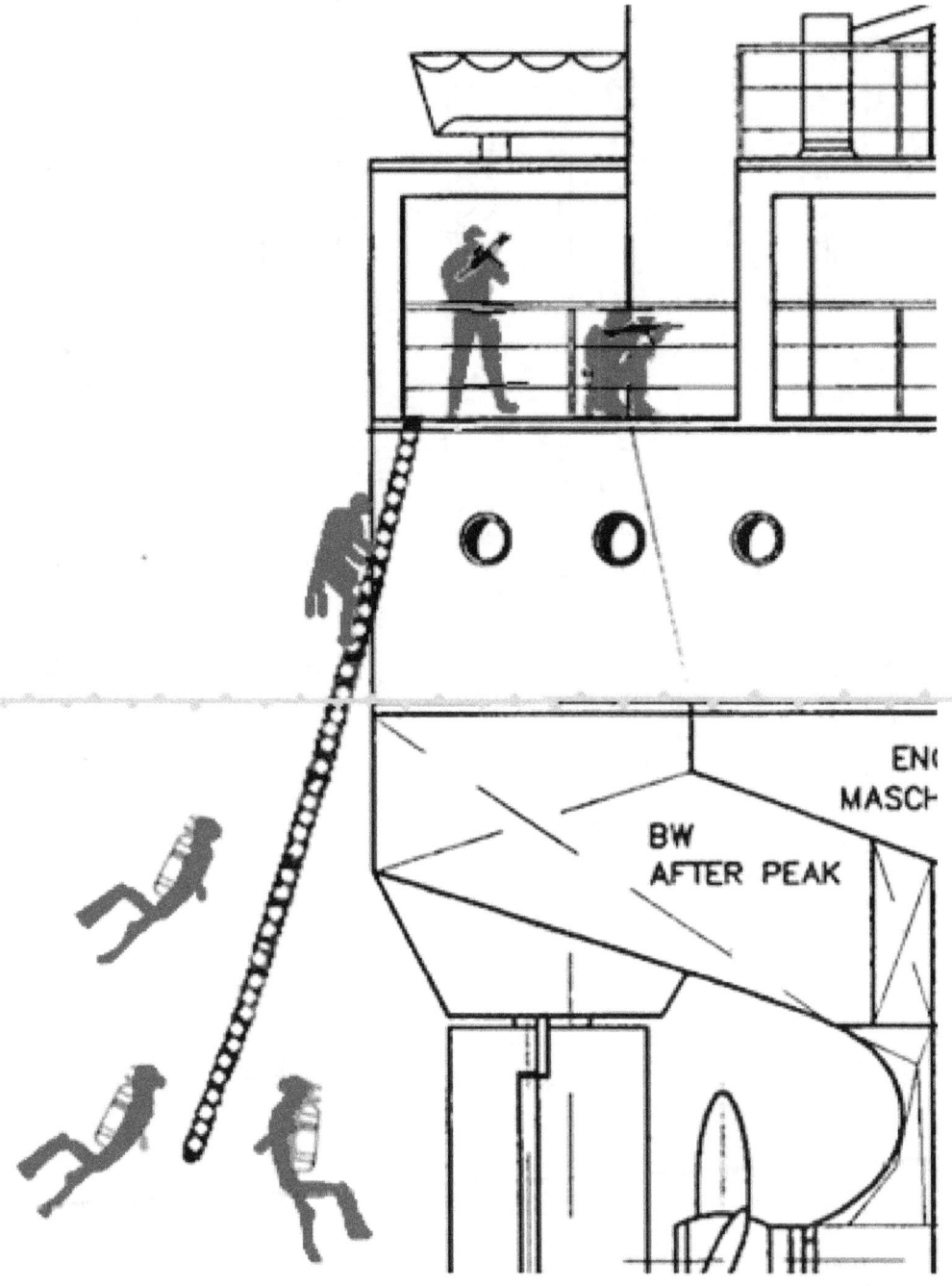

Fig. 6.5

Attack from pneumatic launches

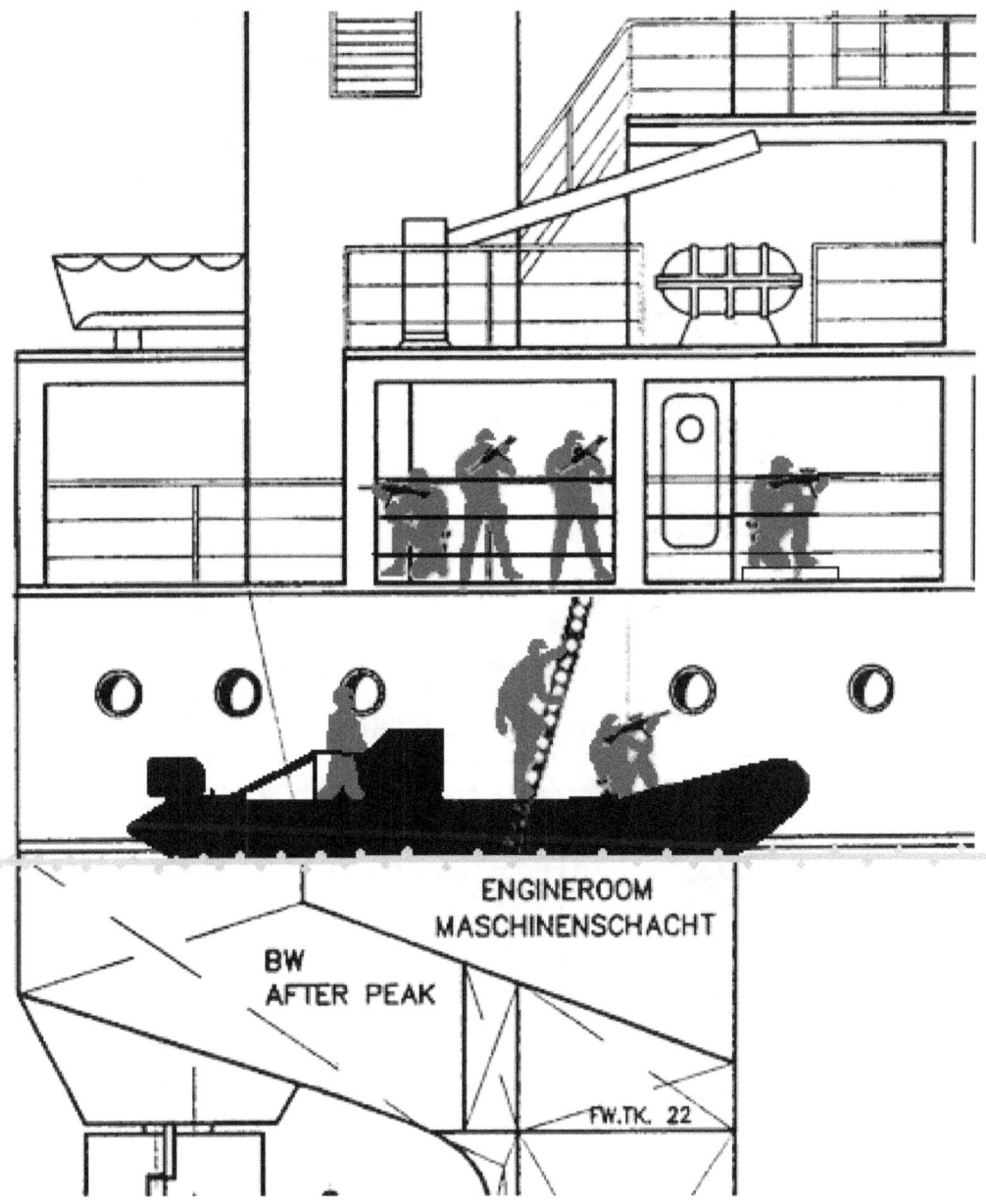

Fig. 6.6

Attack by parachutists

Fig. 6.7

Attack from helicopters

Fig. 6.8

Accesses to the interior of the ship and points of illumination

The red circles indicate the accesses from external decks, while the blue circles indicate the points of illumination on deck and superstructures distributed around the ship to which those installed in the load deck must be added.

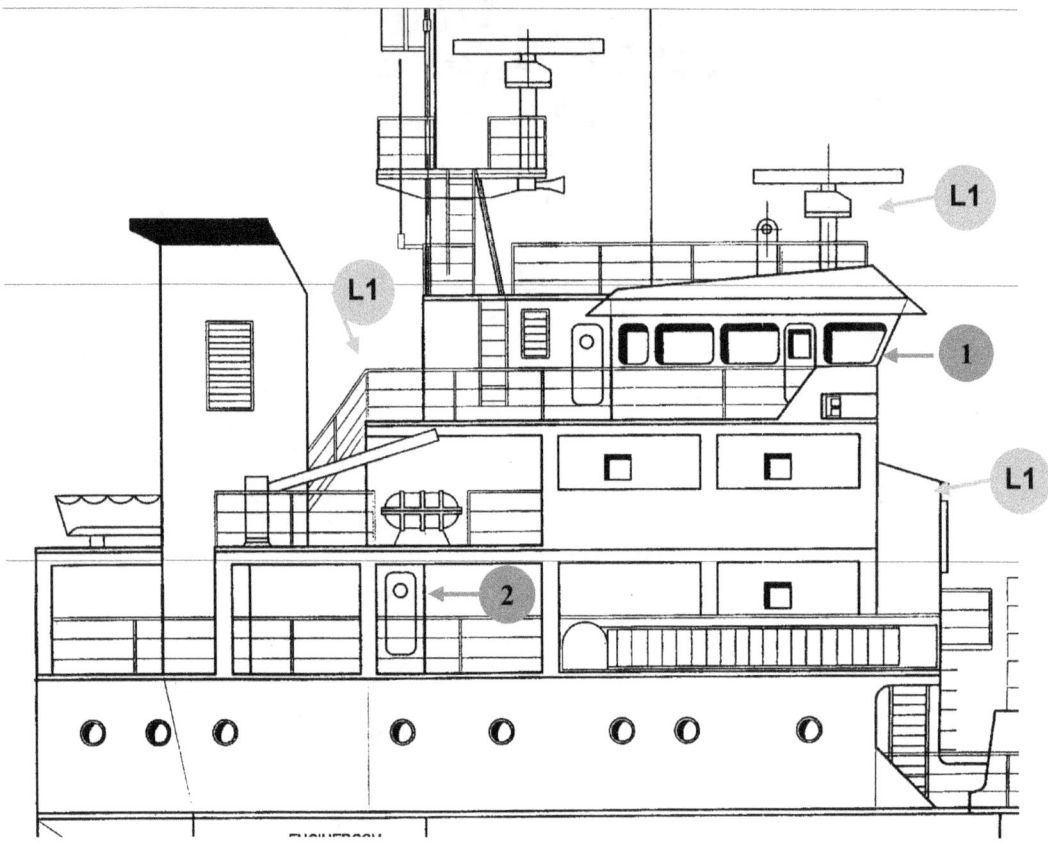

Fig. 6.9

The actions that the crew members may be in a position to take in the moments prior to and during the criminal acts they are facing, foreseeing possible rescue actions by the State security corps and forces, are switching lights on and off and opening or closing access to the compartment.

The most probable outcome is that, taken by surprise, they do not have time for any action that favours possible interventions afterwards and therefore the land assault teams will find themselves on the ship in the conditions prepared by the terrorists and not by themselves. But the use of the first alternative would be positive.

This is the situation if we consider another type of ship affected by the criminal act, the following drills could be used:

a) Considering that the damage they want to cause in the machines room or in the servo.

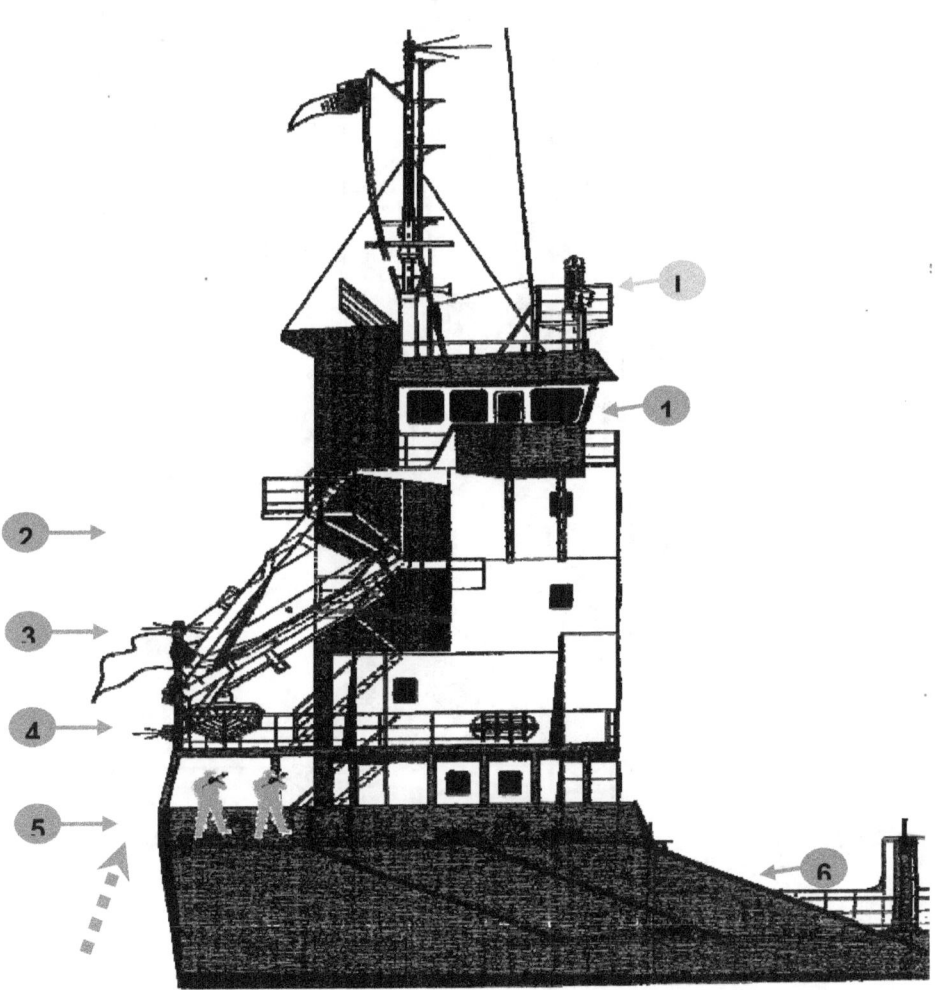

Fig. 6.10 The numbered red circles are entrances and accesses and the blue are lights..

b) Another drill considering they take the bridge.

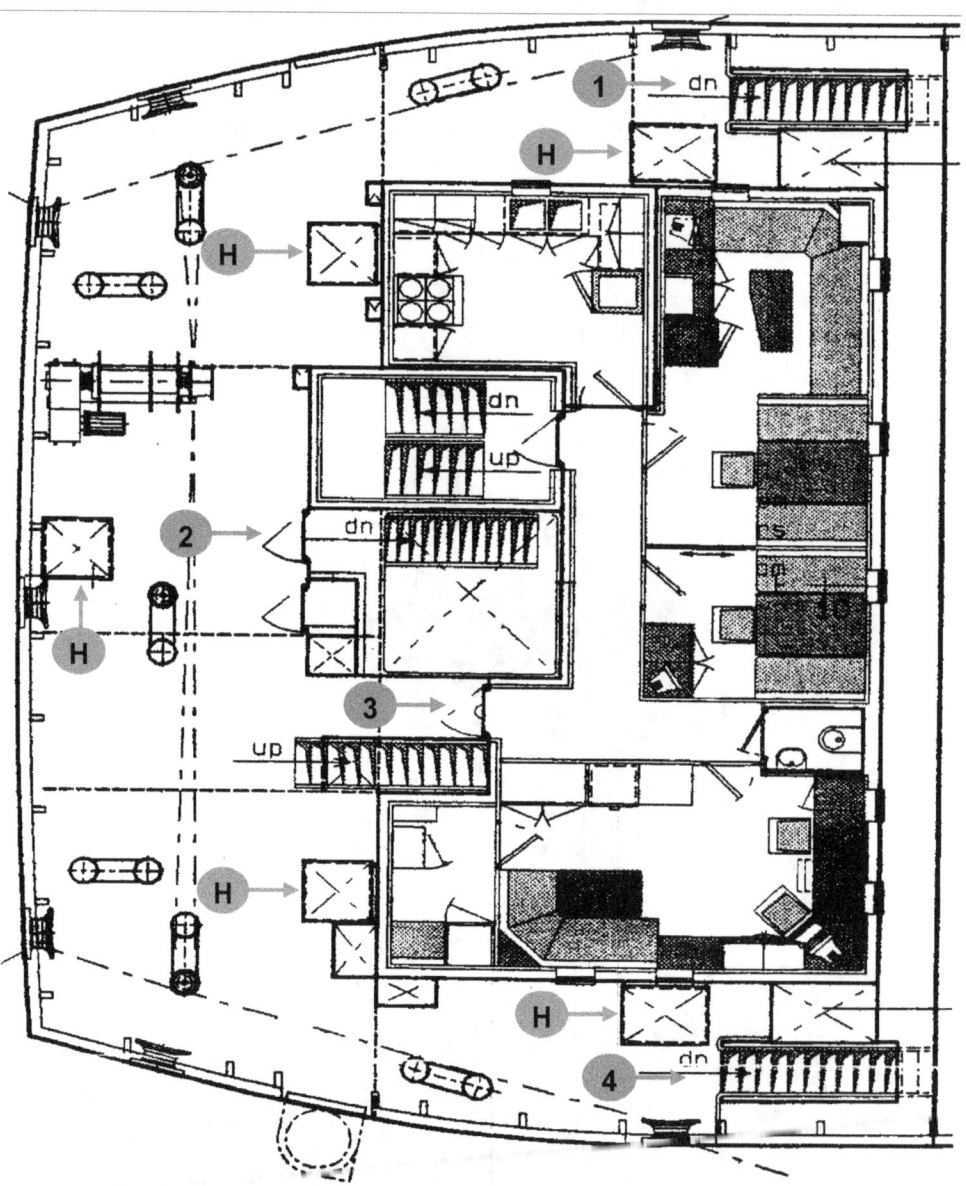

Fig. 6.11 The red circles are accesse and entrances, the gren ones are shed covers which must be taken into account in palnning any control.

6 Ship Intervention simulations

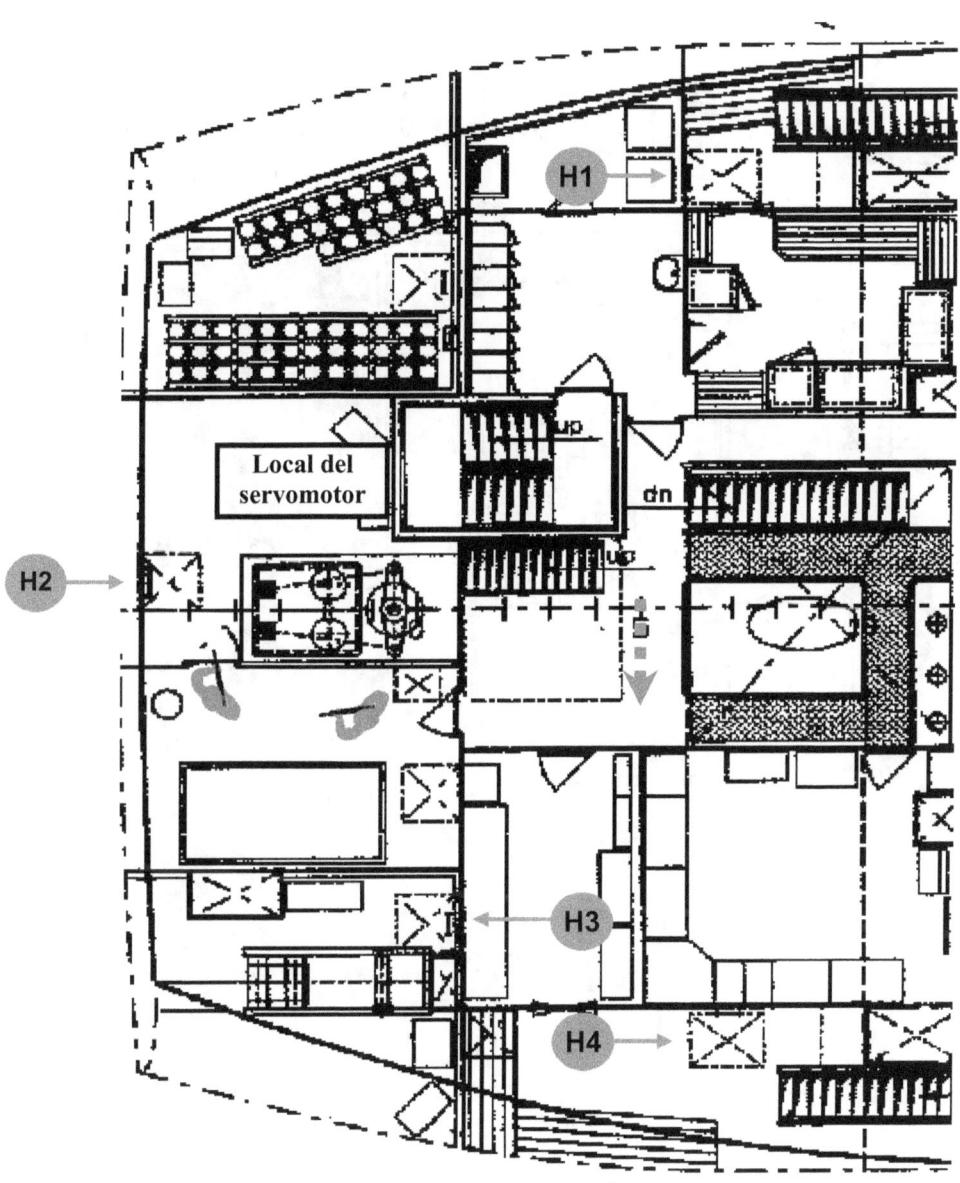

Fig. 6.12 The delinquents go up to higher decks.

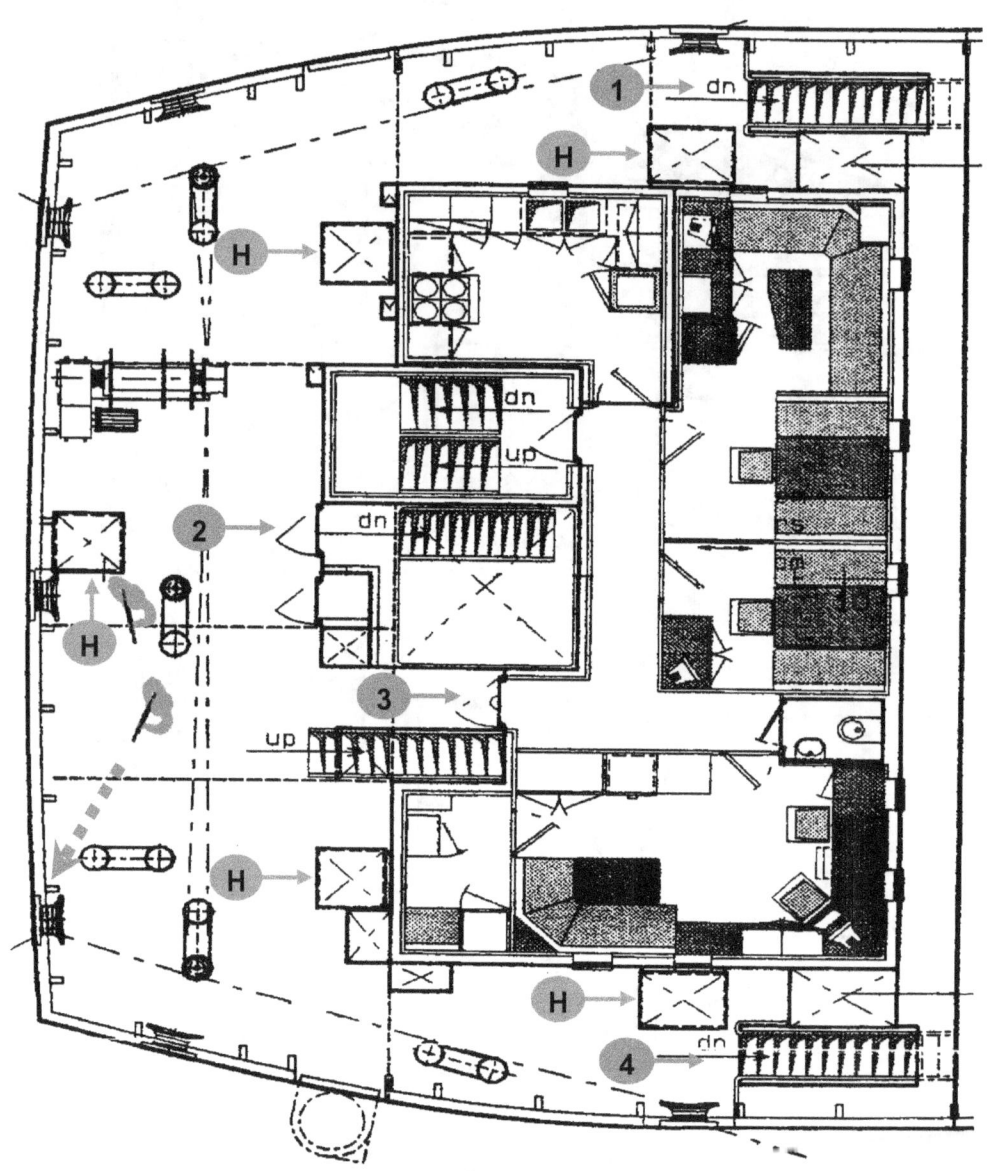

6.13 Escape route if there is no opposition and their objectives have been reached.

c) Attacking the bridge

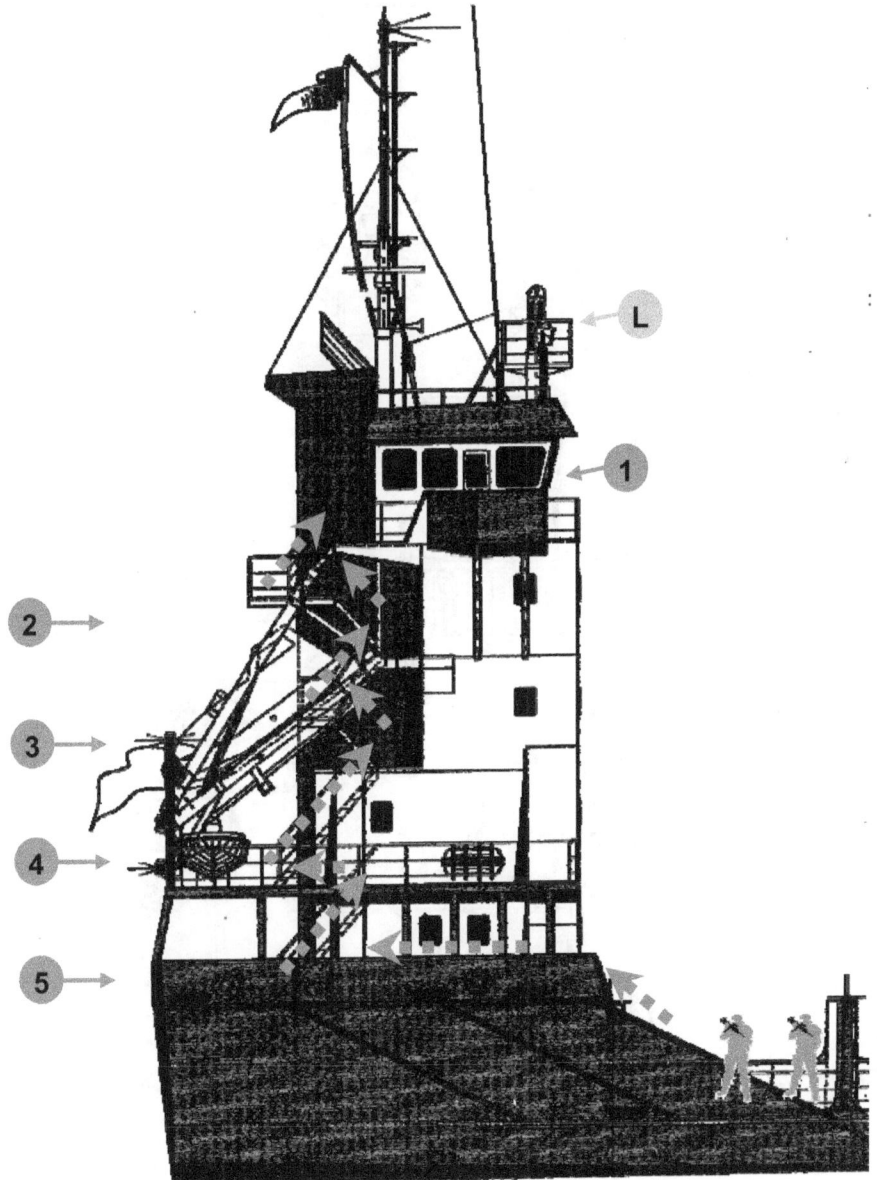

Fig. 6.14

In this case, the delinquents do not use the accesses inside the compartment, either as they intend to control the bridge as their main objective, or because all the doors to the interior of the lodgings are locked.

They use the external ladders to upper decks until they reach the ship's bridge.

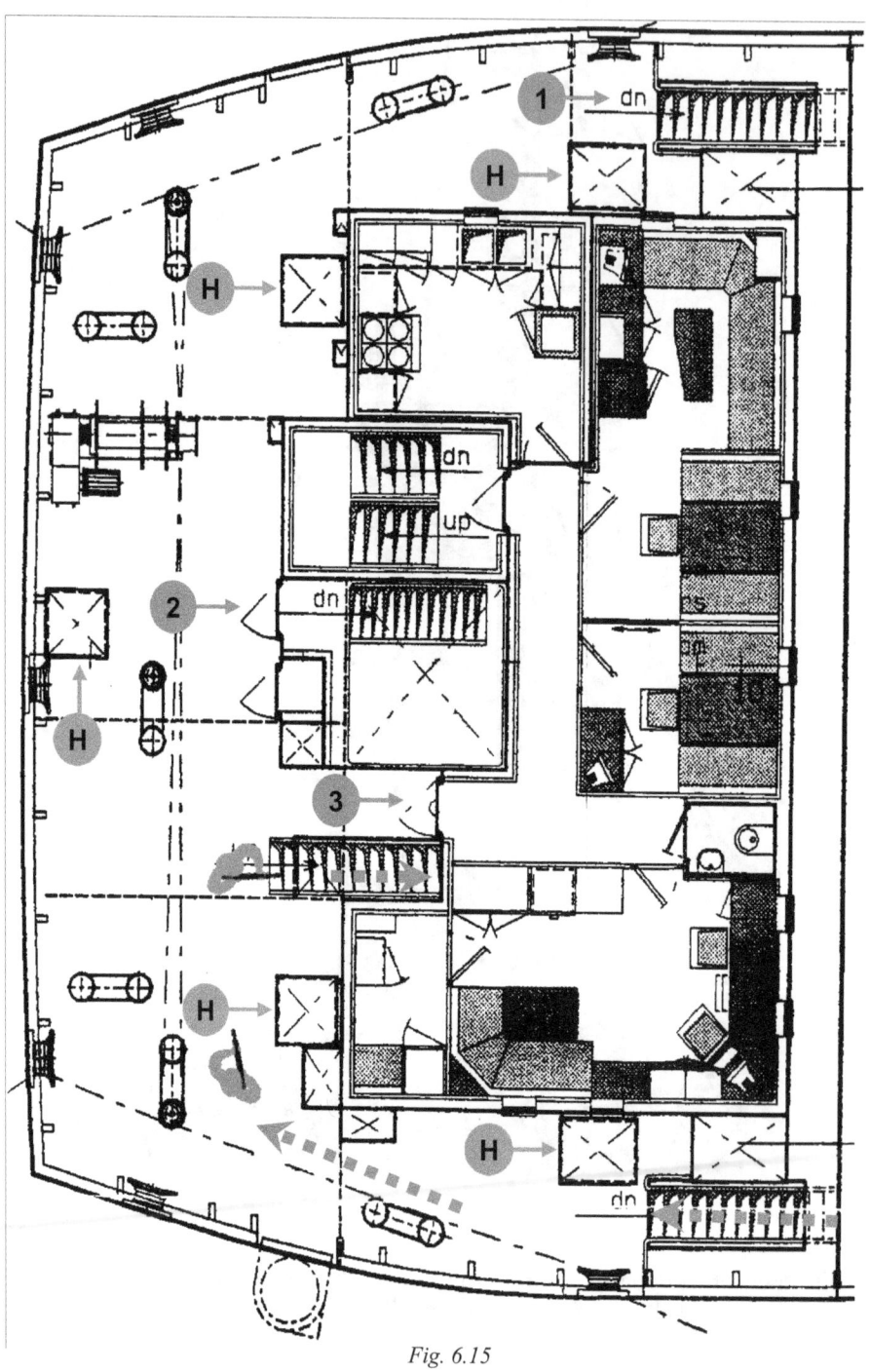

Fig. 6.15

6 Ship Intervention simulations 233

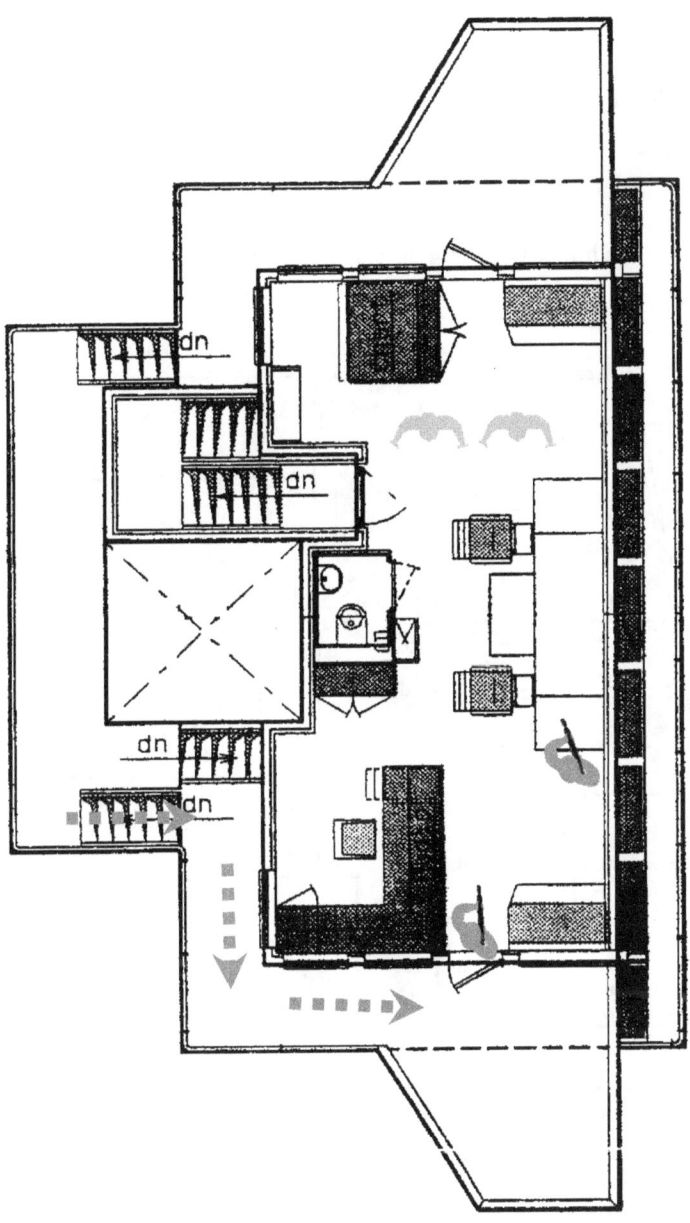

Fig. 6.16

When they reach the bridge they take the officer and sailor on guard as hostages.

Attack by the special forces.

Following procedures used by the SEAL commandos, the intervention on the ship will consider two actions:

    a)   A hostage rescue action from the lower deck of the compartment.

    b)   A direct action on the bridge to control the ship's neuralgia centre from the beginning.

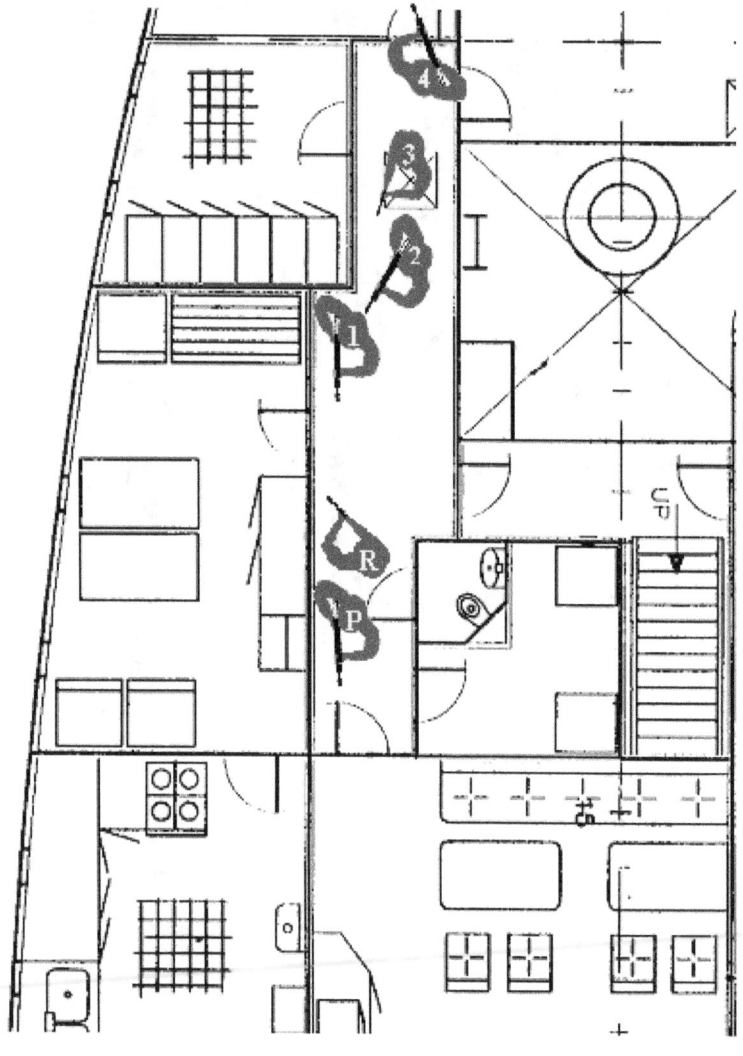

Fig. 6.17 Positions of the commando members to enter a cabin

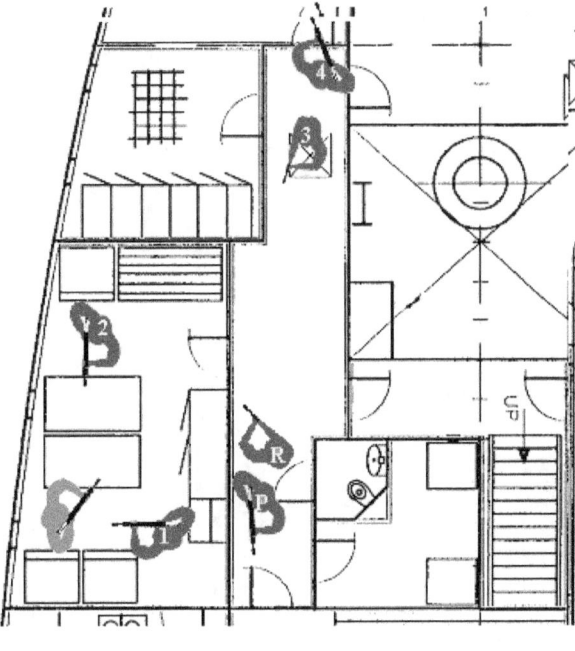

Fig. 6.18

They arrest the first terrorist and prepare to advance until they take complete control of the lodgings area.

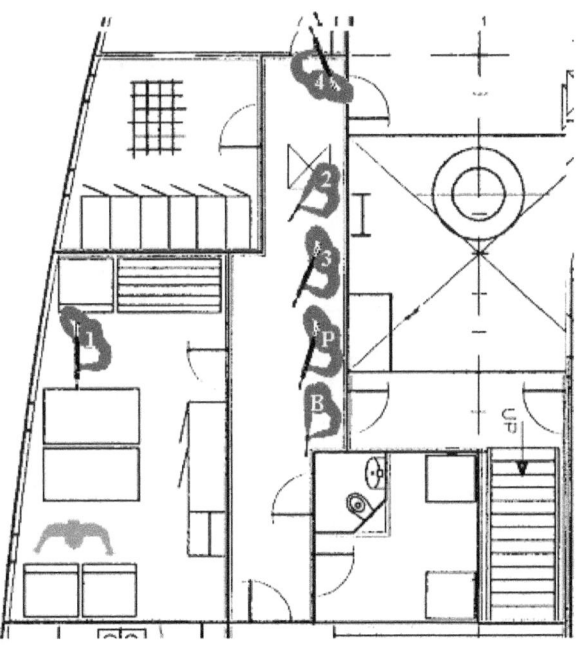

Fig. 6.19

They reorganise in to prepare the next step of their intervention

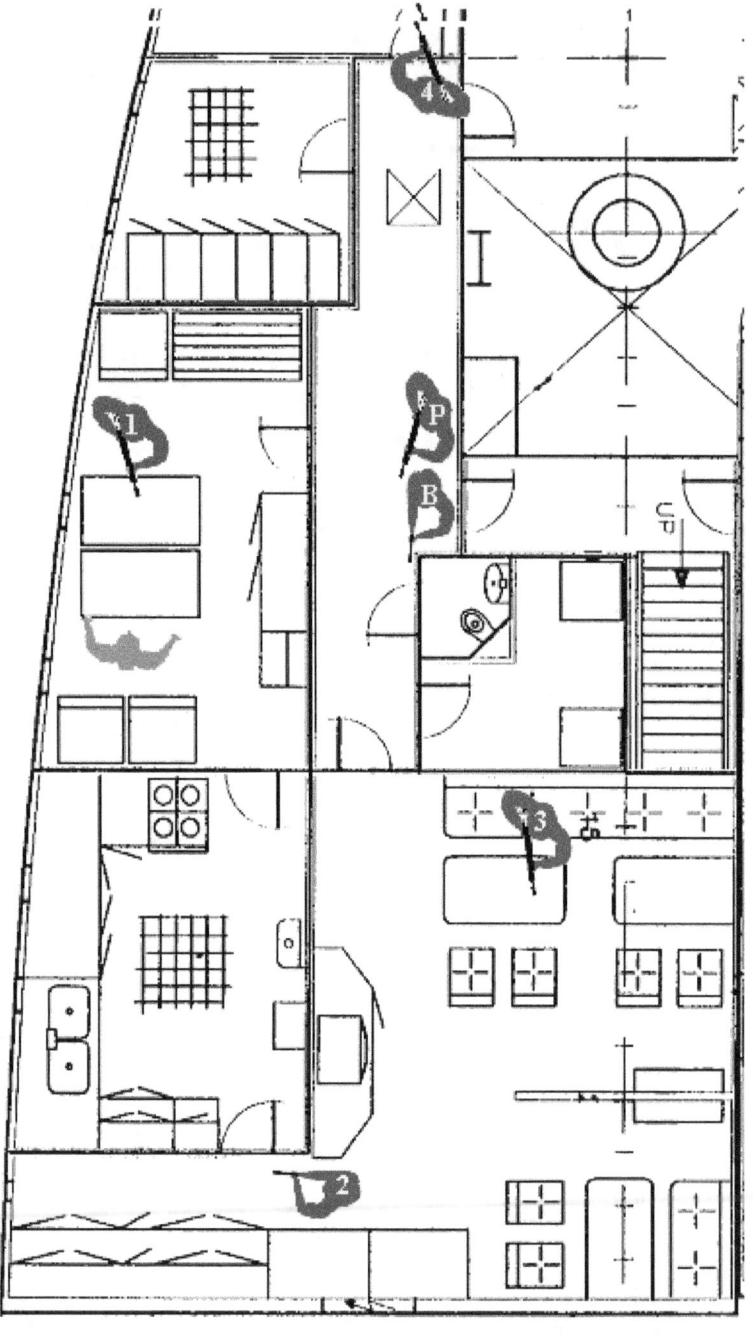

Fig. 6.20

They continue to control the deck on which they are keeping the arrested delinquent under control.

As for control of the bridge, we have:

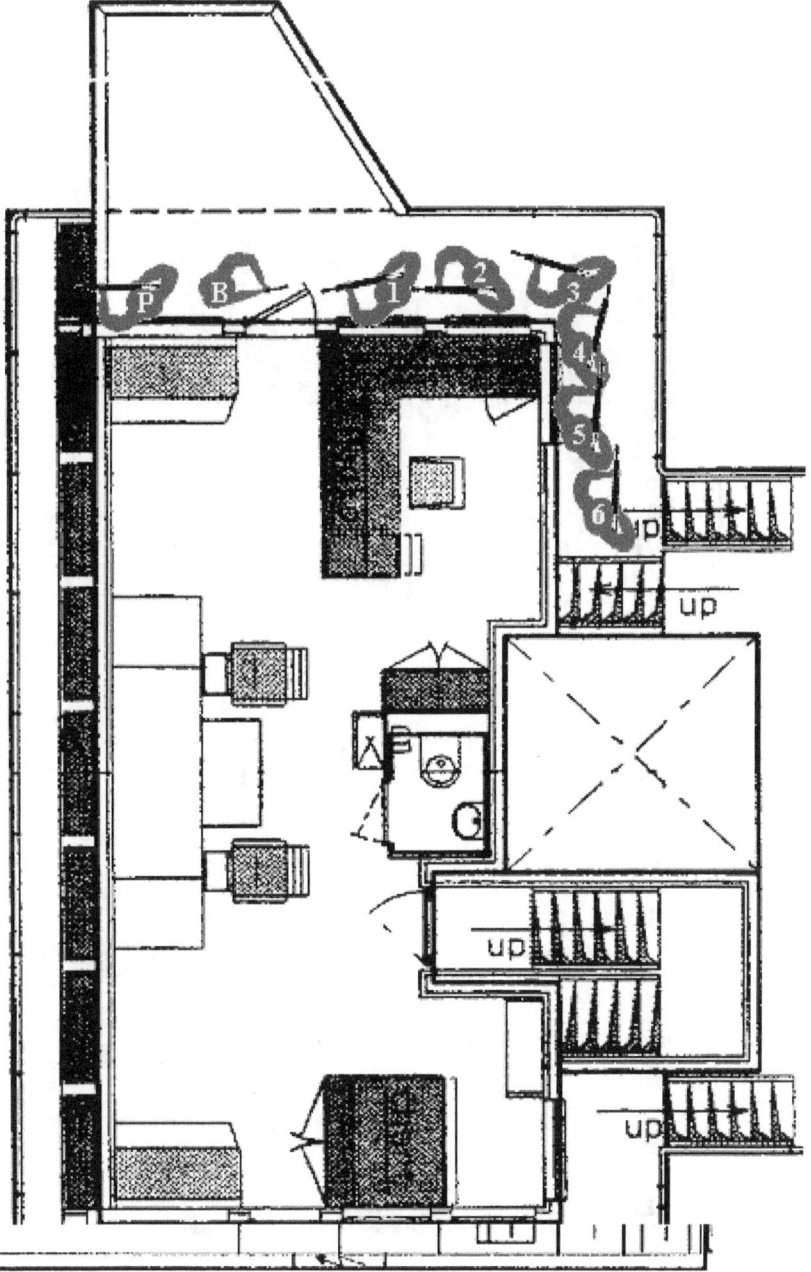

Fig.6.21

Maintaining the classical assault formation, they reach the bridge deck and get into position to enter through the aileron door.

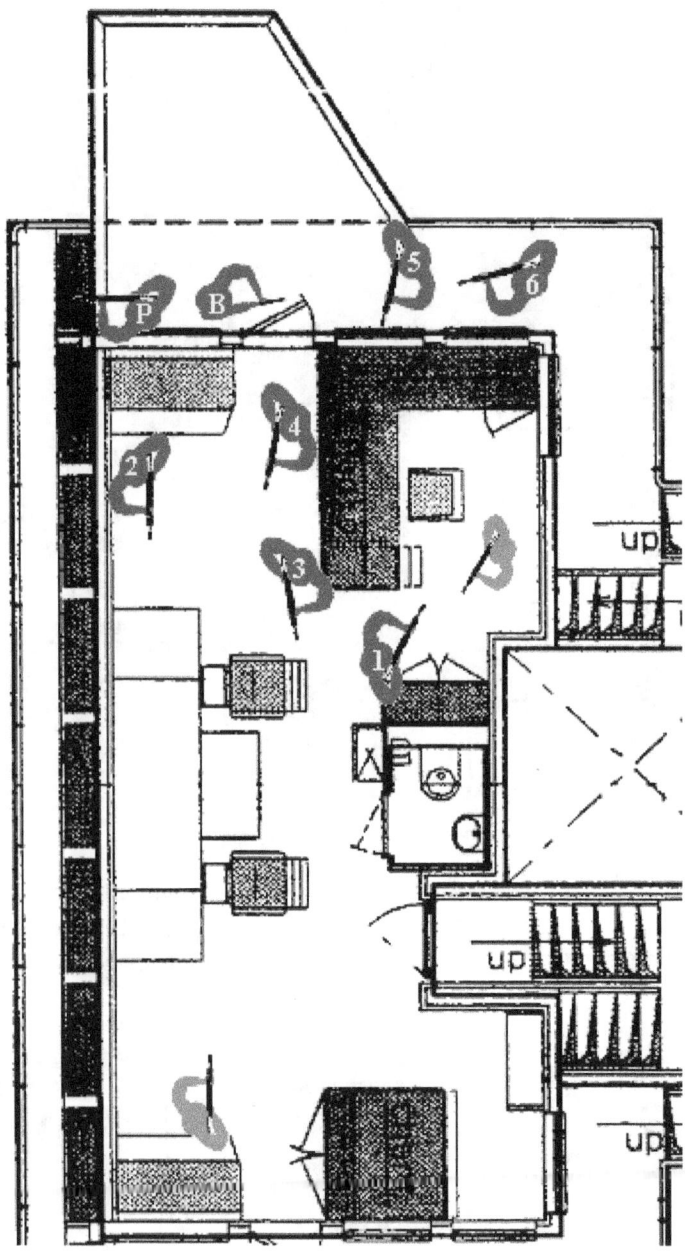

Fig.6.22

As they enter they take control of the situation and of the hijackers.

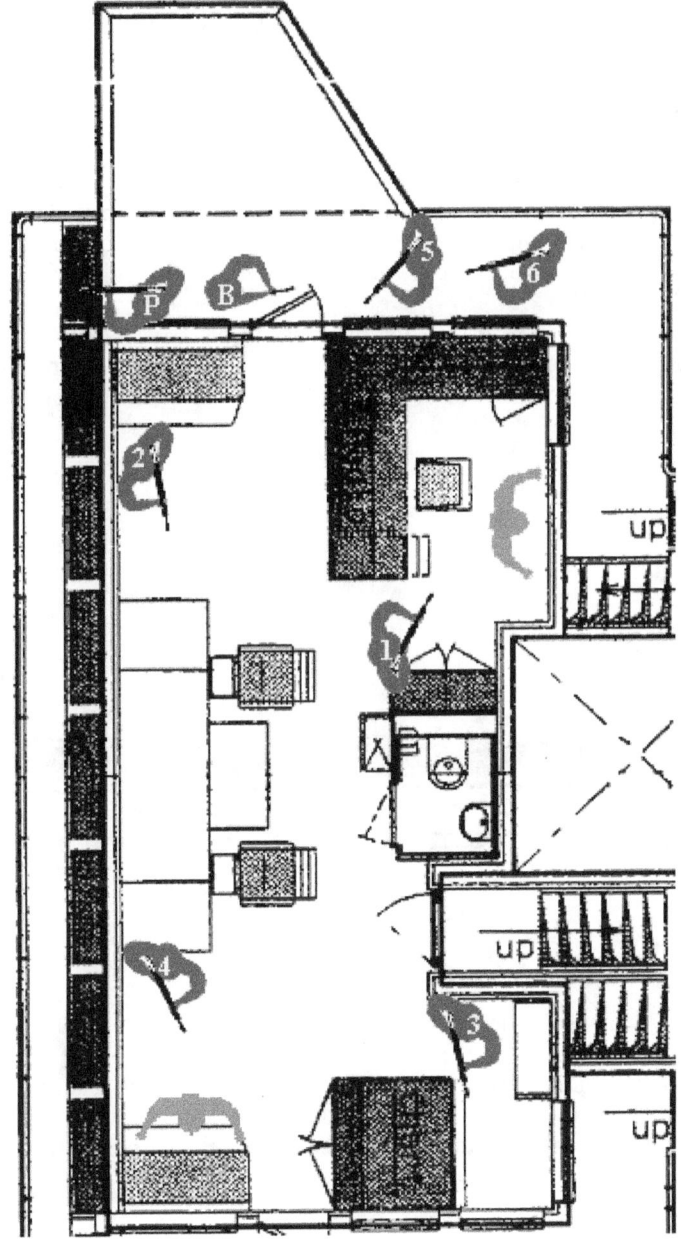

Fig. 6.23

They take control, verify positions and arrest the hijackers.

The rescue actions of the two commandos, one from the lower decks and the control of the bridge confirm the security of the ship. The next step is that of reconstruction, taking declarations, indices, samples and registers to obtain a true picture of the events and to take conclusions for their application in later situations that could be developed in similar circumstances.

Possible actions of the isolated crew

In most cases, the intervention of the special security forces will not be immediate, nor at times possible, at least in the time span desired, either due to the distance of the ship form the coast and the help it could receive or because of the denouement of the events which could lead to taking actions to improve the possibilities of survival of the crew.

In any case, it will always be necessary for the crew to have received instruction and to have participated in it, so that the procedures that may be carried out are not completely new, they know what actions to take in the course of time and what might contribute to controlling panic and its negative consequences.

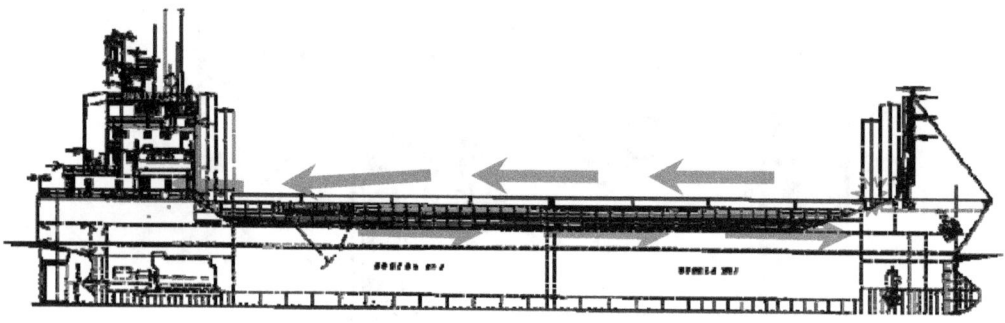

Fig. 6.24

The times required to complete the length of the ship must be taken into account.

Knowing that the ship is going to be attacked by pirates or other delinquents, it may be a good measure to group all the crew in a meeting point and start the control actions and closing of accesses, registering the spaces on the ship and preparing combat measures (fire hoses etc.) from there.

6 Ship Intervention simulations

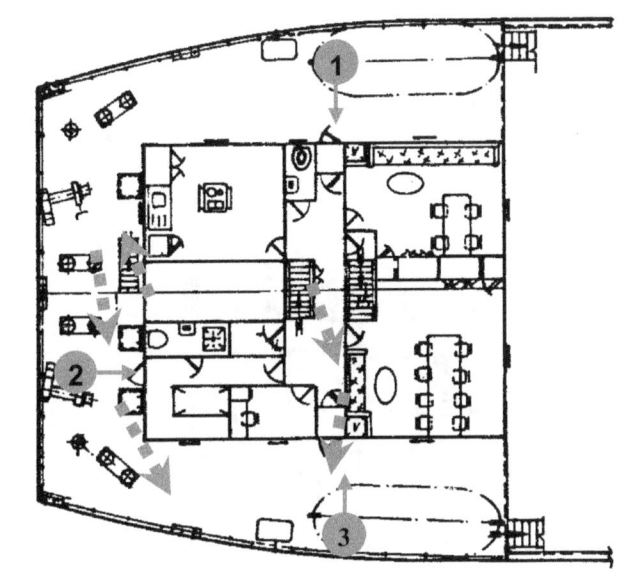

Fig. 6.25

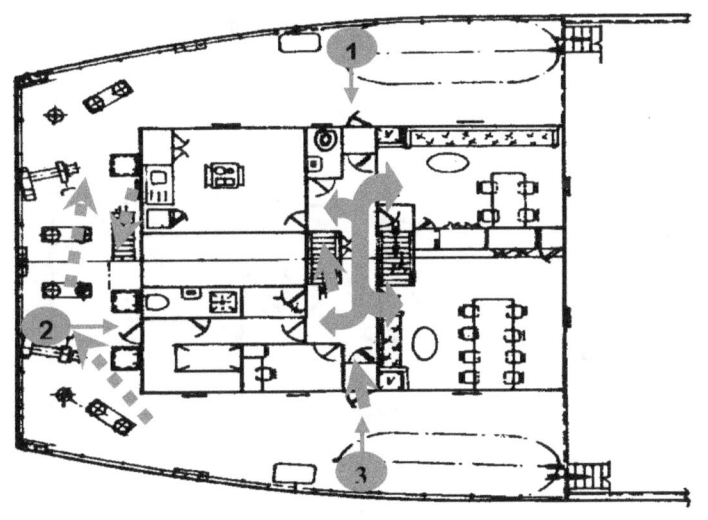

Fig. 6.26

Internal and external routes to be taken by the groups, led by the 1st officer and the lead Engineer officer and other lodgings.

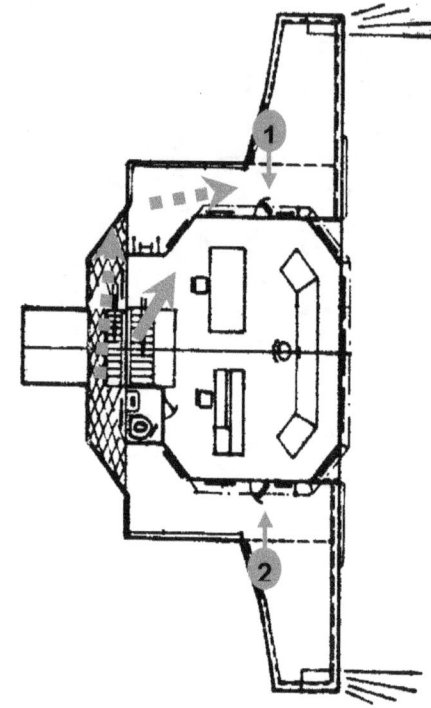

Fig.6.27

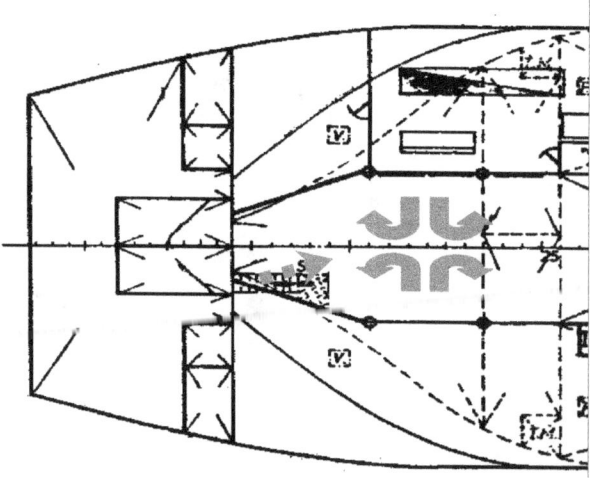

Fig. 6.28

6 Ship Intervention simulations

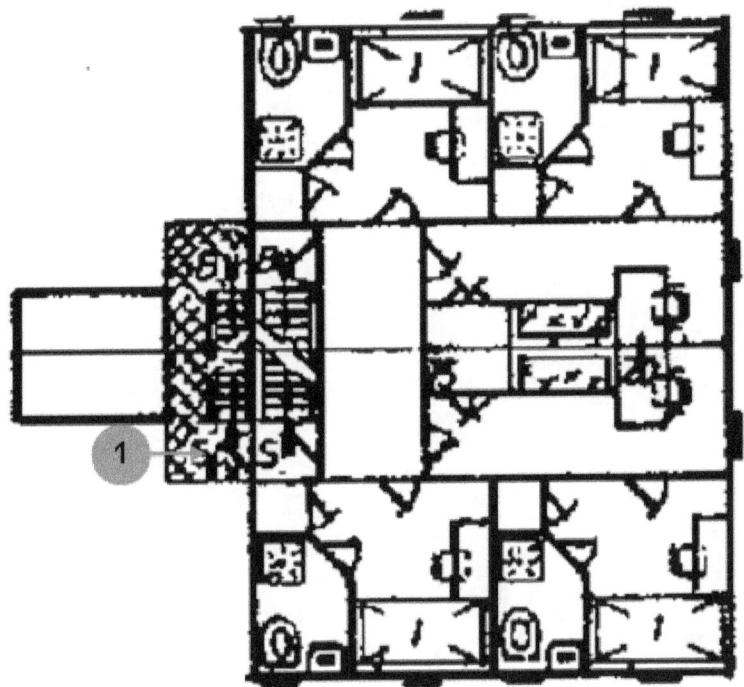

Fig. 6.29

7. Conclusions

Throughout the study it has been possible to ascertain the complexity involved in the violent resolution of a situation covered by the term *security*.

As an independent unit, the ship, without a physical location in space or in time, may be found at sea, near the coast or within the space of public dominion of a port, but always perfectly defined by the form of the ship and its dimensions which makes it special and isolated from other conditions. .

In most cases, the crew will suffer the first consequences of the criminal act without being able to receive the necessary help and moral support which is given to the same type of situations on land.

The faculty and good use of improvisation that the people of the sea must apply in the most varied situations that distinguishes the maritime adventure from other activities is well known but in these cases the crew has a purely and strictly civil base knowledge, with few resources to be right in the actions they take, with the best of intentions, to fight with guarantees against the groups that are highly prepared for criminal acts or to have protection and attack teams as is usual in the security forces commands.

In these circumstances and conditions, the treatment that must be given by the crew to any event that could occur on board will be that of maximum caution and precaution.

Despite what people may think to the contrary, the ship is an unknown place for most people from outside the maritime activity and enormously so for the members of the security forces who are going to intervene to save the lives of the crew members taken as hostages and at the same time to safeguard their own lives.

As has been extensively analysed in the different chapters of this study, the need arises for a strong and important approach of the security forces to the ships so that they can get to know them better, not just partially, but in depth, through the joint performance of drills where they can exchange knowledge, more so form the ship to the security forces, but in a process of identification of objectives and of responses that can be beneficial for one and the other without any obstruction or added complexity.

While it is true that the marine community has not provoked the situations that the international intelligence services classify as a threat to ships and the consequences for the population and assets involved in the ports, it is not logical either that the crews are only expected to accept the responsibility that arises from the ISPS without receiving any feedback with respect to their own safety.

The conclusions extracted from the consideration and the response of the human factor are vital in the balance of the expected results. This balance can only be achieved through training and instruction in the risk situation contemplated in the security scenario and carried out with maximum rigour and with the maximum contents and cases. The materialisation of a criminal event on board should not be received by the crew with surprise or ignorance whether or not they are capable of carrying out support actions in resolving the case.

The control of the human factor may make an external intervention all the more efficient, by giving confidence and by knowing what might happen and not only the tragic and well known events that are learnt in the cinema and novels. By controlling the moments of shock and panic, which necessarily have to appear in these situations, they must be overcome as soon as possible to avoid inadequate response that could endanger the success of the intervention made form the exterior.

It could be considered that in the near future, the ship will have to adapt to the needs that may be required of it by the external security forces, which means that naval construction should take them into account and include them in the designs and new projects for ships.

In this sense the following aspects may be necessary: improved loudspeaker systems adapted to internal communications: removing the shadowed areas inside the ship which do not allow to cross the limits of a Faraday cage, improving the communications that are accessible to passengers for the communication prior to the emergencies or of the emergencies themselves, the possibility of accesses with lighting that varies in intensity, standardised systems in types of ships and ports so as to reduce the variability and increase knowledge of their interior distribution, decks free from boats and points of anchor which are easy to use for the security forces, evacuation routes that take into consideration the direction in which doors open and the type and quality of the locks, illumination in accesses, staircases and corridors as well as the installation of active (not passive) signaling, the elimination of decorations and complements that hinder a safe and regular passage for evacuation and finally the design of the superstructures of the ship along the perpendicular form poop to bow, reducing the places that make it easy to hide people, leaving less dark spaces, without 90° angles and any improvement that favours the detection of intruders during pirate attacks and others.

The intermodality of maritime transport, which assumes all of them, and the internationality of the growing activity make it an enormously complex situation which means that all the preventive measures possible must be taken to make it impossible for delinquents to gain access to the ship and its installation to use it as a mobile weapon against civil interests in any part of the world or to create panic and destroy the sustainable growth.

Therefore it is desirable that such control measures are strict in the port facilities and help to dissuade people form committing criminal acts on board the ships and that their crews are not used for the interest of anyone.

In any case, the training of all those involved, breaking the barriers that prevent a mutual knowledge between the security forces and the crews, understanding and assuming the role that each one has in society and the loss of fear from archaic approaches will substantially improve the precarious conditions that ships still offer today and in the near future to those who wish to harm others through them.

Bibliography

Publications

MARÍ, R.. *Crisis situations in passenger ships*. Barcelona, Edicions UPC, 1998. I.S.B.N 847653 6852

MARÍ, R.; LIBRÁN A.. *Public safety in passenger ships*. Barcelona, Edicions UPC, 2003. I.S.B.N. 84-8301-692-3

MARÍ, R. "The ISPS And the challenge for naval construction". *IPEN Journal (Pan-American Institute of Naval Engineering),* n° 28 of September 2003. ISSN: 1011-5951.

MARÍ, R. "Influence of the Maritime Environment on the casuistry or organised crime". *International Congress on Maritime Technological innovations and research.* University of Cadiz. Publications Service of the UCA, recorded on CD, 2000.

Research work

"Identification and analysis of the influence of the maritime environment (ports and ships) on the casuistry of organised crime". *European Commission. Task Force for Cooperation on Justice and Home Affairs. Police and Customs.* October 1998/April 2000. Main researcher: RICARD MARÍ SAGARRA. UPC

"Methodology and programme framework for the development of the port facilities security plans." Public Entity Ports of the State. November 2003 /March 2004. Main researcher: RICARD MARÍ SAGARRA. UPC

Specialised magazines

TOM ICHNIOWSKI. "Domestic security defence covers multiple fronts: transit, seaports want bigger share of federal aid". *ENR*, New York. 2004

DAVID HUGUES. "Still in deepwater: congress may boost funding further as USCG adjusts the program for counterterrorism". *Aviation Week & Space Technology*. 2004

KERRY E. JULIAN. "Trucking Security". *Professional Safety*. 2003

AILEEN CHO. "Containing container risks and connecting modes intermodal infrastructure planners take on security". *ENR*. 2003

ROBERT WALL. "Coast guard nears decision on maritime patrol aircraft". *Aviation Week & Space Technology*. 2004

KIEFER, K. "Establishing a port security committee". *Proceedings of the marine safety council*. 2004

APPS, J. "International port security programme". *Proceedings of the marine safety council*. 2004

MERRITT, M. "TSA administers grants for port security improvements". *Proceedings of the marine safety*. 2003

Websites

Defense Security Service:	www.dss.mil
Federation of American Scientists:	www.fas.org
Global Defence:	www.global-defence.com
GlobalSecurity:	www.globalsecurity.org
Marine Corps Doctrine Division:	www.doctrine.usmc.mil
MI5:	www.mi5.gov.uk
StrategyPage: http:	www.strategypage.com
Navy Warfare Development Command:	www.nwdc.navy.mil
Naval Magazine	www.revistanaval.com
Special Operations:	www.specialoperations.com
Specwarnet:	www.specwarnet.net
US Coast Guard:	www.uscg.mil
The Free Dictionary:	http://encyclopedia.thefreedictionary.com
About.com:	http://usmilitary.about.com
Control Electronic Security:	www.controlelectronic.com
Insight Security:	http://www.insight-security.com
Security Worx:	www.securityworx.com
Autonomous Solutions:	www.autonomoussolutions.com
US Marine Corps Training and Education Command:	www.tecom.usmc.mil

www.ingramcontent.com/pod-product-compliance
Lightning Source LLC
Chambersburg PA
CBHW081349230426

43667CB00017B/2771